Remember

THE GOOD OLD DAYS ???

Van C. Duling & Jerry Mapes

5 4 3 2 1

Printed in the U.S.A.

ISBN 0-934904-45-6

www.leebooksellers.com
e-mail leebooks@radiks.net
1-888-665-0999 Toll free

On the Cover

22nd & J Street looking east,
May 3, 1921, courtesy of James C. Seacrest.

Contributors

STATE OF NEBRASKA

OFFICE OF THE GOVERNOR
P.O. Box 94848
Lincoln, Nebraska 68509-4848
Phone (402) 471-2244
mjohanns@notes.state.ne.us

Mike Johanns
Governor

I came to Lincoln in 1974 when I was hired by the Nebraska Supreme Court. I have vivid memories of that time and the excitement I felt to be starting a new job in a new place. I remember driving through the streets of Lincoln on one of those first days, and I remember being taken aback by the tree-lined streets and the simplistic beauty of the city. I remember going to work my first day at the State Capitol and being in complete awe of the immensity and grandeur of the building. Most of all, however, I remember being impressed by the warm, outgoing, and inviting nature of the people of Lincoln. They made me feel at home and made me want to stay for awhile.

Twenty-seven years later, Lincoln is still my home. It is the place where I have raised a family and built a career. I have served the citizens of this community as a county commissioner, a city council member, as their mayor, and now as their Governor. I have a special place in my heart for this community and the people who live here, and I look forward to making many more memories here in the years ahead.

Mike Johanns
Governor of Nebraska
August 13, 2001

August 29, 2001

Dear Van and Jerry:

My thanks to you on behalf of the people of Lincoln for your work on *The Good Old Days*. For those of us who have grown up in Lincoln, Nebraska, or spent many years here, remembering our past is a pleasure. My family moved to Lincoln from a farm near David City in 1959. I was 5 years old. I started school in Lincoln and completed my education through the Lincoln Public Schools and the University of Nebraska–Lincoln where I graduated in 1977. I was elected to the State Legislature in 1978. After 20 years in the Legislature I was elected as Mayor of Lincoln in 1999.

It was in the 1970s that I became active in the Lincoln community. Over the three decades of the '70s, '80s and '90s, Lincoln has gone through a remarkable growth spurt. In many ways similar to growing from adolescence to adulthood, as we changed from a town to a city. While achieving this change, it is my hope that the special qualities that have made Lincoln so wonderful will remain a vital part of our community.

I remember growing up in the Bethany neighborhood where our neighbor across the street was an elderly woman living alone. My parents made it clear that we had a responsibility to help her whenever we could. I and my brothers would scoop the snow off her sidewalks in the winter and clear her leaves in the fall and run errands for her when she needed help. It was like that in our neighborhood. Each of us looking out for others. I still remember climbing a tree in our backyard and getting my leg stuck. An older boy in the neighborhood came over and helped set me free. There was always a sense that you weren't alone, that there was always someone looking out for you. It is a wonderful feeling I hope everyone in Lincoln has a chance to experience. I remember the empty lot next to our house and all the neighborhood kids gathering there almost every day during the summer to play a game of football or baseball. There weren't many organized sports aside from Little League. We didn't drive across town to play games. Our neighborhood was our world. A world filled with kids who wanted to play together and adults who cared about us and watched out for us. I often share my story as a Northeast High School student when I skipped school one spring day with my friends, only to arrive home after school to find my math teacher waiting for me in my family's dining room. When I and my friends had called in sick that morning, he had called my mother to see how I was feeling. My mother thought that I was feeling fine and had gone to school. This extra effort on behalf of Robert Wohlers, my math teacher, caught me in my one act of truancy. I never did that again because he took the extra step of waiting at my home for me to arrive and then explained how irresponsible I had been to miss school that day. It was an act of caring that went above and beyond the call of duty and makes Lincoln special.

When you have that sense of community in your neighborhood and in your school, you grow up with a sense of responsibility about your role in society. If people care that much about you, it is your responsibility in turn to care about them. If you want people to help you, you in turn must be willing to help them. It is my wish that Lincoln retains our concern for one another and never loses our sense of responsibility and community.

It is my hope that your book will help people remember the special history of Lincoln and cherish even more this wonderful place we call home, Lincoln, Nebraska.

Sincerely,

Don Wesely
Mayor of Lincoln

Foreword

A few months ago when Van and Georgia Duling were in Raleigh, N.C., Georgia noticed in the paper a bit of publicity concerning a book, *The Raleigh Boys*, written by Russ Reynolds, a local college professor. The book dealt with many of the memories of the male citizens of Raleigh, some of which were a bit ribald. Georgia brought it to the attention of Van who immediately contacted Mr. Reynolds to "pick his brain" on the best way of going about this. The rest is history. Van enlisted former journalism major Jerry Mapes to join in the project. Both Jerry and Van have been Lincolnites all their life. Van and Georgia went off to Florida after sending out about 500 letters to longtime Lincolnites asking for their stories, vignettes, etc. The letter asked people to direct their stories to Jerry who would assimilate them in the absence of Van.

The project proved an enormous success, particularly when Pam Thompson, of the Lincoln *Journal Star* did an excellent article for the paper and generated a lot of additional interest. The result is a compilation of stories and events spanning over a century, and not limited to the "good ol' boys' club" but open to everyone, young, old, male and female.

After reading and hopefully enjoying the memories, one can't help but get caught up in the inescapable fact that these were indeed "the good old days." "Mom and Pop" small enterprises abounded. Keys were left in cars, houses left unlocked, concerts were held in the park and people acknowledged each other on the street. There was enough dirt around to get up a marble game and bicycles could be parked in front of the theaters and would still be there two hours later.

There were scads of little grocery stores, which would put one about every five or six blocks. People ate dinner together, talked together, listened to the radio together, and when Junior came home with a little welt on his hand applied by a teacher who didn't like to be sassed, dad usually applied an additional welt instead of hiring a lawyer to sue everyone in the school system.

Acknowledgments must also go once again to Georgia Duling; and thanks also to the inimitable Jim McKee, Lincoln's noted historian and publisher, for rendering his assistance to this fledgling effort.

Finally, thanks to Tami McLaughlin for hours of editing, typing and assembling of articles.

A noble effort by all involved.

LINCOLN
PREWAR

27th Street Was Wide Enough

By Lou Carter Ganz

I grew up at 3175 Sheridan where the house had a vacant lot next door. Before the days of any little league, Dad and Dr. George Misko (to the west) helped with the "workup" baseball in the spring and summer, tag football in the fall, all co-ed. Carolyn Roberts, Gates Minnick, Billy Jo Misko, Joan Corveth, Jayne Carter and others wandered over, also.

On hot summer nights after it was too dark to play we often went to the Windmill on Cotner and O for a root beer or ice cream.

We sometimes walked down graveled Melrose to 31st and South to the Bishop's farm to buy eggs and/or cream. It was then Bishop Road (now Calvert) a graveled, dead-end (before 27th) and known as "lovers lane." All the homes on the east side of 31st south of Woodsdale had lots extending to the Rock Island Railroad, most had livestock—horses, a cow, chickens, etc.

Smith's Windmill, later simply the Dutch Windmill, stood on the southeast corner of Cotner Blvd. and O Street. The building served briefly as the first home of Gateway Bank before they moved to the Gateway Shopping Center. The windmill, which actually rotated, was lit with various colored light bulbs.
Photo courtesy Nebraska State Historical Society.

A Look Back

By Chan Tyrrell

My dad, Delzon L. Tyrrell, worked for Frey & Frey Florist and Greenhouses at their range of greenhouses at 22nd & Randolph Streets. Their greenhouses were from 22nd and Randolph Streets to 24th and Randolph and from Randolph Street south to Alpha, 22nd to 24th. Alpha is now vacated as it was between F Street and E Street. This property was later sold about 1935–1936 to the Catholic diocese for their new high school. A depression came along, they ran out of money and the building stood empty for many years until Lincoln Public Schools bought it for administration offices. LPS finished the building and stayed there for many years until it was combined with Lincoln High School at which time they closed Randolph Street and built the gym and swimming pool to connect the two buildings.

My dad worked for Frey & Frey at their downtown store at 1338 O Street, which is now a parking garage. The neighbors of the store were Acme Bakery, Schwartzman Cigar Store, Priga Jewelry, and on the corner of 14th and O Street was Acme Chili Parlor owned by the Christopulos family from Greece. On the west side was the Blackstone Restaurant owned by the A. A. Andros family, also from Greece. Then came Hardy Furniture Store, Rialto Theatre, and a drug store on the corner of 13th and O (northeast corner). While my dad worked for Frey & Frey, they had another larger range of greenhouses at 35th and Lake Street. That parcel was from 35th and Sewell to 38th and from Sewell to South Street, they called it "Glass Acres." After the sale of the 22nd and Randolph properties, they grew all of their own cut flowers and plants at Lake Street. My dad oversaw all of the shipping of flowers to the western part of the state by Railway Express. The Frey's oldest daughter Irene was married at "Glass Acres" to Mac McDonald. They later moved to Scottsbluff and opened their own flower shop.

Mr. and Mrs. Irwin Frey built the beautiful house at 27th and Van Dorn (southeast corner). Irwin Frey was buried from that house that was laden with beautiful fresh flowers. He laid in state for three days.

My brother, Clement Tyrrell and myself, Chandler Tyrrell, were both born at 22nd and Alpha, in a house owned by Frey & Frey.

The Catholic diocese moved that house to 28th and Calvert beside the Bishop's house for a groundskeeper, that property is now owned by the Abel family. The Catholic diocese owned all the land in that area, Calvert to Woods Blvd., 27th to 33rd, known as Bishop Heights and on the west side of 27th was Crystal Rae Orphanage, now known as Bishop Square.

A Texan Remembers Lincoln

By Worth Winslow

A few years ago when I was doing a "Remember When" column for the *Capital Times*, Max Speidell sent me some recollections from a Mr. Worth Winslow of Tyler, Texas. Apparently Mr. Winslow was an old friend of Max and obviously lived here in the '20s, '30s and '40s. He labeled his paper "A Texan Remembers Lincoln" (for senior citizens only).

Remember?

Alex Candy Kitchen—best smell in the world
Horse-drawn fire wagons at 27th and Vine Street
Jack Matthew's long yellow racing car
Electric Park, out near Epworth Park
Fall opening downtown, crowds, crowds, crowds
Mayer Bros., Eli Shire, Pres.
Ben Simon—Ben Simon himself
Herpolshiemers—with a name like that it had to be good
Nick the cop at 13th and O Street
Heavyweight Officer Major Gross and his motorcycle—mean and tough
The beautiful lavender touring car that someone drove to the bank every day
Nick at the Acme Chili Parlor—fabulous memory
The man who drove the 5¢ taxi from the Acme every night
Capital Beach—great bands and dancers
Antelope dance pavilion—great bands
Lindell Hotel party house—U of N collegian band
Cornhusker Ballroom—"dance her over the lights in the floor"
Linoma Beach—Sunday dances
Liberty Theatre—vaudeville

A Tribute to Ray Becker:
One of Lincoln's Legends

Raymond Becker was born in Grand Island, Nebraska on December 7, 1905, to Emmanuel and Elizabetha Becker, the youngest of five children. Ray's parents were living in Grand Island while his oldest sister was attending college in Grand Island studying for a teacher's certificate. Soon after his birth the family returned to their farm located four miles north and three miles west of Sutton, Nebraska.

Ray grew up on the farm and attended the one-room school in School Creek Township through the eighth grade. Going on to high school in Sutton, he rode his horse on nice days, tying the horse in the back yard of his oldest sister and her family during the day, or when mother came to see him and his sister's family weekly, bringing home-grown fruit and vegetables from their personal stores, along with different kinds of meat that they had processed. During his time at Sutton High School, he enjoyed an exciting sports career playing right tackle on the football team. The love of football still stays with Ray and he is in the stands whenever the Nebraska football team is at home.

It was during his early years that the banking business attracted Ray. On many occasions he came into Sutton, going to the local bank, while his father transacted business. He always thought he would like to work in a bank, sitting at a desk, and making loans to the customers. After graduation from Grand Island Business College, he and his father came to Lincoln to see if he could find work. They bought a Lincoln newspaper and scanned the want ads. Here they found an ad for someone to work in the City National Bank. The two of them went to the bank, and Ray got his first job, as a collector, visiting various business to get the cash on returned checks.

In 1928, after working at his job for about two years, the bank merged with the First National Bank. He was then given another position, working in the Discount Department until 1937 when he was elected assistant cashier and transferred to the Commercial Loan Department. His work remained in the Credit and Commercial Loan Department after he became vice president in 1946.

In 1960 the Continental National Bank merged with the First National Bank. At the time of the merger, the merged banks located in a new building on the corner of 12th and N. In 1969 a new structure on the corner of 13th and M was built, and completed in March of 1970. In December of that year Ray retired from the bank.

Ray was married to Sue Marie Scott in September 1940. Sue Marie had attended the same business college at the time that Ray had, so they were friends prior to their marriage. Marie Becker was an employee of the state of Nebraska when they were married, and later went to work for another banking firm. In 1960 she and Ray opened "Gifts by Marc," a gift shop in Meadow Lane Shopping Center. She operated this until 1967, when failing health intervened. Mary passed away in February 1987.

In late November 1995 Ray celebrated his 90th birthday, with numerous guests at the Lincoln Country Club. Four of the five grandchildren, along with his daughter-in-law, who lives in Fort Wayne, Indiana, and one great-grandchild helped him celebrate the occasion.

Still a very active and virile individual, he appears to be one of the people we hear about once in a while, being able to reach the year 100 and beyond. He continues to play golf at Hillcrest Country Club, where he has been a member for many years, trying to play at least three times a week, whenever the weather will let him. While interviewing him, he mentioned a couple of incidents that he was inordinately proud of in his golf games:

• He played on the Antelope Golf Course when it was still a nine-hole course; today it is an eighteen-hole course, reserved primarily for teenagers.

• He once made a hole in one.

• He won the Hillcrest Country Club sweepstakes in 1954.

• He doesn't beat any golfing world records, but he scores low enough that he still counts the strokes.

A Youth of Dreams

By Evelyn Egley Pollard

I moved to Lincoln from Holdrege at the age of eleven, the day the sower was being hoisted atop the capital.

Things that stand out in my mind:

The little muscular vegetable man and his sons who came to our door with fresh vegetables from their horse drawn cart. His name was Tony Scolaro.

The Meadow Gold and Roberts milk men who also had horse-drawn carts and left cream topped milk in glass bottles in wooden boxes at our door.

The Omar Bakery man who left fresh baked goods at our door twice a week.

Children playing in the evening on street corners under the street lights, with wild bats dashing at the lights. Tin can hockey and roller-skating were favorites.

One of my first dates was with a young aspiring aviator who roomed across the street and attended Lincoln Flying School at 24th and O Street. We went out to the airfield on north 48th Street and I had my first plane ride in a Ford Tri Motor. My parents would have grounded me for life had they known.

Attending NU football games with a knothole ticket that cost 25¢.

Driving to Linoma Beach to swim.

The wonderful music of the best-ever bands at the Turnpike and Kings at Capital Beach, as well as the University Coliseum.

The sad loss of my young brother who drowned in a boating accident at Oak Lake during World War II.

Meeting the train at the depot. My father was a railroad employee and mother and I met his incoming trains at the Express Office north of the depot. One they called the Canary—it was a little yellow motor car that ran to Manhattan, Kansas, and back.

Sitting on a stool at the basement counter of Miller & Paine, enjoying a 25¢ serving of delicious bread stuffing for lunch in order to save enough money to purchase a 59¢ pair of rayon or nylon stockings. After graduating from Lincoln School of Commerce, my first job as an office secretary paid only $8.00 per week. The school was at 14th and P.

Attending a birthday dance on the big veranda of the old Governor's Mansion—how grand it seemed!

Spending 10¢ to ride the bus out to Bethany for my first permanent—a French curl for 99¢ and a coupon.

Those were the days!

All for 24¢

By Norman Vermaas

In the year 1937 my father, Ed Vermaas, an employee of the Lincoln Water Department, which had only three employees in the department, gave me 25¢ for allowance. On a Saturday I would take my quarter and go the Colonial Theatre, which was at 15th and O Street, catch the trolley in College View for 5¢, a movie for 9¢, popcorn for 5¢ and a trolley back home for 5¢, leaving me with one penny left. Now that's high class.

Al's Inn, the Forerunner of Lee's Chicken

By Bob James

In the early 1930s, my uncle and aunt, Al and Lizzy Remaly, operated a small restaurant on the site of Lee's Chicken. It was called Al's Inn. They sold hamburgers and other short-order items plus beer.

Al would go out to the parking area and take orders. Lizzy would prepare the food and Al would take it back to the customer's car. Al may have well been the first car hop but we can't verify that.

My mother, Nina James, was Al's sister. We visited Al's Inn many times.

Antelope Park

By Don "Fat Fox" Bryant

After more than 50 years of excitement during a career in sports journalism, I can't shake the memories of a rousing childhood in the depression/drought-ridden 1930s. How lucky I was to live near Antelope Park. Huck Finn had nothing on our neighborhood because we had Antelope Creek, a fine zoo, herds of buffalo and elk, a wading pool, and a giant fountain complete with a huge statue, all awaiting our arrival after school and on weekends. We also had a big pond south of Randolph School, which produced fine crawdads and a nice adjacent area for a cave.

In the spring we could build a raft and cruise down the creek, even crash over the sandstone dam, before wading out of a pool to carve our initials on the surrounding rock banks. We would venture into the greenhouse building to watch the alligators, before moving on to visit wolves, foxes and mountain lions in outdoor cages. We could also help Earl, the crippled man, who tended the large animals in the huge pen at 30th and D Street. We saw buffalo, elk and deer (they later moved to the new Pioneers Park viewing areas), and sometimes got to ride ponies. As we grew older, we would even take flashlight tours of the storm sewers that extended from Antelope Creek for countless blocks to the north, but that took real courage that Tom Sawyer never had to test.

We also had the reservoir. We loved the winter snowstorms so we could sled, ski and slide down the slopes of that wonderful playground. And what fun we had in the fall with those tough sandlot football games. There were never any parents on hand to cheer or officiate. We handled all that ourselves, and there were rousing home-and-home games between Antelope Reservoir teams and those from Bradfield and Piedmont. No helmets, shoulder pads or face masks—just fun, and many of those sandlot games produced future Lincoln High School teammates.

Suffice it to say, there was adventure and excitement aplenty in the days before World War II, rocket ships, moon shots, national football championships and, of course, television. Heck, we had crystal radios and programs like "Jack Armstrong, the All American Boy," "Don Winslow of the Navy," "Dick Tracy" and "I Love a Mystery" coming through our earphones.

'Apple Blossom Time'

By Jack McMaster

Some people remember the popularity of miniature golf before the Great Depression. My father owned the Apple Blossom Miniature Golf Course at 48th and Van Dorn Street, where McDonald's and Walgreen's are now in the Van Dorn Plaza. Before the stock market crash, people lined up to buy tickets to play. A year after the crash only sixteen people played at the beginning of the season and we had to close the course.

Sheridan Boulevard had a streetcar running down the median strip from South Street to 42nd and Calvert. I lived at 48th and Van Dorn Street and went to school at Prescott Elementary and Irving Junior High Schools. The neighbor children and I rode the streetcar to and from school. If we had spent our carfare at lunch we had to walk home.

As a prank, boys would shake the guide wire that held the trolley line for the streetcar. The trolley would come off its line and the streetcar would stop. The conductor would then have to get out and reset the trolley before he could continue on his route. The prank was most irksome to the conductor when the streetcar was on the narrow bridge at 33rd Street that went over the old Rock Island Railroad tracks. If the trolley derailed while the streetcar was on the bridge, the conductor would have to walk forward to the end of the bridge, cross under the bridge and reach the rear of the streetcar from the other side of the bridge. He would return to the cab by reversing his walking route.

The streetcar that went to College View also went north down 48th Street, then turned east toward a community called Normal at approximately 56th and South Street. An old story recounts that sometime in the early teens, the owner of the house at the northeast corner of 48th and Van Dorn Street had a grudge against one of the streetcar conductors. The homeowner greased the tracks so that the conductor was not able to stop the streetcar at the corner or slow sufficiently for a turn. When the streetcar came to the greased area, as planned, the car jumped the track, but not according to plan, the streetcar hit the perpetrator's house and moved it three feet off its foundation.

Capital Beach

By Jack Campbell

(ERA 1930–1950)

Capital Beach was a cornucopia of delights for the Lincoln citizenry. Something for everybody. Wandering the ground was a pastime for the family or couples even if they couldn't afford the 5–10 cents per event tickets or to carefully determine where to spend their limited funds.

The midway was perhaps not Disneyland, but it had great offerings for the participants. Starting with the appropriately-named Fun House, the ticket holder had unlimited use of the tumbling barrel, a series of mirrors with body-altering reflections, a slide with gunny sacks to make the descent faster and more exciting, a shifting floor walkway, and a darkened entry to set the mood.

At the end of the midway was the awesome roller coaster, Jack Rabbit. This wooden structure was imposing to look at and frightening to ride. It should have been, as it blew down one windy winter day. No wonder it felt like it was moving in several directions at once! This wonder of questionable engineering was a forerunner of the many esoteric variations found in national theme parks of today. A real thriller.

At the park entry was the unique Capital Beach Pool. This featured the only saltwater pool in the Midlands and had sand beaches. Fifty yards long and equally as wide, it was a huge expanse of aquatic pleasure. In the middle was a large wooden platform—but no diving from this. Instead were the high and low boards for the fancy divers or just for a cannonball and splash. The major-domo was Ralph Beechner and a large corps of lifeguards monitoring the many rules for safety and comfort of the pool users.

Then there was the huge roller-skating rink. It was used by groups and individuals who used the rented skates to revolve around the floor to piped-in music. Church groups, kid groups, school groups and singles or couples participating in "open skating"—skating in smooth rhythm and more than occasionally a spill and slide. Enjoyable and innocent exercise and social enjoyment.

There were various assorted rides, central among which was the merry-go-round with the traditional painted ponies, a small train on a track to appeal to young riders, sometimes a hoop toss in the arcade. These generally eroded over the years until a gradual shutdown in the late '50s or early '60s with King's Ballroom being the last bastion to fall.

Who could forget King's Ballroom? This house of joy could be the focus of several papers. During the World War II era the ballroom was the local hangout of G.I.s from the airbase. Window flaps open to the outside to offer some ventilation but also allowing the music to waft out into the midway. Also, it attracted onlookers from the outside to have a gander at the fancy dancing and listen to the bands.

The bands were superb aggregations called "territory bands." Generally from Kansas City migrating to Lincoln and King's Ballroom for month-long gigs, the bands were led by such as Snookum Russell and the fabled Jay McShann. Jay's band at the time featured a young alto sax player named Charles "Yardbird" Parker—later foreshortened to "Bird." It is probable that for the $1.00 entry fee the dancers and onlookers were hearing many other future stars, as the Kansas City jazz scene was spawning many who went on to stardom.

The G.I.s and locals came to dance, listen and imbibe a little strong liquid (if it could be found in those days of limited availability). It was "bring your own bottle" as Lincoln had a dry liquor policy with set-ups served by the waitresses. The combination of varied audience and music, which raised the emotional level and drink, encouraged an occasional fight, all part of the entertainment.

When things settled down after the war, King's refurbished and cleaned up their act and the venue. An occasional "big band" was booked, but generally these played the larger crosstown Turnpike Ballroom. King's more often featured the "sweet bands" of the area, termed by the band followers as the "Mickey Mouse" bands, Wayne King being the head "mouse."

As the nation reverted to a more normal existence, the operators of the ballroom changed the marketing focus. Heavily promoted was "College Night at King's." Friday night became an event to attend. Mostly cokes and popcorn and slow dancing. The room even included the traditional revolving mirrored ceiling fixture—with the interplay of sparkling lights on the room as the band closed the evening playing "Goodnight Sweetheart."

This postcard aerial view of Capital Beach was taken in the 1940s and is looking to the northeast.

11

Chicken Pot Pie and Other Lincoln Memories

By Kathryn Reed

When I arrived in Lincoln in September 1926, to enroll as a freshman at the University of Nebraska, Lincoln was a city of approximately 60,000. This was a large city to me, having come from a rural community in South Dakota with my hometown having a population of some 1,200 or 1,300. The stores I remember especially in Lincoln were Miller & Paine and Hovland Swanson on O Street, and a large store at 12th & N Streets called Herpolsheimers. My memory of Herpolsheimers is of a noisy and very noticeable overhead system with channels through which tubes were directed, sending money to a central office. My first impression of Miller & Paine was when a new friend, who had been in Lincoln several times before, took me to a "very special place to eat"— Miller & Paine tea room, and told me to order a chicken pie and cinnamon rolls. I did exactly as she told me, and that became a favorite lunch for me, as it was for many other people. Miller's cinnamon rolls were well known far and wide.

The process of registering at the University took place in the Coliseum. The tuition in those years was $1.50 per credit hour in the College of Business Administration, where I had decided to enroll, plus a small out-of-state fee. I believe tuition is now some $92 per credit hour, and out-of-state tuition is $250 per credit hour!

There were few girls in Bus Ad College at that time and I do not remember anyone ever suggesting that a girl could become a certified public accountant. Times have changed. Now there are names of many young women on the rolls of new CPAs. The total enrollment in 1926 was 11,718, which included the Medical School in Omaha and the Extension Division. The enrollment on the Lincoln campus alone in the year 2000 was some 22,000.

There were no dormitories on the campus at that time, so out-of-town students lived either at a rooming house or in a sorority or fraternity house. University life in the late '20s was fun, just as it is today. We stood in line in September to get good tickets for our group for football games, we danced at hour dances, spring parties at the Cornhusker or Lincoln Hotel ballrooms, went to Antelope Park in the spring and fall to dance, and for a big "Ball" to the Coliseum. There was no television then, we had radio (it was still rather new), and I remember one day in April 1927 when word came of Charles Lindbergh's non-stop flight to Europe. Lindbergh had done some training in Lincoln. One afternoon I went with several other girls to a flying field south of Lincoln. Four of us (for a fee of $1.00 each) took a short (very short) ride in a little open plane. We asked the pilot to do some stunts. He did not do that. The next time I was on a plane I was flying to Europe.

There were few cars driven by students in those days, so parking was not a problem, we walked. I can remember only two cars owned by girls who lived in my sorority house. One of these girls had a father in the automobile business. We walked to church at St. Paul's downtown, or took the streetcar, which ran along the brick pavement, to First Plymouth, Westminster, or other churches.

We went to the Coliseum to hear the opera *Aida* or to see dancers from the Bolshoi, even though the seating and acoustics were far from perfect. Later we could drive to Omaha to see Helen Hayes in *Victoria Regina*, or Mary Martin in *Annie Get Your Gun* and others. Today we have the beautiful Lied Center here in Lincoln, with its great auditorium and sound system, which brings many wonderful programs to Lincoln.

With graduation, it was time to find a job. I went to work in an accounting office and was fortunate to have work all throughout the 1930s when times were hard and thousands of people were jobless. My work in the in the accounting office was in the secretarial department, even though I had earned high grades in accounting in college. In time I would have small assignments in accounting. As I said before, girls were not supposed to be accountants.

The equipment in an office at that time was very simple. There were no computers, only adding machines and manually-operated typewriters, some with wide carriages, which were heavy to operate. By the end of the '30s there were small calculators on many desks (it was pure magic that the machine could multiply and divide) and there was some talk in our office of buying a copy machine which had come on the market, thus eliminating the use of carbon paper and the great concern that each copy was legible.

I married Eugene C. Reed, a Nebraskan, who had received a degree from Nebraska in 1923 and had gone to southern Mexico, then to Venezuela, to work as a petroleum geologist, and eventually to become chief exploration geologist for Lago Petroleum (later purchased by Standard of Indiana). They found oil, lots of it, but the thought of an advanced degree eventually brought him back to Nebraska and the Conservation and Survey Division of the University, where he worked in the development of Nebraska's natural resources, particularly in the fields of oil and water.

The discovery of oil in southeast Nebraska, near Falls City, came in 1939. Ten years later oil was discovered near Sidney, and still ten years later wells around McCook began pumping. Some oil is still produced in these areas.

The work of the Conservation and Survey Division in the field of water and its availability is well known in Nebraska and far afield. The test drilling program and other research in that office enables the citizens of Nebraska to receive valuable information about this resource. The knowledge of the location of a well supplying drinking water for a family or for a business is invaluable. An overhead sprinkling system operating in a field of corn on a hot summer day in Nebraska is a beautiful sight, and is a reminder of this great resource, and the resourcefulness of its citizens.

Lincoln has continued to grow and prosper since I first saw it, and it is a wonderful city in which to live. There have been many fine men and women who have worked to keep it that way, and there will be others who will continue to do the same. One may travel to far-off places, but the best part of a trip is to be headed home to see the capitol dome in the distance and know we are coming home to Lincoln.

Curb-Hopping

By Dick Marshall

Every time I tried to make an extra buck back in the mid-'30s I usually turned to a curb-hop job, the one most likely job available for a teenager. Lincoln had a number of drive-in establishments and I worked at several over a period of a few years. My earliest serious job was running a root beer stand located at Holdrege Street and Idylwild Drive. The stand sat on an old man's property, Tilman's Books and Sundries. A mug of root beer was 5¢ and my pay 1¢ per mug sold. Most afternoons would net me anywhere from 15¢ to 50¢—an occasional tip "swelling" the total (the postman was a steady customer). Flies were a menace, so much of my time was spent perfecting a freehand catch-and-destroy technique—not a popular maintenance routine with the Health Department, but I apparently didn't think to ask the boss for a fly swatter.

I moved up to better conditions at Stover's Candy Store and Soda Fountain just off O Street. They provided fountain and curb service and a job for me, for part of one summer, with better pay and nighttime work only. One night after closing, a fellow employee, and good pal, suggested we ride our bikes to Camp Strader in Crete—23 miles. We pumped all night on gravel roads, arriving at dawn. A return trip was out of the question, but we were lucky enough to have a camp counselor loan us a couple of cots to sack out on. My pal's mom drove down from Lincoln to retrieve us. The friend was Don Hilgert, later a World War II pilot and casualty in North Africa.

One summer job was at Cliff Alvord's Pharmacy and drive-in at 33rd and A Street, but the curb-hopping memory that sticks with me most is during the year 1939 when I ran malts, shakes, sodas, cones, etc., at the Iceberg, on the corner of 14th and N Street. The facade was, as many Lincolnites will remember, in the shape of an iceberg. I received my social security card that year and at 10¢ an hour, 40 hours a week, got a check every Saturday for $3.96 after deductions, enough for an occasional movie date or two.

The Dutch Wind Mill at 58th and O and the Mug at 33rd and O escaped my service but had my patronage for many years. Ditto for Harley Drug, that famous pharmacy and soda fountain across the street from Golds. Harleys, at 11th and 'O,' was part of the business center of downtown Lincoln for many years, and a highly-esteemed and long-lasting operation for four generations. My father had his dental office on the second floor, over the drug store, for several years. It was a great spot for viewing parades and activities on O Street when I was a young kid living with the family in rooms next to my dad's office. Many will remember Nick the cop, who was a regular fixture patrolling the street and a good friend to the kids. Movie houses like the Strand, Colonial, Rialto, Lincoln, Orpheum and Stuart, along with the YMCA, occupied much of my leisure time—lots of good westerns and serials. While money was short in those years, I've always agreed with an old friend when he said again and again, "We were really lucky to have all the carefree times."

Drug Stores and Saloons

By Jerry Mapes

In researching the history of the drug store in Lincoln, a lot of memories have been resurrected and refreshed. A lot of opinions have been expressed as to which drug store was the most interesting or the most memorable.

One indisputable fact about this research is that the Harley Drug was the first such establishment to grace the main street of Lincoln. In fact, J. H. Harley and his descendants occupied the southeast corner or 11th and O Street from 1874 until approximately 1950. Harley Drug underwent several facelifts during this period but it remained in that location. According to Harold Ledford, a long-time Lincoln citizen and real estate developer, the Rehlaender Drug started on O Street on the side between 11th and 12th approximately nine months later. Mr. Ledford's late wife's grandfather was the proprietor of this fledgling business.

It was several years before drug stores began to proliferate in Lincoln and its suburbs. Another apothecary-type drug store was O. D. Rector who did business on the northeast corner of 14th and O Street. In about 1912, Walter Scott became the owner, and this was documented in the Lincoln newspaper as follows: "By a sale made late yesterday afternoon, W. P. Scott who has been engaged with O. D. Rector in the management of the Owl Pharmacy at 14th and O Street for the past three years, becomes sole owner and proprietor of the store."

According to Mrs. Paul Rodwell, Lincoln resident, her father, Mr. Scott, then located in the Owl Drug on the southeast corner of 14th and P Street where the Wooden Nickel is presently situated. Mr. Scott continued this location until about 1947 when the Diamond Bar and Grill moved there from 13th and P Street.

Another pioneer in the drug store business was R. E. Fenton. According to Dave Fenton, son of the long-time druggist, and Lincoln resident, Fenton opened a store at 19th and O Street in 1918. In 1925, he opened a store in the southeast corner of 17th and South and later at 33rd and A Street and 12th and N Street. About 1927, Mr. Fenton sold the store at 11th and South to Guy Butler. Harold Wagey from Crete joined the firm and the store became Butler-Wagey and was the forerunner of the Wagey Drug Store chain, which dominated the drug store market for several years.

Other prominent drug stores of the era spanning the first part of the twentieth century was landmarks such as Baker Drug in Havelock, Barth Drug in downtown Lincoln, Boydens at 13th and P, Gulley Drug in the old Cornhusker Hotel, Bradfield at about 29th and South and Rupperts at 13th and N.

Van Dorn Drug, owned and operated by Claude Adderson, was a unique store also. "Andy" was famous for his "Victory Sundaes," a special concoction of vanilla and chocolate ice cream, chocolate and marshmallow syrup and the piece de resistance—malt powder sprinkled over the whole mess. Curb service was offered as well as some sage "Andy-isms." To anyone growing up in southeast Lincoln during the thirties and forties, Bradfield Drug was very special. Teenagers and younger, gathered every evening both inside and outside Bradfield to plot their evening's forays. Bradfield was definitely the social mecca.

Murphy Drug on the northwest corner of 27th and O was a full-service drugstore according to former Lincolnite Carreton Flynn of Novato, California. "It was a popular stop for kids coming home from Lincoln High School and a great hot chocolate stop in the winter."

Historical taverns and saloons of Lincoln past

In attempting to document the first taverns in Lincoln our reliance on the old city directories betrayed us initially. Nothing could be found listed in the early years of Lincoln under bars, beer, whiskey or tavern. It was only after a knowledgeable librarian suggested "saloons" that our searching came to fruition.

There were about eight saloons in the city of Lincoln in 1876. They were for the most part gathered between 9th and 11th streets, N to P. The prominent names in the business at that time were L. Hahn, R. N. Hodskin, August Hoppe, Simon Kelley, Bill McLaughlin, George Mohrentecher and a tavern owned by Neubauer and Fischer.

By the year 1900 there were 33 saloons and again they were primarily located in that general area. From 1900 until Prohibition a couple of saloons that stood out from the rest were The Two Johns Saloon at 915 O Street and the Little Gold Dust Saloon at 125 North 11th.

The Two Johns Saloon was a popular establishment, handsomely fitted in solid oak and resplendent with fine large mirrors and cut glass. The name was derived from the owners John Wittorff and John Rosenstock as opposed to the possibility of "his and her" plumbing, which naturally didn't come until much later. The Two Johns prided themselves on keeping the finest brands and qualities of imported and domestic wines, liquors, brandies, sherry, mineral waters, imported and domestic cigars etc. ... they were both natives of Germany as so many early entrepreneurs were.

The Little Gold Dust Saloon under the proprietorship of Emil Dahl was originally at 125 North 11th St. in the early part of the 20th century before Prohibition and survived into the year 1950 when it was located at 901 O St.

Another interesting bit of the history of tippling in Lincoln was given to us by Marie Guest and Jean Stauffer, the daughters of Adolph Hock Sr. Mr. Hock came to Lincoln from Russia in 1910, started in the shoe repair business and later with his son, Adolph Hock, Jr., owned and operated the Bismark Tavern at 1330 O Street in the year 1935.

The Bismark was later sold to the Dinges family and moved to the north side of O Street between 15th and 16th. The blue ribbon for longevity in the business by one family would probably go to the Jelsma family who have operated the Royal Grove tavern for about 50 years. Other family names that were prominent in the business through the years were the Easleys, Abbie and Heinie Klein of the old Harmony Bar, Vane and Lee Franks, Francis Ellsworth, the Grasmicks, Leo and Bud Kelly, John Schwindt, Studnickas, Stumbaughs, Weilers, etc. etc. The Little Bohemia at 27th and Cornhusker also qualifies for its 50-year pin.

I have more than a passing interest in this bit of history because of his involvement in the old Diamond Bar and Grill at 14th and P St. This tavern which was rather famous or infamous with the college crowd, had its inception in the late 1940s at 13th and P. Mr. Frank Piccolo, Sr., was the proprietor. Mr. Piccolo sold it to Alfred Stroh who moved it to 14th and P Streets and in approximately 1952, I owned it until 1955, selling to bill Blockwitz who in turn sold to Reuben Worster. "Red," as he is affectionately known in the trade, later purchased the Little Bohemia location and ultimately the Tam O Shanter at 24th and O Street.

Other taverns that could be found flourishing in 1940 were the Brass Rail at 1436 O Street, the Bismark at 133 O Street, the Lodge at 2135 O Street, the Gold Dust at 901 O, Grasmicks at 1119 P, the Hurdle and Halter in the old Lincoln Hotel, John Schwindt at 930 P Street, Ways Inn west Lincoln and Wilhelm's tavern at 1412 O.

As far as a tavern with a personality, nobody can come up with an entry like Lebsack's. The reception one got at Lebsack's might be sour, but it was definitely a reception. Many uninitiated made the mistake of asking the Lebsack boys for coffee, water or some other potable unavailable in this unique place. You may have heard, "If you want a cup of coffee, go to a restaurant." This kind of answer would be appropriate only if the Lebsacks were in a good mood ... otherwise, you could expect anything. Hank, John and Eddie held forth for many years down by the train depot and later at 12th and P Street. They dispensed beer, great chili and beef sandwiches along with assorted grunts and epithets. The beer came by hand to the bar or booth and the sandwiches were usually nestled in Hank, John, or Eddie's armpits (wrapped in waxed paper, of course).

Bear in mind that all of these aforementioned taverns had to meet expenses and payroll through the sale of 10¢ glasses of beer. Liquor by the drink, of course, did not come onto the scene until the '60s and at the end of prohibition, all Lincoln taverns could serve only beer. Tapping in the neighborhood of 100 half-barrels (16 gallons) of beer was usually the mark of a successful tavern.

Eating Out in the '30s and '40s

By Frances Amen

Having been a Lincoln resident all my life, I occasionally like to reminisce a bit about some of the charming little restaurants and popular eating places in the city during the 1930s and 1940s. Some were rather obscure—perhaps few people even knew about their existence. Nevertheless, for the depression era, they provided a little charm and atmosphere on the one hand and just plain good eating on the other.

Few Lincolnites probably remember Oak Hall Tea Room that was located in the old F.M. Hall residence on the northeast corner of 11th and D Streets. Mrs. Lulu Kennard Holden, who was a daughter of the Thomas P. Kennard family that, in earlier years, had occupied the Kennard House at 1627 H Street, managed it in 1931. She served dainty luncheons and teas for society ladies who enjoyed the privacy and exclusive atmosphere of its location.

Another small dining room in the late thirties was Edith's Tea Room at 1231 F Street. It was neat and cheerful and away from the downtown area. She served "Good Home Foods at Moderate Prices."

In the downtown area around 1942–1944, in a graystone building at 345 South 14th Street, was Mauel's Bake Shop. It was managed by Mrs. Julia B. Mauel who baked delicious breads and rolls, and served lunches and dinners in a small apartment-size space. It was especially convenient for business and career women who were employed downtown.

Town Talk Bakery and Luncheonette was tucked in an old building next to Hardy's furniture store at 1310 O Street. A new building formerly housed by the J. P. Penney Company now occupies that space. There were only a few booths but they served such good homemade soups and bakery goodies. It was a handy place to get a quick snack right after work, especially if you planned to go to a movie before 6:00 p.m. in order to get in for the matinee price.

Colonial Cup Tea Room was a more elegant place to dine in the 1950s. It was located in a stately white house at the corner of 56th and Cotner. I remember the lovely see-through glass top dining table and fresh flower bouquets. Their pastries and rolls were also baked in their own kitchen. It was truly a pleasant place to take a guest.

The charm of lovely table settings and soft music graced the service at Beaumont's Dining Room at 226 South 12th Street, the block later occupied by Cengas and a parking building. They served lunch and dinner specialties from 1936 to 1940. It was also convenient to the downtown business area.

Last but not least, the Lincoln business men's favorite stop for breakfast, lunch and snacks was Bob's Coffee Shop which was located in an old building on the southwest corner of 14th and O Streets. It was popular from 1932–1942 and operated by Robert H. Burns. I presume many sports and political issues were discussed over several cups of 5¢ coffee.

There were others too, which indicate that the food service industry has always been an important part of Lincoln's economic history.

Famous Friends and the Y

By Larry Jones

When you grew up in Lincoln, Nebraska certain opportunities just came your way. Oh yeah ... the older kids said there was nothing to do, they roll up the streets at nine o'clock and on Sunday after church they take the car for a drive. How lucky we were.

Mother took us to the YWCA ... yes, when you were not yet nine years old boys went with the family to learn to swim at the YW and lots of times we would stay and eat our evening meal at the YW cafeteria. I remember so well that the lights had such a glow from all the chlorine in my eyes.

Happy days at age nine because I could join the Young Men's Christian Association, which was then at the current location of the Douglas 3 Theatre. A building old before its time with big windows on the upper floors where you could hang out and drop paper cups of water on unsuspecting passers-by. The daylight basement was remodeled into a boys club and Chile Armstrong, a pure example of wholesomeness, was the director. He was more like Charles Atlas or Jack Armstrong that we read about in the comics with his muscles bulging from his tee shirt. Chile was talented at demonstrating boxing, tumbling on mats, pommel horse, rings and parallel bars, and of course basketball and swimming. We also had lessons in crafts, woodshop and braiding those plastic laces into all sorts of shapes. We had culture also with books to read, records and films.

During the week the Y was a bus ride downtown and a place to hang out after school ... and a chance to get a chili dog near the Varsity Theatre while waiting for the South 37th Street bus. Saturday was a full day of fun at the Y and sometimes a hamburger at the lunch counter on the first floor.

I remember a particular day after school at the Y, I was sawing a board on the 8" table saw and working on a Christmas present for my folks. Guys were horsing around throwing sawdust and yelling and I made the grave mistake of looking up when someone shouted. Immediately I felt something wet and warm on my face and then I realized I had sawed the board and my right thumb. Quicker than an Indian Tom Tom message, Ted was there calming me, turning off the saw and carrying me to the lobby where he elevated my feet and had my hand wrapped in a cold towel. I didn't feel bad, but the oh's and oh my gods from the crowd convinced me that I was in trouble. It was winter and Ted picked me up and carried me across the street to the Stuart Building, where the Lincoln Clinic was located. More comments ensued in the elevator and I was getting worried. I was sweating and it was winter. Medical attention was at hand and that signal you get when the white coats and ether smell are near triggered that it was going to hurt ... and it did! Ted was nearby on the phone to mother who recalled my screams coming over the telephone. I was sure they gave me drugs but when the thumbnail came off with a pair of pliers I knew the Nazis had me and I was undergoing torture.

Reassuring Ted was there mopping my brow and helping hold me down and convincing me I was OK. Some stitches and some TLC and I was in Ted's car being taken home to my waiting parents concerned about my welfare. Ted told them the whole story and the were very grateful for his caring for me and I remember father saying, "please tell me your name again" ... "Ted Sorensen, sir ... I am a student at the University and work at the Y part time."

Lincoln, Nebraska, the Holy City with 110 churches give or take a few, produced some pretty famous people with words that reached around the world, for Ted Sorensen was President John Kennedy's speech writer and now an elder statesman living in Washington.

Growing up in Lincoln has been an opportunity. I don't remember what kind of car Ted drove, or what he wore, or if he had any money, but I sure remember what he did for me. I predict that 50 years from now it won't make any difference what kind of car you drive, what your bank account is, how you dress, or what your handicap is, the difference will be what you did for a child.

From the Belmont Perspective

By Pat (Hamer) Kitchen

We lived in Belmont ... my brother and I and our friends used to walk across 14th Street down to Oak Creek and the east side of the bridge to ice skate, the banks of the creek were so tall they broke the freezing wind and it was so warm we could take our jackets off and skate like it was inside.

Also, do you remember the Circle Drive Inn? I can't remember exactly where it was ... seems like about 44th or 45th and O Street. I just remember they had footlong hotdogs with chili and a dill pickle slice on each end ... oh my gosh—I can still taste them.

I remember the Yum Yum Hut, they served a loose meat sandwich that had really thinly sliced onion on it with mustard, sort of the forerunner of the Tastee Inn ... speaking of which, our Dad would load us in the car on Saturday (there were 7 children in our family) and we would drive to the Tastee Inn on 13th and Q to have the Tastee Special which was a tastee sandwich, fries and a shake for 49¢ ... boy that was special.

When I got a little older my oldest sister would take me down to Miller and Paine for the chicken pot pie and cinnamon rolls, the pot pie was 45¢ then. When I got a little older and worked downtown for two doctors I ate my lunch there everyday and had the same thing everyday. The pot pie, cinnamon rolls and iced tea, I never got tired of them!

I remember driving downtown with the family in our '35 Chevy and parking on O Street to watch all the shoppers, that's all we did—just watched. How funny.

I remember when World War II ended there was a siren that sounded from out at the airbase and I ran and got my Dad and he said "the war is over," and we all jumped in the car and went downtown to a traffic jam on O Street ... with confetti, and screaming and whistles and horns honking, it still gives me a chill to think about it.

My dad ran a Phillips 66 station on the corner of 14th and Cornhusker. Mother told lots of stories about how people didn't have money so they purchased their gasoline with fresh farm eggs, warm baked bread, milk and butter, she said we ate very well in hard times. When it came time to fill the gasoline tanks it was very hard for Dad to scrape together the $150 or $200 he needed to pay for it. She said no one felt poor, we were all in the same boat.

Growing Up In Lincoln—Pre World War II

By Tom Harley

I was born August 1, 1929. The stock market fell in October of that year, so I guess it was a bad omen for my future stock market trades. I lived with my older brother, Jim, and my parents, Burks and Zella, at 2310 Smith Street. The one thing that strikes me mostly of the thirties was how hot it was in the summer. We would take our mattresses down to the basement to sleep by a fan. I remember listening to the radio and at midnight the announcer said it was 101 degrees. Along with the heat, came the dust storms. Big black clouds, from the west, would just roll over us. The dust would seep through all the doors and windows, in spite of putting wet towels down around them.

All was not bad though. Empty lots were there for baseball games, football games and most of all digging caves. The biggest one was on the corner of Sheridan Blvd., between Sewell and Park. Must have been ten rooms, connected by tunnels. Twenty or thirty kids worked on that, of course when it rained we had a foot of water in there and lots of mud.

We always looked forward to winter. Ice skating on the Lake Street Lake, Oak Creek Lake and the lakes at the Lincoln Country Club, which are still there on holes 5 and 14. That was also a good time to make money shoveling snow; 50¢ for walks, $1.00 for walks and driveways. No gas blowers then. On a good day we could make one or two dollars. It doesn't sound like a lot, but bus rides were 5¢, and movies 10¢. For a quarter we could see a double feature, serial, cartoons, news, a bag of popcorn and a soda. But to do that we would have to walk at least one way, 3 miles, to save 5¢. Sledding was done at Pioneers Park by the Indian and down Smith Street. We hated it when the city put ashes on the street so cars could get up the hill.

The Lincoln YMCA had a summer camp in Crete, Nebraska, called Camp Strader, on the Blue River. It was really more of a dark brown, but that didn't matter. What a great spot to get away. We lived in eight-boy cabins, seven boys and a counselor. Three meals a day at a cost of $1 per day. They had a 25-yard pool with three diving boards, two low and one high. It was there that I learned to swim. They also had track, tennis, archery, riflery, crafts and canoeing up and down the Blue River in 10 to 14 man canoes. It was great fun. By the time we had campfire at night with stories and songs, it was not difficult to get a good night sleep.

In 1939, things were heating up in Europe and I started to work at my dad's store, the Harley Drug Company, at 11th and O Street. The pay was 10¢ per hour, stocking shelves, marking merchandise and running errands. Later on I delivered prescriptions, by bicycle all over Lincoln. Havelock was a killer trip; usually I'd make that trip once a week. These were good times, even though a recession was on, but everyone was kind of in the same boat. I joined the Boy Scouts, Troop 2. We met at St. Mathews Church, on 24th and Sewell. Mr. Folsom was our scoutmaster and it became a very large group. It was on a Sunday morning, December 7, 1941, that my brother and I were riding Arnott Folsom's horses on a farm west of the penitentiary that we heard of Pearl Harbor. The days of our innocence were over.

World War Two

Rationing everything; gas, tires, food, sugar, meat. You name it, it was rationed. Paper drives, aluminum, metal of all kind drives. To get a tube of toothpaste (made of tin) you had to turn in your empty one. We still went camping, by bike, to Camp Minis Kuya out west, between Gooch's Mill and Pioneer's Park, on the Salt Creek. Hiking out south on 24th Street, the pavement stopped on the south side of the Lincoln Country Club and was gravel from there on south. At triple trestle was Beal's Slough (27th Street and Highway 2), a heavily wooded area where you could spend all day just "messin" around.

In January 1945 our family moved to 2035 B Street, to be closer to our grandparents. My brother joined the Navy, and I went to Lincoln High. Since all of the younger pharmacists were drafted I was working weekends and vacations at the Harley Drug Company, now waiting on customers, running the cash register and any heavy lifting. Winter of course, I shoveled the walks at 11th and O, the whole corner. The Harley Drug had a soda fountain, but my dad never trusted me to be a soda jerk. The soda fountain closed shortly after that, never to open again. High school was great. Latin and English were bummers, but the athletics were what it was all about. The Yum Yum Hut (28th and O) and the Mug (33rd and O) were high school hangouts. In the summer of 1945 the war was over. I graduated from LHS in 1947 and entered the University of Nebraska Lincoln that fall.

A few lasting memories of Lincoln. The parades down O Street for almost any occasion, especially when the circus came to town. Christmas time was shopping up and down O Street. When the sidewalks were jammed with people, the one-cent sale at the Harley Drug, the Corn Popper across from the YWCA, Sunday night dances at St. Mathews Church (always the first dance was Star Dust). Capital Beach with the salt water pool, fun house with the long wooden slide and the "platter," roller-skating, the octopus and the arcade. The knothole section at the NU football games and the Lincoln Air Force Wings basketball team with Goose Tatum. I saw them play and beat the Harlem Globe Trotters in the old NU coliseum. And, last but not least, the final closing of the Harley Drug on January 1, 1951.

It was a great life.

Looking east on O Street about 1939, Harley Drug Store is visible on the right at the corner of 11th and O Streets. *Photo courtesy Nebraska State Historical Society.*

Growing Up in the '30s

By R. C. Guenzel

During the '30s, we measured time not by the ordinary calendar, but by BDL and ADL, standing for Before Driver's License and After Driver's License.

Before Driver's License, our lives were limited by transportation furnished either by the city in the form of busses or trolley cars, or by parents. Attending Irving Junior High School, we customarily took the bus downtown or, in the winter, hooked a ride on the back of the bus holding on to the bumper and sliding on our feet down to the lake at 14th & Lake Streets. There we customarily, in the winter, played hockey. On weekends we played hockey either at the lake at Lincoln Country Club or at the Boy Scout Camp which was then located at about 2nd & Van Dorn Streets.

Weather made very little difference to us at our then ages. We would often spend Saturday night at the camp in lean-tos, with one totally open side. If cold enough, we played hockey on the creek that came through it.

During this period of time, the boys became interested in girls, and girls in boys. However, without a car, dating would be accomplished on roller skates. Frequently, we would all roller skate downtown and go to the movies.

We did not go with the same girl every week, but, generally, we went with the same group of girls and boys.

When we reached 16 and the glorious license arrived, our activities changed substantially. As I think back on it, we did terrible things. Our ordinary activity was what we called "chase." This meant one car starting out and the second car trying not to be lost by it. This led to traveling at high speed on the streets and alleys and, not infrequently, we would use driveways that would end up in alleys as entrances or exits. There were few police and so very few of us ever received any traffic tickets. Unbelievably, now, accidents were almost unknown.

Only one of us in our group had a car, and this was Sterling Mutz, who owned an old Packard touring car which was driven with the top down, generally. This was a large car with so much room in the back seat that two couples could dance on the floor between the front and back seats. Everyone would chip in for gasoline, as it used quite a bit, but at 25¢ a gallon, this did not create much of a problem.

One visible evidence of our activities continues to exist today. On the south side of Auld Pavilion there are, even now, four concrete structures, two on each side of the entrance to the parking lot, with space between the two. This space is now blocked but it was open when we were engaging in these activities and one could drive through it at a high rate of speed if one did not worry about scraping the side of the car. This was not done in the summer, however, because dances were held on the weekends in the Pavilion. One would buy tickets for the dance for each set, which would be several songs long. As these tickets were, according to my recollection, only 10¢, you could spend quite a bit of time and not much money.

H Street Tales

By Ted J. Forke

From the age of seven, my childhood was spent around 38th and H where my mother, brother, Don and I moved into a new house early in 1941, our Dad had died in 1936.

At that time H Street between 37th and 40th was just being developed. Randolph Street to the South and J Street to the north were both established, older neighborhoods, but for some reason H Street didn't begin to build up until the early 1940s. There were still a number of vacant lots that made for great tree climbing, BB gun shooting, etc.

One of the Randolph neighbors had a grocery store in his garage, and there was Shermans Grocery (Hyman and Rosalie) at 40th & Randolph.

There was a small farm on the south side of Randolph with a few cows and a bunch of chickens. We would cut through the farm on our way to Randolph school. The area to the east of Randolph School was a swamp, now called wetland. It was eventually drained, filled and became one of the "Brownbuilt" housing developments.

For Junior High, Irving made a pretty long bike ride everyday but was the only way to get there. I walked to Lincoln High School because bikes weren't cool in high school. We spent a lot of time on our bikes in Antelope Park and at the Rock Island Depot on O Street when the coal-fired locomotives were still coming through town. I remember riding out North 48th to Arrow Airport after the war. Don and I spent several thousand hours in airplanes together when we were in business with Forke Brothers Auctioneers, with our cousins Avery and Dean.

The Yum Yum Hut and the Mug were favorite spots. Later it was Tastee Inn and Ken Eddy's that were hot. When we really wanted to "put on the dog" we would motor out to Emerald to the Lone Oak, a straw bale building that appears now to be a junkyard.

The H Street experience lasted from 1941 'til 1953 when I was drafted at the end of the Korean War, 12 years that seemed to last forever. The 48 years since have gone quickly and get more rapid every year.

The Randolph School rhythm band is shown about 1929 complete with a rather professional leader, probably Dale Babcock. *Photo courtesy Virginia Sharpnack Dzerk.*

Just a 17-Mile Walk to Work

By Walt Meier, Jr.

The Meier family has lived in Lincoln since November 1869. My great grandfather, Francis William Meier, made his home in Lincoln above his shoe shop, on the southeast corner of 10th and O Street. He moved his wife and five children on to an 80 acre homestead in 1871. He kept his shoe shop, and every Saturday he would walk out 17 miles to the homestead, 10 miles south on 14th and 7 miles west. He would walk back early Monday.

My father, Walter senior, was born in 1910, and was raised at 32nd and P Street. In the teens and '20s, kids were just as ornery as now. He told of soaping the trolley car tracks on O Street, east of 33rd Street, as the trolley came up the hill from Wyuka Cemetery. The boys (mostly Walt and his brother, Frank) also tied a rope between trees, derailing the trolley arm. Up to the late '20s only the more expensive autos had bumpers. On Sunday, the kids would rush from church to the hill on the northwest corner of 33rd and O Street, to watch the Sunday drivers crash. There were no traffic controls yet. One incident involved a man in a Model T, who was run into by a Buick. The Model

T driver screamed, "If you didn't plan on running into me, why do you have bumpers on your car?"

In 1925, my grandfather, Otto, and great uncle Henery, bought a touring car. Neither could drive, but Uncle Henery seemed the better prospect. Grandpa insisted that he be given a chance. He managed to get the car moving, but couldn't stop it, so he continued driving around the block till the car ran out of gas.

Lebsack's Tavern

By Jim Haberlan

Some places, like some people, should last forever. But they never do. Some last longer than others, but even those don't last long enough. Then maybe we last too long and outlive the best, and then only live with the memories.

Lebsack's Tavern and Parker's Steakhouse are two places that should still be operating. Why aren't they? What went wrong causing them to both quit operating? Did we stop serving them as customers the way they used to serve us? I'm sure there are reasons, but who cares, they just don't exist anymore and those of us lucky enough to have known the individual owners and thankful for the great food they served, miss those times.

"Hi, John, give me a bowl of chili, a little extra grease, beef cheese onion on dark."

That's all you had to say.

"Hi, guys. What do you want to drink?"

"A draw."

It didn't take long to order at Lebsack's. John took the orders and served the food. He didn't give you a speech he had just learned from the staff meeting, about how the chili was made or how they cooked the beef. The most he said was "Hi," and then, if you paid attention, you would notice he was usually looking out the front windows on P Street while you were ordering. John could write his abbreviations of your order on the small pad without looking at it. The same pants, same shirt, same shoes, same carpenters nail pouch, to carry the soup crackers, the same everything every day, always clean but they always looked the same. He didn't believe he needed to chat or be overly friendly with the customers. John probably figured you came to Lebsack's because you wanted to, his only function was to take your food order and give it to Hank, and give the drink order to Ed, both guys were his brothers. God, wouldn't that be welcome today. None of the bullshit about how the chef adds a little of this, a little of that, gently seared to seal in the flavor and just a touch of Madeira wine to add to the velvet taste. John's honesty was beautiful, he didn't know how Hank cooked the chili; he couldn't give the recipe because he didn't know it. He didn't know what kind of beef they served on the sandwiches because he didn't cook it. It also appeared that the three brothers, either didn't like each other, or they just didn't spend time talking to each other. John may have been the only waiter, or waitress in Lincoln, that never spent time standing at the cash register having a conversation with the bartender.

I saw John smile only a few times, but never when Hank Cech would start yelling when he entered the bar. "Hey, the place down the street is called the Loafenstien, they should call this place the loafing brothers." Everyone in the place would laugh except the brothers and then he would yell at John that he wanted "a piece of cherry pie a la mode." John would then come to the table, without saying a word, and take everybody's order, leaving Cech 'til last. Then John would say, "If you want a piece of pie why don't you go to Miller and Paine's Tea Room and eat with the rest of the girls?" But Hank's food would be served the same as everyone else's. If you wanted some extra crackers, that had been individually packed and stapled in little wax paper sacks, John would reach in his carpenter apron and throw one, from whereever he was standing. Where does that happen today, and wouldn't it be great?

Hank made the chili, bean soup, cooked the beef, whatever kind it was, for hours and hours, until all of the tallow (fat) was cooked out of it. He would then slice the meat with an electric slicer, just thick enough not to fall apart when he put in the pan of hot au jus. They served brick and American cheese, and Braunschweiger and hard salami were the other choices for sandwiches.

Every item served was fresh, because Lebsack's served a lot of each item everyday, not like the other menus today that have several pages of sandwiches. Some of these sandwiches are only served, maybe every third day, at the most. It is impossible for these ingredients to be fresh. At Leb's which was the name used by the regulars, he hand cut only the meat that he thought would sell that day, if he ran out of meat you waited until he cut more.

It was a treat to watch Hank serve up a bowl of chili by the way he handled the soup ladle as he put the last touch of oil on top of the chili. You could tell he was proud of his chili and bean soup. Both soups were made from scratch, nothing Leb's served was frozen or canned. You didn't need to send word to the chef that the sandwiches and soups were good; Hank knew it was good, and if you didn't like it, then that was your problem, because Hank was not going to change anything. He was going to continue using his service fork to pick up each piece of beef out of the au jus and lay them on the bread, the same way he had done it for over 50 years. No one got a larger or smaller helping than the other person, and when a sandwich called for cheese, he went to the refrigerator, opened a wrapper of cheese, took out one piece of cheese, closed the package and put it back in the refrigerator. If the next sandwich called for the same, he did the same thing all over. Pretty simple.

Lebsack's did not exist to impress their customers with anything but good tasty food prepared the way they knew it would taste good and the only way they knew how. From Supreme Court judges to the most common man or woman, all were welcome as long as they behaved themselves, even Henry Cech. Then John died, then Hank, then Eddy and the Lebsacks were gone and no one picked up where they left off. The Lebsacks never thought of franchising their business, that would have been too impersonal, and how would you train anyone to be like them, they were as much a part of the taste as the food itself.

When you sat at the bar, you didn't bother to tell Eddy your problem, he didn't care and he wasn't interested in serving you another drink just to get you to stay around. He served you the drink you asked for, as long as it wasn't a fancy cocktail. Ed never learned to mix the fancy stuff, and he wasn't going to change. "They serve those martinis and Manhattans across the street." Eddy's specialty was getting the same size head on each glass of beer he drew. He cared about that. When was the last time you saw a bartender that cared about a little thing like that?

So, now we have only the good old memories of noons and Saturday lunches at Lebsack's, and with that, those kind of people, that kind of attitude existed today. So, one more time, "Give me a beef cheese and onion on rye, chili, easy on the grease."

Life Was Good

By Rena Forsyth Dean

I remember sleeping in the back yard before such things as air conditioning and spending time in the basement to stay cool in the hot summers. I also remember hobos coming to the back door to ask for food after they had jumped off the Rock Island train. We fed them and they were always polite.

We didn't lock our doors in those days. In the winter we went ice skating on the pond at Lake Street or, for special treats, we went out to the Blue River. My father and Mr. Lahr had the old-fashioned clip-on skates.

I also remember riding the streetcar downtown on Saturdays to eat lunch at Miller and Paine or the True Food Shop. The chicken pot pies and cinnamon rolls were so good and also the hot ham sandwiches and mashed potatoes and yellow gravy. Sunday rides were the entertainment of the day and we would go see where the gypsies were staying out in the country where 70th and A Street is now or farther away where there had been a flood or derailment.

My grandmother lived with us and we got up very early to go hunt mushrooms on the golf course of Eastridge Country Club or pick violets in the Penn Woods.

For money to buy fireworks for the Fourth of July we dug dandelions from our yard. My grandmother also cooked the dandelion greens, which I really didn't like. There are so many good memories from the past and it amazes me how little it took to make us happy.

Lincoln In August, 1941

By Roger Bacon

When the 96th Women's Amateur Golf Championship was held at Firethorn Country Club in 1996, Roger Bacon, the current manager of the Lincoln Country Club penned this article.

Prior to this year's U.S. Women's Amateur, the 1941 U.S. Amateur had been the only USGA championship held in Nebraska. That event, held in late August at the Field Club in Omaha, was one of the last of its kind held before this country entered into World War II.

In 1941, the citizens of Lincoln were still getting used to their new capitol (completed in 1932), which was being praised as one of the most beautiful government buildings in the country. The summer had been unmercifully hot and dry; the threat to Nebraska crops brought back a faint feeling of dread to those who had been treated so viciously by the Great Depression. Then August brought rain, and the air cooled. By the end of August, agricultural prices were high, unemployment was low, and there was cause for cautious optimism. One hundred seventy new families moved to our city in August 1941, and only ten heads of family were unemployed at the time of their arrival in Lincoln.

Lincoln was then, as it is today, a vital and sophisticated prairie capital. An interesting combination of bucolic midwestern town, bustling seat of government, railroad hub and education and business center.

The U.S. Amateur received daily press coverage in Lincoln, but was overshadowed by the grim news coming from every corner of the world. The citizens of Lincoln were preparing for war in the summer of '41, but held hope that America could avoid another A.E.F. abroad. Charles Lindbergh, who learned to fly in Lincoln, was traveling the country, urging America to stay out of the war.

As the college football season approached, Nebraska coach Major "Biff" Jones had to deal with the fact that the military exacted a heavy toll from the squad of Huskers that had traveled to the Rose Bowl the previous year. Of the Big Six schools, Nebraska contributed the most athletes to the U.S. Army.

In local sports, Alex Lutze successfully defended his city horseshoe title, Harry Meginnis won the Lincoln Newspaper's Annual Junior golf title, and Dizzy Dean played with the governor in a celebrity foursome during the City of Lincoln Golf Championship. "Monk" Wilson won the title.

Golf was enormously popular in Lincoln, as it is today. Lincoln golfers followed Ben Hogan's game, who led the money winners on the tour with $13,933 in August, 1941—as well as that of Joe Louis, who sometimes talked more about golf than about his upcoming bout with Lou Nova. They also followed the antics of the players, officials and gallery at a wild U.S. amateur in Omaha.

But in August 1941, there were gasoline shortages—a sure sign of things to come. The government, in an unprecedented move, banned the $1 down, $1 a week financing practice that small business used to sell everything from clothing to jewelry to furniture during the lean times, had just ended. With the agony of the depression fresh in the minds of most Nebraskans, and growing uncertainty about the future, golf was as much a diversion as a passion for many.

Lincoln's municipal tennis courts were rated the best in the nation in 1941, movie tickets at the Joyo or the Stuart theatres cost a quarter, and fashionable women could, and would, buy a dyed opossum jacket for $58.

As autumn approached, the people of Lincoln, like all other Americans, were trying hard to be hopeful and optimistic while preparing for a war that might never come.

Lincoln, The 'Good Life'

By Bob Martens

I was born October 27, 1923 on the 300 block of South 25th Street. My father in 1925 built a new home on 36th and F Street, then two years later we moved into another new home on South 37th Street between Randolph and F Street. He felt the stucco exterior of the first home would not be durable. We lived in this home for the next fifteen years. It was a great neighborhood extending from 33rd Street east to Piedmont and from J Street south to A Street. All of the kids living in this area were pretty well acquainted, as practically all of them attended Randolph Grade School at 37th and D Street. From 37th Street east to Piedmont were cornfields and just a few houses, and of course dirt streets. Behind Randolph School we had a pond, which we used for many winters for ice skating and hockey. In the summertime we had organized playground activities that consisted of baseball games, marbles, soccer, etc. This was during the terribly hot drought years of the '30s and I remember lying in the shade of Randolph in the summer and watching the sky which was nearly black with the hordes of grasshoppers flying over.

We improvised most of our daily activities. Bob McCracken, who lived at 40th and H Street, had a pony named Dynamite. Bob would bring the pony to our house, where he would charge a nickel to ride the pony around the block—just once. We had large cottonwood trees standing in the fields, and we would build tree houses in them. We would hang a large rope from the tree house down to the ground. Then attach a gunny sack to a pulley and the pulley to the rope, and away we would swing—fun, fun, fun. We build two and three room caves in the vacant lots, assuming the role of pirates or whatever. As we grew older, we started organizing our own Olympic games consisting of the javelin, shotput, discus and track. Needless to say, none of us ever became Olympians, but we sure had fun. I also remember standing on the lawn at my great grandmother's house on 25th Street and watching the Sower on the capitol being raised to its majestic position at the top of the dome, probably in 1932. My aunt worked for the Rudge & Guenzel department store at 13th and N Street, and at Christmas we would go to the fifth floor, where they had ponies waiting to take us for a ride around a circle—hay on the floor, but lots of Christmas finery.

Our education was enhanced by the fact that we had very good teachers as well as new school buildings—both Randolph and Irving Junior High were practically new. In Irving I participated in the homeroom teams in basketball and football. From Irving I went to Lincoln High were I graduated in mid-term, December 1941. I became Harry Kuklin's sports assistant in my senior year, having bypassed organized sports to enter the work force.

I entered the University of Nebraska in January, 1942, and spent one year in college. WWII had begun, and the draft was fast approaching, so I joined the Enlisted Reserve Corps in December 1942. We were told we would continue our schooling and perhaps enter officer's training, but instead we were activated into Infantry Basic Training at Camp Roberts, California, and sent overseas in August 1943 as infantry replacements to New Caledonia. I was extremely lucky when I arrived and because I had had typing in high school, I was transferred from the infantry to Admiral Bill Halsey's headquarters in the Adjutant General Radio Section, while all my buddies were sent to the front lines on the island invasions. My job was to take all radio messages, many of them top secret. In April of 1945 I was transferred to General Douglas MacArthur's headquarters in Manila to the A. G. Radio Section, where I read the advance plans for the invasion of Japan. I was able to qualify for a furlough as I had more points than anyone else in the office. We were on the boat ready to set sail for home when the atomic bomb was dropped. We were so afraid our furloughs would be cancelled, but we came home as scheduled and did not have to return because the war ended, and I was discharged in November of 1945.

I enrolled again in the university in January 1946, and pledged Alpha Tau Omega fraternity where I met many lifelong friends. In September 1946, I met the love of my life, Miss Mary Cox, at the Tri Delta house. We dated, went steady, and I gave her my ATO pin first, then a diamond in the spring, and we were married in August of 1947. Mary was president of her sorority and Junior-Senior Prom Queen. I was Prince Kosmet in 1947, and had to share the spotlight with Johnny Carson, who was Master of Ceremonies. In 1949 I was graduated from the university with a Bachelors Degree in Bus Ad and a Second Lieutenant's commission in the Air Force.

Upon our return from the service in 1945, Lincoln was a comparatively small city, with everything east of 40th Street still mostly farmland. The south part of the city extended to the Lincoln Country Club. Today Lincoln has developed into an ever larger city, but still maintains its desirability as a great city to reside in and raise a family. I enjoyed having my own business for 35 years and Lincoln has been very good to me and my family.

Long Journey—Short Distance

By Jack Mapes

A short story about a long journey over a short distance.

In the summer of 1942 I was a 16-year-old kid enjoying my first (legal) car—a 1935 Ford. When I first got it the tires were bald. I would have had them recapped but under wartime rationing no tires, new or used or recaps were available to a teenage high school student. I therefore drove on the bald tires until, one by one, each tire wore through to the tube. I tried to concoct patches, some of which would work for 20 to 30 miles at 25 miles per hour city driving. When patching would no longer work, I "rescued" junk tires from the wartime scrap rubber drive. None of these were much better than my own but if I cut the bead off the scrap tire (no easy task) I could stuff it inside my own tire, being careful that holes in the junk tire did not line up with holes in my own tire.

It was with four of my five tires in this precarious state that I set out for Grand Island, Nebraska early one morning. The results were about what a mature adult would expect but since I was a fool kid, I did it any way. The wartime highway speed limit was 45 mph so I tried to start at about 50. The shaking and vibration from all that totally unbalanced rubber was so bad I dropped back to about 40. This was better, but not good enough. A few miles down the road a tire blew out. It didn't just deflate, it exploded. I replaced it with the spare and drove on for a few more miles to the next blowout. Now things were getting difficult. With no spare, I decided to remove the blown tire and pull the car halfway off the paving so the bare wheel could ride on the dirt shoulder and not be totally ruined. Having forgotten my tire iron, I struggled and fought and kicked and cursed getting the blown tire off.

Driving with the right side of the car off the road worked pretty well, (except going around culverts) and held the speed down so much that it was quite a few miles before the next blowout. This time it was on the other side of the car so I needed to move a "good" tire from the dirt side to replace the blow out on the paving side. This operation would require two jacks (I had one) or something to hold up one corner of the car while exchanging the tires. I walked the ditches for about half an hour looking for something that would work. Fortunately a farmer stopped and helped, using his jack and mine. Again, the struggle to tear off the blown remains. I set out again with two bare wheels riding in the dirt.

After about 10 hours on (and off) the road I pulled into a gas station on the outskirts of Grand Island very tired, hungry and dirty. Luckily the station owner was a bit of a crook and he sold me a set of nearly bald but sound tires for about five times the wartime ceiling price, and did fake paper work about the price and my occupation.

I've forgotten a lot over the years but I'll always remember that trip.

Memories of 21st and Y Streets

By Susian M. Hadley

In the 1930s and to the mid 1940s my father, James G. Eastman had a milling company there. The Eastman Milling Company was at 1025 North 21st Street. Some of the other businesses in the area were, to the southeast, Nebraska Salesbook Printing Company, they made business forms. To the southwest was Lincoln Steel and to the west of Lincoln Steel was Kingery Construction Company. My father's mill was on the Kingery property just west of 21st and along the Missouri Pacific Railroad tracks. He prided his mill as making whole grain products on stone burrs. He made flours, pancake mixes, cereals and animal feeds. The name of the products was "Life Line" and they were sold to Lincoln grocery stores as well as stores in nearby towns.

In the area the streets were brick and I can remember hearing the Missouri Pacific Zephyr coming back to Lincoln in the late afternoons. To the south of the railroad tracks on 21st Street was Cushman's. They had a foundry on the west side of the street and a manufacturing plant on the east.

Memories of Lincoln

By Bob McCracken

Born in Lincoln in 1923, I am the son of C. C. and Hannah McCracken and have two sisters, Mary and June and one brother, Dale. Because my parents were very active in all Masonic organizations, I was fortunate to become acquainted with their friends' children—Art Pierson, Fred Metheny, Reese Wilson, Paul and Harold Mahaffey, to name a few, and have fond memories of our times together.

One of the highlights of our family fun was when Dynamite, a two-year-old shetland/hackney pony was brought home by my dad who had obtained him from Asa Stuart. Don and Roger had kept him in high spirits and it took a while to get him tamed down for kids. My dad had the knowledge of the effect of this animal would have on me and the words he said on the first night of Dynamite's arrival have been with me ever since as if it were etched in stone. "Bob," he said, "you are about to take on the responsibility of caring for this horse because he cannot do anything for himself. Do a good job and be sure you don't let a day go by without thinking of his needs and give him your love and it will come back to you in many ways. God has a way of repaying for a job well done." I have thought about this experience many times and have often wondered if that is why I've been so lucky all my life.

Because a pony cart came with Dynamite, I would drive all over east Lincoln and give rides to the kids for a nickel. One day we went down Laura Avenue were the Chesins lived and I told Irv he could ride around the block for a nickel and he came out of the house crying because his mother said she didn't have a nickel—so I gave him a free ride. Many years later I was in the Cornhusker Hotel and someone told Irv who I was so he reached in his pocket and pulled out a dime and said "Damn it, I still don't have a nickel, but here's a dime for the pony ride."

Irving Junior High was better than Randolph Elementary because the girls were prettier and friendlier. The next thing was to dance so I talked my neighbor, Betty Ann Heilig into dance lessons. She was a great teacher and I loved dancing so soon I was on the dance floor—it sure beat riding ponies.

During my time at Irving, I was accepted by Bert Faulkner's Southside Midget Football Team. In 1935 and 1936 Dick Chapin was the quarterback and he ran the team so even today when I see him, I still consider him "The General."

Next came Lincoln High and it did take 2½ years before I was expelled. Mr. Otto Hackman caught up with me and it was "turn in your books and goodbye." To put it mildly, my dad was highly ****** off so I spent the summer working for Theisen Brothers Construction Company and surprisingly liked it a lot, even though I was stranded without any transportation and no way to get back to Lincoln.

Although I enjoyed having my own money, it didn't last very long as my Dad enrolled me in Wentworth Military Academy for the next semester—I think he was influenced by Rich Anderson. My first impression was "I'm going to jail" but as it turned out to be one of the best things that ever happened to me, I can only thank him for doing it.

Then to World War II. My three years of military training at Wentworth made it pretty easy for me and it didn't hurt to find out that my C.O. was a graduate of Wentworth. He promoted me to corporal instead of "buck-ass" private and assigned me the duty of NCO in charge of the Officers Club. The club was new to them and I really enjoyed being a gopher for the C.O.

After the war was over and our combat wounds healed, I came back to Lincoln and had several jobs. When I told Mitch Tavlinski I was working for Continental National Bank at $200 a month on an "on the job training" program, he said "hell, you could stand out on the street and catch wild horses and make more than that." So I made application with Continental Oil Company for a service station and was lucky to get the station at 12th and L Street and had such good people with me—Dick Brigham, Bob Linberger, Swede Nelson and Ralph Wilson. We had a good business but, of course, ended up at Lincoln Equipment Company with my dad.

The next fifty years were all pretty neat. I won't go into all of that—only to say I've lived a very lucky, lucky, lucky life.

Miller and Paine

By Alice Frampton Ditman

My remembrances of childhood in Lincoln seem to be linked to the Miller and Paine Department store at 13th and O Streets, the hub of Lincoln. As a child I remember buying shoes in the lower level where you would see people walking on the sidewalk above as the sidewalk had glass bricks. Also it was fascinating to use the X-ray machine to see if the shoes fit and each pair tried on required a trip to this large brown box with viewing ports. I notice they are not in use today. Do you remember when Miller and Paine installed the first escalator from 1st to 2nd floor? What an event. It was always required when I got a new dress as a child to go to the "Ribbon Department" on the first floor to get a matching bow. Of course all of your purchases would be delivered within a day or two to your home at no extra charge. No trip to Miller and Paine would be complete without lunch at the fifth floor dining room. Chicken Pot

Pie was a favorite! And do you remember the ice cream balls rolled in nuts and covered with hot fudge? Oh my ... died and gone to heaven. Lincoln has always been a very special place to live and I'm glad to report that it STILL IS!

Mom Saved A Dime
By Van C. Duling

When I was a preschooler we lived at 40th & H Street in Lincoln. My mother, of her own volition (and my father's I might add), really never learned to drive a car. For this reason she was a devotee of the buses and the streetcars.

Along would come a nice warm day and mother would take "little Vanny," as she like to call me, by the hand and we would stroll from 40th & H over to Randolph Street a block away, then down to Randolph from 40th to 33rd where the streetcar would be at its terminus and turn around.

Often while we were waiting for the streetcar, mother would point toward a nearby large evergreen tree and ask me to go and stand behind the tree. Not knowing any better and not wishing to question the wisdom of Mom, I would dutifully comply.

Inevitably, along would come a Good Samaritan—oftentimes a nice gentleman who would pull over to the curb and ask the attractive "young lady" (my mom was a good looker) if he could offer her a ride. Well, she would blink her eyes and think this was wonderful. With that, she would say something to the effect of "thank you sir, but excuse me just a moment," she would turn to the tree and say, "Vanny, would you mind stepping over here?" and with that I would appear from behind the tree—much to the consternation of the driver. With that, Mom would put me on her lap in the front seat and away we would go downtown.

As noted, mother had saved 10¢. Having a big mouth, I would usually relay this information to my father who would chastise mother for doing this and suggest she never do it again. It was truly "crass" in his judgement, and not something that a lady of good reputation would do. Alas, it never worked. Ah, such memories.

More Memories
By Lois (Severin) Reed

My memories of Lincoln are when I graduated from the eighth grade from a country school near Princeton, Nebraska, Lancaster County. We had our graduation ceremonies from the Stuart Theater's stage in Lincoln. Nathan Gold gave us all free tickets to all the rides at Capital Beach. What a thrill that was for this country girl who only got to Lincoln twice a year to buy clothes.

Later on after marriage I worked for Nathan Gold at his store for two years, he was an astounding man. He called all his employees by their first names.

Lincoln is now my home and I love living here.

'Move Your Gardner'

By Pace Woods

When I was about four or five years of age, my parents drove me into downtown Lincoln for the first time and it was during the summertime. I noticed a pine tree on top of the capital building then under construction. I knew nothing about the topping of a building with a green tree, so I assumed it was up there for Christmas. What really convinced me that it was the Christmas holiday were the green and red electric stop lights which I had never seen before. It's curious what goes through a child's mind when they see something for the first time.

I do not know how many people recall Fredericks' Grocery Store at 17th and South Street. It was located on the southeast corner. The College View street car made a turn at that corner going on south 17th to South Street and then from South Street to Sheridan Boulevard.

My mother had a large French imported Gardner car. It was light green with side tires and mirrors on either side of the front fenders and had yellow detailing on the doors. The cars in those days used angle parking and the car was very long. Every time mother parked on south 17th, the car blocked the street car and the conductor would have to come in to Fredericks and ask her to please move her car so that the street car could make the turn. I remember how embarrassed as children we would be that we were blocking the traffic, but it never seemed to bother anyone else except maybe the conductor.

My Lincoln in the '20s and '30s

By Dorothy Kingery

How lucky I was to have grown up in Lincoln!

In the wintertime, we went sledding at 27th and D Streets, now the Sunken Garden. Lake Street Pond was popular for ice-skating. Someone usually built a bonfire on the island in the middle of the pond, and was that ever a good spot to get warm!

Roller-skating was one of my favorite pastimes. Our skates clamped onto the soles of our "school shoes," as opposed to our "Sunday school shoes." I was lucky—I had two pairs of shoes. The school shoes had rather thick soles, because they had always been half-soled, and we adjusted the clamps with a skate key on a string, which was worn around the neck when not in use. I always had skinned knees and elbows, but the fun we had was worth it. In grade school playing jacks was an all time favorite with girls my age.

On Saturdays, mother and I walked three blocks from our home and caught the streetcar at 33rd and Randolph to go downtown. Some of our neighbors said uptown, but we said downtown. We dropped our streetcar checks into a little box that was next to where the conductor sat. When we got off the street car at Harley's Drug Store near the dime store we walked to Rudge and Guenzel's and Herpolsheimer's department stores where we were "just looking, thank you." Then we went to have lunch a Miller & Paine's tearoom, on the fifth floor of the store.

The elevator ride itself was quite thrilling. The cars were operated by women in navy blue uniforms. On the sleeve of their jacket there was an M & P emblem embroidered in gold metallic thread. I suppose the operators did the best they could, but it was always a bumpy ride, because they had trouble trying to accurately judge the proper time to stop on each floor, on the way to fifth, so the passengers did a lot of head bobbing at every floor.

The standard fare at the tearoom was chicken pot pie and a cinnamon roll. The price of the chicken pot pie was 15¢ so a few years later when it was raised to the exorbitant price of a quarter we usually skipped the cinnamon rolls.

After that sumptuous repast we would sometimes go to the Lincoln Theatre (not the same as the present one) where for many years Harold Turner was the organist and Harriet Cruse Kemmer was the soloist. After that we saw the movie, all for 10¢ if you were under twelve. The movies changed every week at all of the theaters. Another popular theater was the Orpheum, most theaters had vaudeville performances before or after the movie. The most beautiful theater in Lincoln—many years later—was the Stuart, hopefully, someday it will be restored to its original elegance.

Once in a while we would go to a movie on Sunday, but in the really "olden days" in Lincoln, movies were not shown on Sunday because Lincoln was a blue law town, and very strait-laced. The emphasis was on our many churches and fine school system.

For "the world's best hamburger," with everything on it and costing a nickel each or six for a quarter, there was a wonderful hole in the wall at about 12th and O with counter service only, was the Hotel d' Hamburger. You could also have a generous slice of homemade pie for a nickel. Several years later, the Yum Yum Hut at 29th and O was the in spot.

There was a choice of two root beer drive-ins: the Mug at 33rd and O, with a miniature golf course on the lot to the south, or the Windmill at the corner of Cotner and O. Of course you only went to The Windmill if your parents had a car and they could afford to drive way out there, what with the price of gas being 12¢ a gallon.

In the summertime we had Sunday School picnics at Antelope Park, Capital Beach camp grounds, and Pioneers Park. We also went to the Epworth League grounds where we attended Chautauqua meetings in a big tent while our mothers were working with the ladies aid church circles at the dining room on the grounds. The weather was always hot, but we thought that under the shade of the tent we were keeping cool by frantically fanning ourselves with the handheld fans compliments of a local mortuary.

Walking to the corner drug store at 33rd and A on a summer evening to get an Eskimo Pie was a "biggie." If your pocketbook could stand it, you could sit up to the counter and perch on a high stool and be served by a soda jerk at the fountain.

Going to Camp Kiwanis at Milford on the banks of the beautiful Blue River for a whole week with the Camp Fire Girls was pretty exciting, too. The girls whose parents were more affluent went to camp for two weeks. There was no indoor plumbing, but there were lots of flies and mosquitoes and the grounds were always either muddy or dusty, I guess it was hard to grow grass there. There was no swimming pool so we swam in the Blue River. Even though the water was thick and brown with mud, we thought we were having a good time.

Swimming at Muny Pool was fun, and we could stay all day for the price of one admission ticket—a dime. Of course we were always terribly sunburned, but we got our money's worth.

There was a saltwater swimming pool at Capital Beach but it was a long way from our house and besides the price was right at Muny. However, when my out-of-town cousins came to visit for a few days it was a real treat when our families all went together to the amusement park at Capital Beach. It was officially dubbed "The Playground of the Middle West."

In the "something to do" summertime category homemade pop stands ranked up there right along with digging caves in the neighborhood vacant lots and making hollyhock clothes pin dolls. Everybody had hollyhocks growing in their alleys and everybody had permanent clothes lines in their backyards, so of course we all had clothes pins. Where else would your mother hang up the family washing on Monday, or would you hang rugs to beat them with the carpet beater when your mother did the spring house cleaning? In the wintertime she usually hung clothes on lines in the basement to dry, unless she knew ahead of time the coal man was coming that day to fill the coal bin. What a dirty mess that was, but it was nice knowing we would be warm in the winter.

During the summer months band concerts in Antelope Park were very popular. The bandstand was not the same as the one that is there now. We played croquet in the backyard, and put on lots of shows. Admission was one cent, and worth every penny. Sitting on the front porch swing was a good way to keep up with neighborhood activity.

I attended Lincoln High during the thirties, almost everybody did, because there wasn't much choice. I have such happy memories of my high school days: the formal dances in the Grand Ballroom of the real (original) Cornhusker Hotel, always with a ten piece orchestra—the girls wore formals, and most always had corsages—cokes and "shoe strings" in the Tee Pee during intermission. There were wonderful summer evenings dancing at the park (Antelope Dance Pavilion) where Eddie Jungbluth's, Leo Beck's or Johnny Cox's orchestras played.

The Turnpike was wonderful; the grandest ball room between Elitch's in Denver, and the Aragon in Chicago. It was where all the big bands played, being a good stop over between Denver and Chicago.

I am so glad I still call Lincoln "my hometown."

My Most Embarrassing Moment in High School

By Larry Vaughn

The title of this written piece is a misnomer. My embarrassment lasted more than a moment, and the incident, which caused my embarrassment, affected me for many years.

It was the fall of 1938. I was a sophomore at Lincoln High School. When I was at Irving Jr. High the year before, my singing voice had matured to a point where I felt confident that I could perform in public as a soloist. As a sophomore in high school, I joined the Clef Club. This was a club in which I could be with other students who had vocal talent. Early in the fall term of school, the Clef Club was asked to take part in an assembly, specifically for incoming sophomores. It was an assembly meant to orient the sophomore class as to how things "worked" at LHS. The Clef Club was asked to furnish some entertainment for this special occasion. The Clef Club asked me if I would like to sing a solo for my sophomore class. I was flattered, so I said, "Yes." That was the beginning of my undoing.

The day came for the sophomore orientation assembly. I was really excited about it, especially because my girl would be in the audience. I had practiced my solo with the pianist several times. I knew the words and the music of the popular song I was to sing, and all seemed to go well. While that was true in practice, singing this solo before my peers on the Lincoln High School stage was something else.

There I was, standing a few feet from the piano on the stage and peering out over the sophomore class. My girl sat in the fourth row in the middle of the auditorium. Oh me! What did I get myself into? My legs turned to jelly. My throat got dry, and my voice sounded husky. The piano player gave me a hard look and said, "Get started." I managed to tell the sophomore class the name of my song, gulped a couple times, and heard the introduction to my song being played. I wanted to say, "Whoa, I'm not ready," but it was too late. It was put up or shut up time.

I began to sing. My voice quivered. I sang the first line of the lyrics of my song, and then my mind when blank. I panicked. I stuttered and stammered and couldn't think of the next words. My face drained of all its color. What to do? Questions ran through my mind: "What will my girl think of me if I can't think of the words to this song?" "What will my peers think of me; a member of their class?" Finally, after an undeterminable period of time; I gave up, walked over to the piano, and looked at the music. I said to the pianist, "Let's start over." This time, looking at the music and reading the words, I finally got through the song. Whew! What a fiasco!

What I did next is still a blur in my mind. I know I hurried off stage, ran out of the building, jumped on my bicycle, and headed home as fast as I could go. Such humiliation—such a failure—oh, I wish I were dead, were my thoughts as I rode home. I was devastated.

The upshot of this disastrous experience is that I didn't attempt to sing a solo again for the next 20 years. Now that I'm past retirement age, and have lost my inhibition to singing solos, I sing whenever someone asks me. Hooray for old age.

My Neighborhood 1926–1937:
Park Street from 24th Street to Sheridan Blvd.

By Georgia Stone

Starting at 2401 Park: This house was owned by Dr. and Mrs. C.V. Gibbons. Dr. Gibbons was a dentist, and his daughter, Marjorie, was five years old and my best friend. Their house on the corner was a two-story brick house with a large lawn (one of two on the block) on the east side. There was plenty of room for a lemonade stand. Marj and Georgia did a fair share of business thanks to milkmen, garbage collectors, delivery people and a man with a one horse cart that came by once a week selling fresh vegetables.

Going east from 2401 Park. Next door lived the Polsky's. I think he had the Oldsmobile dealership. They had a son and a daughter (who died at a very early age).

Next door to the Polsky's lived Al (short for Alice or Allegra, I think) and Chauncey Kinsey. Mr. Kinsey had a parking garage on the corner of 14th and N or M, I believe. They had two daughters Kaye and JoAnn (younger than Georgia or Marj).

Next to the Kinsey's lived Dr. and Mrs. George (Nellie) Covey. They had a son and a much younger daughter, Georgia (about 5 or 6 years old). Their brick house had a large cement porch with a swing. We would hose it down and slide across the cement on bare feet. This was great fun until a neighbor girl fell, hit her head on the cement, and knocked herself out. Panic! She revived in a couple of minutes and other than a golf size lump on the head, she was OK. That girl was Peggy Weaverling who lived across the street. Today she is Mrs. Cecil Parker of Lincoln.

Next to the Covey's lived the Matchett's. There was the widow Matchett with her two grown children from Ohio. Daughter Kathryn had been superintendent of schools in Ohio, and her younger brother, Foster was at the University of Nebraska. Foster became an MD, married with five children and practiced in Denver. He promised me to wait for me to grow up (I was six years old) to marry me. The cad! My father was Foster's mentor and the families were friends for many years.

Next to the Matchett's live the Sorensen's. Mr. A. J. Sorensen was, I believe, a Lt. Governor of Nebraska at one time. His wife was from the east, I believe. They had four children. Bob, Tom, Teddie and daughter Ruth. Bob became associated with the Voice of America I don't know about Tom and Ruth, and of course, Ted was a J. F. Kennedy writer. Teddie was younger than Georgia and Marjorie and in some kind of fuss he spit on us. So, we took his tricycle and hid it in the Gibbons' garage. Long story short, Marj and Georgia did not get to go out and play that afternoon.

And then the last house (next door to us) on the block lived the Stahls. They had one son, Ed.

Pill Hill

By Virginia Coleman Buckley

I was born and raised on Stratford Avenue, a short four block street in a brand new housing development. It was called "Pill Hill" in the 1930s because in this small area lived my father Dr. Fred Coleman, Dr. W.C. Becker, Dr. Floyd Rogers, Dr. George Walker, Dr. Hancock, Dr. Wm. Orr, Dr. Everett Angle, Dr. Clarence Moyer, Dr. "Red" Munger and Dr. Hummel.

My childhood was great!

Potpourri of Memories of Lincoln

By Jerry Mapes

My first recollection of living in Lincoln that is not fuzzy from the effects of pre-pubescence is living at 745 Elmwood which is about 30th and Randolph. North of Randolph was a huge "grove" stretching from J Street north to almost O Street and about 29th to 33rd. There were homeless people inhabiting these groves. My mother referred to these people as tramps and bums which was in direct defiance of today's attempt at a kinder and gentler assessment of those less fortunate. In any event, "I want you to stay out of the grove or those people will eat you."

The streetcar ran down Randolph but we were too young to pull trolleys. Instead we contented ourselves at guessing whose dog would be run over first. My dog survived (or maybe I didn't have a dog).

There were three small grocery stores within three blocks of my house (which we rented for $35 monthly) at which I could spend my nickel per week allowance. For a penny each one could buy bubble gum cards which could very easily have pictures of Babe Ruth, Lou Gehrig, Charlie Gehringer or Hank Greenberg. You could also buy bubble gum with pictures of vivid massacres of Chinese in Manchuria. I usually chose the massacre pictures (not a good sign). Also for a penny, the stores offered "sixers" which were cheap caramels packed six to a package and selling for a penny.

When I was about six or seven we moved to 2401 St. Mary's Avenue which was definitely a blue-collar middle class neighborhood. Strangely enough, there were a lot of families on that street who rose above the "working stiff" designation. The Tooheys, Parsons, Russell Brehm's family, the Joe O'Gara family were just a few.

The neighborhood was predominantly Catholic so we all went to Blessed Sacrament School. There was a seven-inch slanted ledge around the whole school above the windows and with the proper new tennis shoes, I could negotiate the whole damned distance inching my way. One had to be careful to not fall on one of the nuns when trying to get across the front entrance.

My *Liberty* and *Photoplay* magazine route netted only about 20¢ a week and that came only after freezing my tail off every evening at the entrance of Lincoln General hospital trying to sell nickel magazines to people visiting patients. A good evening was five magazines at 1½¢ profit each. I supplemented my meager income by snatching an occasional empty glass milk bottle from the front stoop of peoples homes. They would leave the empties with a note stuck in one of them telling the milkman what to leave. The bottles had a 4¢ deposit so this could have been a serious felonious misappropriation if abused so we held it down to a few cents a week.

The neighborhood would break out in spontaneous football games (touch) on both Park and St. Mary's Avenue right in the street. The hazards were not automobiles (about one an hour) but more likely the droppings from Tony Scholaro's horse as he made his rounds through the neighborhood selling fruit. These games were invariably broken up by the most hated man imaginable, the motorcycle officer Campbell who the kids called "Soup Campbell." He would not only break up your game but would confiscate your football. No one knew what ultimately happened to all those footballs. Maybe old "Soup" opened a sporting goods store in his retirement.

When they built the addition to Lincoln General, we would climb around on the second- and third-story framework and in the winter would actually jump from as high as the third story into snowdrifts. Sometimes after the spring thaws we would notice that there might be a wrought iron fence with sharp posts right next to the drift.

I survived this era of my life and moved to a home at 2827 South 27th which my father purchase for about $5,000. That was in 1943 and I noticed a for sale sign on the home not to long ago with a price tag of $119,000. Everyone over 65 or so has a story like that.

Pull the Trolley

By Reese D. Wilson

In the middle 1930s on summer nights, my neighborhood buddies and I would pull the trolley. The street car (trolley) ran down South Street and turned on to Sheridan Boulevard going south and east on Sheridan to College View.

We would wait until it slowed down and then run behind it and pull the rope that removed the wheel from the electric connection. The streetcar would then come to a complete stop in about 50 to 100 feet, the conductor would come out and put the electric connection back on the line. It was frustrating for him. It finally got so easy that we would go to about 33rd and Sheridan where the street car would go over the bridge and try to time it so when we would pull the rope and disconnect the electricity, the street car would roll to a stop in the middle of the bridge. That really frustrated the conductor.

My first memory was when I was three or four years old, about 1929 or 1930. My grandfather Charles Wilson and his brother-in-law George Dana, had a wholesale poultry and egg firm called Wilson and Dana. The farm trucks would come in carrying wooden crates of chickens—with slats on the sides and the chickens would squawk and poke their heads through the slats and look with one eye head cocked. The next thing I knew they were killed and drenched in boiling water, then they were held against a rotating wheel that removed all the feathers. Between the boiling water and chicken feathers the memory was enough to stay with me all my life.

Randolph Leaves Legacy in Lincoln
By Theodore F. Randolph

Theodore F. Randolph was born August 24, 1872 at Germantown, now called Garland in Seward County, Nebraska. The family left Germantown in 1876 and settled in Frontier County (Stockville) and lived there until 1877. We later moved to Red Cloud and then back to Seward County on Plum Creek. We lived there until 1880 and it was at this time that the family Bible was given to my mother Susan Siddens Randolph. In 1880 we moved east and in order to get the wagon across the ferry on the Missouri River it was necessary for my father to sell our old yellow dog for $1 for fare to cross the river. Our family decided to go to Colorado. The snow had melted and the team could not pull the wagon through the mud. Dad put me and my sister Olive and mother on the train and we went as far as Atchison, Kansas. A man asked me to watch his valise in the train station and that was the first quarter I ever made. Mother, Olive and I went by train to Trinidad, Colorado. Dad sold the team and wagon in Iowa and joined us in 1881.

After living in Colorado and Missouri for several years Uncle Tom Siddens, my mother's brother, sent money for all of us to come back to Seward County. This was 1884. Uncle Tom worked for the Griswold Feed and Seed Store. We all stayed in Seward and mother got a check from the federal government granted for Civil War Veterans. Her father Tom Siddens was killed in the Civil War. We went to the north west part of Seward and bought a house and some ground. The Northwestern Railroad came through and cut right through the property.

Dad went to Lincoln in the fall of 1885 to do lathing. I helped him. I was 13 years old at the time. He had done some lathing in Neosho, Missouri, to help make a few dollars. Dad and I boarded and mother and the girls stayed in Seward and in the fall of 1886 the whole family went to Lincoln after the railroad had bought the Seward property. We first lived on C Street between 7th and 8th and before winter we moved to 23rd and O Street.

Dad put me in the Q Street School in 1887 and in 1888 I was put in the fourth grade on reading and arithmetic and in the second grade for grammar.

In the blizzard of 1888, school was let out at 2 p.m. and I just never did return. I guess I stopped about the fifth grade.

I helped Dad build a house on 24th and Sumner Street for us to live in. Building fell off in Lincoln in 1888 so Dad went to work in a butcher shop. I took orders in a team and buggy and then I would go down to the butcher shop and help fill orders and go back and deliver them.

In 1889 I got a job at the stove factory and walked from West Lincoln to home in the bitter cold winter. I would skate across Salt Creek. The foundry was in the old Burlington Railroad yards. I worked in the winter of 1889 and all of 1890 and 1891. In April of 1892 I went to Belleville, Illinois to work for the Bridge and Beach Stove Company. In September of 1892 my dad and I went to work for at stove factory in St. Louis and came home to Lincoln for Christmas. While Dad and I were working in St. Louis they moved the stove foundry to Lincoln at the State Penitentiary. After three salary offers by the owner, Dad decided to stay in Lincoln and work at the Penitentiary. He worked 10 hours a day, helping convicts learn to build stoves.

In 1894 I went to work for James Rivett on the Burlington Railroad doing carpentry work. I stayed with the Burlington until 1905 and married Alice Shofield in 1899. I was a traveling carpenter on the railroad. I helped build Bridgeport and Alliance depots on the line, Alice went along to cook; we lived in bunk cars.

We came back to Lincoln in 1901 and lived upstairs at 23rd and O Street. Roy was born there. I went to work in the carpenter shop in Burlington yards. I helped build the round house and shops in Havelock, now Lincoln. I rode a bicycle to work in Havelock from 23rd and O Street. Later, we moved to 2128 O Street. We bought the place for $600 which included the house and two lots. Floyd was born at 2128 C Street. The owner flipped a coin to see if I could buy it for the $600 and I won. My mother died in 1902.

When Roy was nine months old I went to work for a carpenter named Harry Dobbs. We moved in 1906 to an acreage in University Place, now part of Lincoln. I had bought the 15 acres previously in 1903 and built a house on it and we moved there in 1906.

Agnes was born there in 1908. I worked in Lincoln as a carpenter and went back and forth to work. The boys tended the cows, garden and had a milk route. Our house was right beside the Burlington tracks. We lived there until March 1, 1917 when we moved into Lincoln and lived at 13th and A Street. My dad died in 1917.

A parade on O Street in front of the then U.S. Post Office, later Lincoln's City Hall.
Photo courtesy Nebraska State Historical Society.

Red Feathers

By Gates Minnick

I remember taking the College View streetcar (the one that we used to pull the trolley on as it went across the bridge at 33rd and Sheridan Blvd.) to downtown. The trolley went out to College View, then back down Sheridan Blvd. to South Street, down 17th Street to N Street, then along N by the Lincoln Theatre and the old Bauer Drugstore (Bauer's Russian Mints) to Gold & Co.

We would go to the movie at the old Lincoln Theatre which was a beautiful old place then get something to eat at either Baner's Pharmacy or go up to Boyden's by the Stuart Theatre (extra thick malts) or sometimes go to Bricks (really thick malts—you got the full mixer and then some).

Since we are discussing food, don't forget the wonderful Yum Yum Hut at about 29th and O or the famous Mug at 33rd and O, and since we are talking about O Street we must never forget Decoration Day (Memorial Day) with the street being lined by people selling peonies.

Well, I could go on and on, but will end with just two other memories, the fall opening with all of the downtown stores Hovland-Swanson, Miller and Paine, Lawlors, and last but not least, Gold & Company, where my mother worked for fifteen or more years. Do you remember the Red Feather that Gold's gave out before the football games, the ones with the white Ns?

The wonderful 10¢, never-duplicated, Yum Yum sandwich was one of the most remember bits of Lincoln's past. *Drawing courtesy Bill Schlaebitz.*

'So Earnest, Yet So Gay'

By David Johnson

My grandmother, Marie (Meisinger) Dittenber, arrived in Lincoln in 1921 at the age of 15. From the age of sixteen until she was 32 she worked at the Rudge and Guenzel's Cafeteria downtown on 13th Street. A German-Russian immigrant who arrived in this country in 1909, she remembered those occasions when she took the streetcar to work downtown from her mother's home on A Street in the South Bottoms area of Lincoln. She spoke with fond memories of Rudge and Guenzel, her job at the steam table and the many friends and acquaintances gathered through sixteen years working there. She seemed particularly to enjoy the bustle of the many different peoples that frequented Rudge and Guenzel.

Apparently, one of the frequent patrons of Rudge and Guenzel's was Marie Macumber, best known today as Mari Sandoz. As Jim McKee related in a July 1996 article on Sandoz in the Lincoln paper, Sandoz, like my grandmother, was also a recent arrival to Lincoln. During the decade of the 1920s Mari Sandoz attended UNL, working in various capacities at the university.

Exactly what sparked a friendship between the erstwhile writer and my grandmother is difficult to say. Though a full decade older than my grandmother, the two Maries shared several commonalities: German spoken at home, educations terminated with 8th grade, and harsh—yes, even abusive—fathers. Whatever the source of their friendship, Sandoz proudly presented a first edition of *Old Jules* upon its publication in 1935. Sandoz captured the essence of my grandmother and the spirit of these young immigrant women from that era, in a simple, yet moving inscription.

"To Marie Meisinger, because she is so earnest, and yet so gay too, like no one else on earth—Mari Sandoz"

The Best of Summer and Winter in Lincoln

By Mary Frances Danley

I was born in 1926 and grew up at 4724 A Street where we had 10 acres of ground in what was considered suburban Lincoln. During the 1930s my father, W. Bruce Shurtleff let the W.P.A. and the state prison have gardens out behind our house, I still have a billy club from those days that my dad found out in the field. There was a large stone gazebo east of our house, and Dad had a screened-in "sleeping cottage," big enough for two double beds, two singles and a covered pot, built on top of it. Every night from approximately early May to late September we would walk outside and up the steps to the sleeping cottage and spend wonderful nights sleeping up in the treetops, enjoying what breezes we could catch. During those hot, hot summers we would close all the windows in the house early in the morning and pull down the shades in an effort to keep the house cool, and then would circulate the air with table fans. That was our air conditioning.

Summertime treats were root beer floats at the Root Beer Mug at 33rd and O Streets and swimming at the Capital Beach salt water pool, and oh how we enjoyed the amusement park there! On days when I couldn't talk my Mother into taking me to the pool I would fill a laundry tub with water out on the front sidewalk and scrunch myself down into it, even at the age of 13, and now I'd be lucky if I could just get my feet in it.

Winter treats were going for a sled ride down south 48th Street my sled tied to the rear bumper of dad's car, or sledding down the hill on A Street between 52nd Street and Cotner Blvd., or digging tunnels with my younger brother in the snow drifts in the cornfield where Christ Methodist Church is now.

Sunday evenings almost always found us at the counter in the Yum Yum Hut at 29th and O Street, where my brother Bruce could easily put away half a dozen Yum Yums.

In 1944 my Dad stunned us all by buying the second largest house in town, the old Raymond home at 2464 Woodscrest. This house had a swimming pool in the basement and a fireplace in nearly every room of the house. Now this part will make every prospective home buyer cry: he paid $19,000 for it! That's enough to make even me cry for the "good old days."

Of course south 56th Street and South 70th Street were both just gravel roads in my youth and were not traveled enough that I was able to teach my children to drive on them as late as the 1960s. Where Wellington Greens is there was a field with cattle in it, and I used to stop my Studebaker and "moo" at the bull just to see him get mad and start snorting and pawing the ground. This was when I was old enough to know better, and since then I've hoped he didn't take his temper out on the poor farmer later.

When my mother was growing up in Elmwood and my Aunt in Eagle, a trip to Lincoln by horse-drawn wagon was an all-day excursion. My Aunt said they always bought groceries and the like in Havelock so my mother probably did too.

Havelock's main street looking east from the corner now occupied by the Joyo Theatre, about 1890. *Photo courtesy Nebraska State Historical Society.*

The Birth of Bethany

By Jim McKee

In looking through available historical data in an attempt to document the "birth of Bethany" we find, as usual, the best authority on much of Lincoln's history is Jim McKee. So, as we have often done before, we quote directly from *The Prairie Capital.*

Bethany, like University Place, was created around a denominational school. In 1886 a group of businessmen bought the Hawley farm and several smaller parcels of land to the total tract of 321 acres. They then offered a major portion of the land to the Baptist Church, on condition that the church build a Baptist college on the site. The plan, like many others concocted by speculators, assumed that as the school grew and prospered a support community would grow up around it, making the remaining land considerably more valuable than the original purchase price. Unfortunately, the Baptists felt that their resources were being strained by their existing Nebraska institution, and they rejected the offer. J. Z. Briscoe, representing the Nebraska Christian Missionary Alliance, quickly asked that his group be considered for the land offer. Almost at once, the Christian Church was offered 500 acres of land southwest of Lincoln by a similar investment group. With the inclusion of an additional 18 city lots, said to be worth in the excess of $4,000, the eastern package was accepted in 1888. The area was called Bethany Heights in honor of Bethany College in West Virginia, the Christian Church's first university.

On August 30, 1888, a group of nearly 200 people gathered at the Missouri Pacific depot in Lincoln for a trip to Newman's Station (now about 66th and Vine Streets). After a ¾-mile walk north, they were met by a group of about 50 others who had arrived by wagon for a picnic in a small grove and the official cornerstone laying for Nebraska Christian University. An auction of city lots was held to raise construction funds, and $8,315 worth of the $100 to $400 lots were sold the first day. O. C. Placey's design for a building to cost $85,000 was chosen, and while classes started in 1889 in the Demarest home, construction began. The five-story stone and brick building, built by Thomas Price, contained 32 classrooms, 7 offices, a 500-seat chapel, a library, and a study hall. At the first commencement in 1890 spirits were high, and it was predicted that by 1924 eight additional buildings would be needed. On November 10, 1890, the village of Bethany was officially incorporated. A gymnasium was built in 1907, and a short time later a 16-room women's dormitory was built at a cost of $4,373. Unfortunately, the school found itself in financial trouble almost from the opening day. Samuel Cotner, one of many benefactors over the course of the school's lifetime, donated more that 50 acres of land, helping to save the school during one of its acute financial crises, and the school was renamed Cotner College in his honor.

The Gangs

By Robert Hillyer, MD

I have fond memories of my childhood in Lincoln. That period would have to be most reminiscent to me. Later, I lived in New York the ten years that our generation was forming.

Ours was a very active social group of young people. We had "gangs." Our gangs were in no way comparable to those of the present era. One of these little social groups had their shack on the Hardy property at the southeast edge of town. Bill Thornton was their leader. Another of the socially prominent shacks was on Dr. Harry Everett's yard on Woodscrest. Young Harry Everett was a leader there and the likes of Bill Beachley, Harold Bookstrom and Ralph Luwick hung out there. Our place was in the back yard of the Buntings on Van Dorn just west of Sheridan. Jim Bunting was our leader and we had Herb Walt, Fred Webster, Norm Shaw, Jim Bunting and myself there. We had friendly competition between these shacks. The most we ever did was swipe each other's Whiz Bang and Police Gazette magazines. One time, Ann bunting came down and confiscated all of those terrible Police Gazettes. Their mother didn't give us much flack over it though.

We certainly never had any fights between the shacks. In fact, we were all friends, and it was somewhat of a social station to be in any one of them. The most terrible thing we ever did was pull the trolley on the electric streetcars as they approached the "penny bridge" at Sheridan and 32nd. Passengers had to pay an extra penny to go over that bridge.

If we ever had any guns in our shacks our folks would have taken them away from us. We were great hunters though. Jim Bunting was the greatest of all. He and Herb Walt and I would hike out into the south woods and beyond with our big shot guns and trapper's revolvers. We read how the Three Musketeers had a feast of choice red breasts and thrushes. We tried it but the pigeons off the barn were much better. Our folks never worried about us spending nights camping in those south woods because I had a giant Airedale dog that went with us.

Buntings had some horses on a farm north of town and we learned to ride on them. There was an alley between Sheridan and 27th a half block south of Van Dorn and Seacrest's had a couple of ponies up near Sheridan and they let us ride them down the alley. The Magees had a couple horses in University Place and we rode them too. Ours was a very full and happy childhood in South Lincoln during the depression.

We played in various bands when quite young. My father was a school principal and later in life I asked him how our bands were and he said, "terrible." I asked him why I was first trombone over the likes of Don North, Kenny Anderson and Bob Pierce. They had much better tone quality. He said, "You were the loudest."

To my knowledge, every one from each of those shacks went on to amount to something. We all went to college and some scattered to far away places, but each to some good.

In my own surgical profession it is noted that Lincoln has gradually progressed to be quite a medical center. Each medical and surgical specialty is well represented and all practitioners in major hospital centers are Board qualified. An example of this progress is in Dr. Steve Carveth taking over two years out of his practice time to work with Dr. Walt Weaver to form the Lincoln Heart Center. Dr. Carveth also developed the very fine first aid system for our Nebraska football stadium. We hope his retirement in real estate development and skiing is enjoyable.

The Growth of the Drive-In

By Jerry Mapes

In-car eating was popular in Lincoln before the word "drive-in" was even coined.

In the late 1920s Lincoln began seeing food and drink vendors experimenting with serving patrons in their cars. It is difficult to determine exactly which one was first, partially because some were outside the city limits and were not in city directories and none advertised.

As near as I can determine the first drive-in was probably the Dutch Mill, which according to records was incorporated on October 1, 1928 by J. V. Robinson. Robinson had designed the building to look like a Dutch windmill and commenced operation at Cotner and O Street, which was "way out in the country." According to the newspaper files, the Mug was incorporated by Chester Ager, R. A. Russell and Dr. Carl Kail and commenced operation April 1, 1930 at 33rd and O Street. We know that these two locations served root beer and perhaps also served sandwiches from the very beginning or at least not long after the opening. The mug was particularly interesting because it was a tall cylindrical structure that looked like a root beer mug. It had large eyes that moved from side to side and the mouth was the dispensing counter.

Again, according to newspaper articles Albert Nebelsick became involved in both the Windmill and the Mug and eventually acquired them. The probable dates of acquisition were the Dutch mill in 1930 and the Mug in 1933. At this point, things became a little bit confused because Bob Smith, the son of B. J. Smith the owner of the Smith's Home Dairy which started in January of 1933. On Mr. Smith's menu, he shows a location at 33rd and A, 58th and O, 21st and G and 14th and South. Nebelsick must have bought the Windmill from Smith and the Mug from Messrs. Ager, Russell and Kail.

Somewhere in this time frame, probably in April of 1931 Leon Addleson founded Leon's Lighthouse Barbeque at Normal and South Street. This was a tiny building that looked like a lighthouse and later became a filling station. It was on the northeast corner of Normal and South and was across from the old tennis courts. According to early advertisements Leon also provided "good music to dance to." It is not easy to see how this all took place under that little roof. As most readers know, Leon later went into the grocery business at 14th and South and wound up with Leon's Food Market in Rathbone Village. Leon's still serves the area. A place called Stork's Barbeque Drive In also popped up at 14th and High street. This location has been the home of many drive-ins throughout the years.

Along toward 1932 the Yum Yum Hut at the northwest corner of 29th and O Street became the meeting place for almost every teenager that had access to an automobile. The Yum Yum was a concoction of ground beef and other assorted and secret ingredients and sold for 10¢. This wonderful sandwich concoction has had many imitators but no one has successfully duplicated that elusive family recipe. The Yum Yum Hut lasted through the '50s and on weekend nights required uniformed policemen to help direct traffic in and out of the miniscule lot.

Leon Adelson opened the Lighthouse on the northeast corner of Normal Blvd. at South Street about 1930 and later owned Leon's Grocery. *Photo courtesy Nebraska State Historical Society's MacDonald Collection.*

From the late 40s through the 50s and 60s, there were a number of drive-in restaurants that sprouted up. The notable ones would seem to be the Circle Drive In at about 45th and O Street, Ken Eddy's at 48th and O, and of course the ever popular King's Restaurant with the first three on North Cotner, 40th and South and 10th and South.

Perhaps Lincoln's first drive-in was Smith's on the northwest corner of 33rd and A Streets as shown in this 1935 photo. Mr. Smith is at far right. *Photo courtesy Nebraska State Historical Society.*

The Ideal Story

By Gardner Moore

I was working for H.P. Lau Company for $175 a month. Art Meyers also worked for Lau's on the road and lived at 27th and Randolph. One afternoon he invited me to go to dinner with him at his house. When we arrived, his wife Nellie asked us to go to the store for some small item. It was the Ideal Grocery and Market, owned then by Bill Vidlock. The storeroom was about 25 by 25 feet. Bill said he would like to sell the grocery department. He was a meat man. We talked to him for a while and made a date for after dinner that evening. Well, about nine o'clock we had a key to the only door, the front. Art and I each gave him $50 to bind the bargain. The price was $2,500. That was for everything, which was not much by today's standards.

After a year or so Bill wanted to get out so we took over the market. We had several butchers but none were very satisfactory even though we paid them $25 a week.

We decided to hire a full time delivery boy, Harold Stanley. About this time on a hot summer day with a good south wind, Pauley Lumber Company caught fire. It was a dandy. Sparks were flying everywhere, in fact, our awning caught fire and also the room and we were two blocks away. Of course we did no business that day because the street was blocked off. I remember we took our truck to go to the firehouse for more hoses; which reminds me, the city still owes me for the run.

In the mean time I had met Ruth. I fell for her right away, but I am afraid she did not fall so quickly. She was still in school. Art and I decided I should have the store all by myself since we were to be married.

53

It was then that I decided to go cash and carry. We were not getting any-place as it was. What little business we had was mostly on the books and we did not have the store paid for after several years. Of course we had bought the market and that cost money. The first day I think we did about $30 in sales and the days that followed were about the same. Then I decided to run a big ad in the paper. It was a big flop. The ad cost $350 and we took in a little over $300. We put up a big front and told everybody how well we were doing.

Then I ran across Lynn Pantier and sold him the meat end of the business for no money down. Things started to go a little better. I finally had a $50 day in the grocery side then a $300 week. However, it was some time before we hit a $500 week. We put out handbills and hired kids to deliver them. I caught one of them stuffing them all down the sewer. I think the bills cost around five or seven dollars.

We tried anything and everything to get a little business. One time I bought a couple hundred honeycombs of honey to sell, three for 25¢. I just got them all in a nice pile when a bunch of bananas, which were hanging over them, fell in the middle, of course spoiling about half. What a mess!

I got the idea that I should start an egg route. I started out in the country and bought eggs from the farmers who were then supposed to come and buy groceries from us. Well, it was a perfect flop and soon I had enough of that. Then we got the idea to start another store at 27th and R Streets. We put in a butcher there and Ed Harris, who was working for us to run it, just a two-man store. It broke even after we had it for several years. Then we got the idea to open at 9th and O Streets. We were going to get all the farmer business. Well, we got some of it. People would bring in eggs, which we had to candle, and then give them merchandise or cash.

I moved the office to 9th and O which was about a desk and a checkbook and left Lyle to run South 27th. I would go to all three stores every day and was doing most of the buying for them all. We were making a living and get-ting our bills paid, but not laying up much treasure. I had a man, Ed Gibbson, running 9th and O. We got in with a lot of Bohemian trade from up north, so I hired Henry Reback who could speak Bohemian, as many of them could not speak English.

Then came the big mistake. Earl May was putting a branch at 7th and Washington, which looked pretty good. We had the use of KFOR in Lincoln and KMA at Shenandoah, Iowa. 7th and Washington was the old Country Club before they moved to South 24th Street. The building had a big porch across the front; this was enclosed and that was to be the grocery department. We were up to $500 a month rent in Lincoln and $750 in Iowa. The price was close to $50,000, most was in merchandise, very little in fixtures. Carl Weil let me have $35,000 and Earl May carried back $12,000 and we had to stock 7th and Washington. I hired Curley Wagner and Jock Worster for $18.00 a week and opened at 8 o'clock and closed at 10 o'clock. You see they had a radio studio, which was going all the time. There was no network, so they had their own entertainers. I would use 15 minutes in the morning and 15 minutes in the afternoon and evening to sell groceries. Then we had a country school act for 30 minutes which I was the teacher and then I worked on the grocery floor.

I would make a trip to the other stores some time during the day. We sold several carloads of green bananas and several carloads of peaches. We were doing pretty good. I had bought a carload of canned corn, peas and peaches with the Earl May label on them. Thought I made a pretty good deal, along with other things.

Then one fine morning I got out of bed and found that the bottom had dropped out of everything, and I was under the whole pile. We did not do enough business to feed a few birds, in fact, we hardly took in enough to pay the rent. I went to see the bank and Earl May. I got the rent reduced to 5% of the total sales and Mr. Carl Weil of the bank offered to let me have some more money. That was what saved me. I would never be able to thank him for what he did for me. Strange as it might be, I was later on the board of his bank for twenty years.

About this time I took a one-day vacation and took Ruth, Margaret and Jack to Kansas City. I think Jack was about four and Margaret two. We left early in the morning and got home late at night. A Mr. Milgram had opened a store there about the size of our present store and going to town. More business than I had ever seen. After we got home I found out we could buy the two lots where our present building was for $5,000. I thought this is it. I went to see Mr. R. C. Lau and told him what I wanted to do. I was just ready to leave when he said, wait a minute, I will build a building for you. He offered to buy the lots and put up the building and charge me 1% a month rent and an offer to sell anytime within three years at a profit of 10%. That was all there was to it. Well, away we went.

My biggest pleasure is looking over the many, many fine customers that have been with us from the beginning and helped to make us a success. There were times when I wondered if it all was worth it. Let me tell you, it was. The wonderful people we have waited on over the years and the fine people that I have worked with. I want to list these people as they came to us. These are the key people and I want to thank them all for their loyal support. It has been a pleasure working with you. Here they are. Hope I didn't leave anyone out.

Harold Stanley was the first full time. He drove the old Model T car, delivered the few orders we had, did the sweeping and cleaning up. Then Lynn Pantier, Henry Krougher, he worked in the morning in the groceries and in the afternoon in the meat. Lyle Hans, he worked full time in the grocery department and Henry then worked in the meat. Ed Harris, Ed Gibbson, Henry Rehak, Curly Wagner, Jake Worster, Homer and Leland Van Boskirk, Don and Dick Simon, Dick Bartow, Francis and Bob Kelley, Veronica, Elizabeth, Edith, Bruce Shear, Henry Schuldies, Bryan Tatman, Crewsdon, Everett Evnen, Bob and Bill Ellenwood, Henry Frisbe, Muriel Rice, Dave Sims, Tom Saunders, Howard Boyd, Jack Moore, Gary Starck, Paul Minning, Larry Moats, Ray Stimbert, John Jewett, Dale Bettenhousen, Elmer Rinehart and Marge Fehr. And our most recent additions; Jim Moore and Rob McMaster. I could go on and on telling the fine things that have happened but these are the highlights.

An Ideal Grocery ad from December 31, 1936, shows some amazing bargains by today's standards.

The Old Neighborhood
1934–1944

By Dale Capek

From South Street to Lake Street along Sheridan Boulevard, anchored by Westminster Church at Sheridan & South and by one of the Woods mansions at Sheridan and Lake. East/West the neighborhood went from 24th Street to 27th Street.

On South Street Bev Williams lived just east of Westminster Church and later married Bill Kimball. Bill Gold lived at 24th and South his father was in department stores. At 24th and Ryons were Jim and Molly Woodward. Jim became a M.D. like his father, and Molly later married Don Cunningham. Across the street were Pete Keene and brother Dave.

At Sheridan and Ryons, just south of Westminster, lived Mrs. Wishardt. This was important because the word was never get in her yard. When we were 13 or 14 we jumped the fence on the north side and ran across the yard and started to climb the tall gate on the driveway and when this nice voice spoke out "Can I open that gate for you?" She was very nice and we spoke after that experience.

Two houses east of Sheridan and Ryons was the Weaver family. Walt, Art and John all doctors and Jim the youngest was a banker.

One the east near 27th and Ryons was Bob Simon of department store fame. At 27th and Ryons, on the northeast corner lived Jack Heckenlively who was know for his expertise in golf even at a young age. On the south side of Ryons lived Bob "Shorty" Pierce of Nebraska football fame. Dr. and Mrs. Reese and their daughters lived two houses west, their daughter Margaret married Burt Folsom, Kathryn married Joe Marvin. Next door west was Dwight Evans. His father was with the University of Nebraska. The Reeses and Evans each had two stall garages with the driveways connection. This made the best basketball court in the area.

Next door lived Adele Coryell who later married Don Hall of Hallmark Cards. One door west lived Don and George Albin their father was in the insurance business.

Back on Sheridan, on the east side second from the corner lived Mary Ellen and Ramey Beachly, their father had a grocery store on O Street around 15th. One door south lived Carol, Dick and Dale Capek. The lot south was a vacant lot and held the famous Capek caves. Other caves showed up in the lot from time to time. Some of the neighborhood also started pole vaulting on that lot. On the corner of Sheridan and Sewell lived Jane and Buffie Carpender. Jane married Beaky Jamison. The first house east on the north side lived Patty Burt. The family moved while the neighborhood was still playing "kick the can." Next door were Nancy and Bob Howey. Bob made the first water skis in the midwest and was an insurance entrepreneur. East one door was Chubby Burlingame. Chubby was a great storyteller including stories where you had to bleep words.

Across the street was Velma Hodder and her three children, Don, Bill and Kathryn. Bill went from IBM to CEO of Donaldson Corp. in Minneapolis.

West of Sheridan on Sewell on the south side lived Charley and Sam Haupt in the first house. Their dad was with Miller & Paine department store. West three houses were Giles and Dolores Henkle. Their sons were Bill and John. Bill Ran Henkle & Joyce for years and John now lives in Seattle.

Back on Sheridan Dr. Whitham lived on the eastside. They had a daughter Ann and a son Miller, Miller excelled in tree climbing at a young age.

Abel's lived across the street west from Sewell to Park Street. The Abel children were older, but some of the boys in the neighborhood played cops and robbers in their yard. It had a grotto swimming pool, wading pool and lots of bushes and shrubs to hide behind. Much fun.

Park Street on the south side on the corner was a vacant lot where a lot of the boys of the neighborhood played football in the fall. Two doors west lived the Sorensen family: four sons, Robert, Tom, Ted, Phil and one daughter. But you would almost never see any of them. They were all reading books and all became brilliant. Ted Sorenson was best known at the speech writer for President Kennedy, Robert as a lawyer in New York City. Two houses west of the Sorensens lived Frank Jacobs. Frank, a fun person going through school in Lincoln, became a writer for *Rolling Stone* magazine. On the corner of 24th and Park lived Jack Phillips who later married Jo Selleck. On 24th and Lake Street behind Phillips lived the McCulla family. Herb the son was a banker.

Next door east on Lake Street lived the Don Stewart family. There were three sons, Don Jr. (Bud), Jack and Roger. The best story on this street was that Don Jr. and Robert Sorensen were good friends. One afternoon Don, Robert and other buddies decided to bury Robert up to his neck. They did this on a vacant lot at 24th & Lake and then all went home for dinner. An hour later Mrs. Sorensen showed up at the front door of the Stewarts to ask if they had seen Robert. Robert had not shown up for dinner. Jack, who answered the door, said "Oh yes, they buried Robert this afternoon." Mrs. Sorensen turned white, but Jack and Bud quickly explained that it was only up to the neck in the vacant lot less than a block away.

The Onion Caper

By Marilyn Maude

Visualize South Street from 7th St. to 56th St. in the mid 1930s as a sleepy two lane brick street lined on both sides with huge elm trees that shaded the entire length. Only one stop sign on South St. at 27th St. slowed the few cars that navigated this lovely street. Of course the trolley car tracks went east and west, connecting with the tracks to the west and 17th St. and to the southeast at Sheridan Boulevard, slowing traffic during the scheduled runs of those wonderfully punctual conveyances. Otherwise, South St. was a very quiet street, so quiet my dog regularly napped on the cool bricks during hot summer days.

I grew up in a house on South Street near 27th, close to the unique stop sign. Our big side yard was the neighborhood field for all the kids who wanted to play baseball in the spring and summer and football in the fall. The south branch of the city library now occupies that hollowed ground. The street was so quiet that when the big kids wouldn't let the little kids play in the game of the day, we little kids sat on the curb with our feet in the gutter hoping for a car to go by so we could wave at the occupants. One hot day we heard a truck coming from the west and as we excitedly looked toward the noise we saw a big open farm truck loaded with a mountain of onions. As it started down the hill from the crest at Sheridan Boulevard the driver must have seen the stop sign because it appeared that he jammed on this brakes. To our astonishment we saw his huge load of onions come over the cab of the truck and tumble onto the bricks, smashing, bouncing, and rolling in all directions. They got under his wheels, mashing them into slick muck that caused the truck to slide uncontrollably down the hill. Ultimately it crashed head-on into the telephone pole that was beside the stop sign. At the sound of the crash my mother swooped out of the house, grabbed us out of the gutter and scurried us to the front porch. By then our front yard was covered with onions, the street was littered with them, and some had even rolled all the way down to the bottom of the hill at Bradfield Drive, a block away.

Someone apparently phoned for the police (no 911) because soon a police car came from the north on 27th St. When the policeman saw the situation he came to our house to call the ambulance and a wrecker. The excitement of the situation escalated as the neighbors gathered to watch the injured driver get loaded into the ambulance. Then the wrecker went to work attempting to dislodge the truck from the post.

It was exciting to all the children watching to see the wrecker driver attach his chain to the back of the onion truck and connect several hooks. Then he crawled into his little cab and shifted gears with a loud grinding noise. We all held our breath as he tried to go up the slippery brick street. When the chain became taut between the wrecker and the truck, the wrecker made no more progress ... his wheels just spun. The wheels spun faster and faster and smoke rose up to the shading tree branches. Then the smell of burning onions permeated the warm air and many on-lookers ran to close windows against the stench. Finally the spinning wheels stopped, the wrecker backed a few feet, took another angle up the street and tried again. The same scenario repeated again and again for what seemed like hours before the onion truck was finally pulled free of the pole and dragged off to somewhere unknown.

The street was black with burned onions as well as the garbage of broken onion pieces. The grassy parking along the street presented a monumental job for everyone to clean up the onion debris or forever after be tracking bits of onion everywhere. As I remember, my thrifty grandmother found a few whole onions to cook for dinner that night. I don't believe I ate any that night, or for years after, because the horrible smell stayed for weeks until a big thunderstorm washed it all away.

Then we little kids sat on the curb with our feet in the gutter again waiting for something exciting to happen.

The Sounds of Lincoln

By Jack Stewart

I remember the sound I heard while growing up in Lincoln during the 1920s. At 6:30 on winter mornings, Dad's shovel scraping the basement floor told me he was tossing coal into the furnace. That's how we heated our home; houses didn't have gas furnaces then and most people had not converted from coal to oil. Nobody, of course, had air conditioning. When summer came, his scraping was replaced by the sound of steel chains clanking against a metal scoop across the street from us, where the basement for a new house was being dug. A team of horses pulled the scoop to dig into and carry away soil. Their whinnying and the clanking of the chains were supplemented by the curses of the team's owner, who swore loudly, vividly and frequently—sounds my mother (usually unsuccessfully) tried to shield me from.

Our ice man and garbage man had replaced their horse-drawn wagons with trucks by then, but the Roberts Dairy man hadn't: the rhythmic clippity-clop of his horse's hooves could be heard half a block away and was fun to listen for. Even more fun was hearing fire engines. They had sirens much like those today but also had a brass bell, which the driver or his assistant clanged by hand. Once, when I was downtown, they roared down O Street to fight a fire at the Colonial Theater. At many intersections there were traffic signals whose electric bells rang continuously during an emergency like this, which added to the excitement; usually they rang only briefly, when the light changed from red to green or from green to red.

The sounds that steam locomotives made were also exciting to little boys—at least to me. They huffed, chugged, whistled, expelled steam and banged noisily when coupling freight cars on a siding. By pressing my ear to the ground near the Rock Island tracks at 33rd and Sheridan Blvd. I could tell by the sounds the rumbling transmitted that a train was coming in from the south. You could also hear the rumble of streetcars going across the bridge above.

A sound I heard once, and never again, because my parents immediately put a stop to it was the screeching of automobile tires in front of our family home at 2418 Lake Street. The branches of a big elm tree stretched over the pavement. My brother Bud and I often climbed it. One day we stuffed a pair of coveralls with crumpled newspapers to make a lifelike dummy, which we hauled up in the tree and then dropped (intentionally) in front of an approaching car. The driver slammed on his brakes to avoid striking what he thought was a person, got out, and when he was finally able to speak gave us a lecture like we had never been given before. I learned more swear words from him that day than from the guy across the street in a whole summer. Dad gave us a powerful lecture, too, but later admitted that he and his friends laughed about this for weeks.

As the years went by, many of these sounds disappeared. Some, however, remain: babies still cry; Methodists still belt out hymns as if God were deaf; the plaintive song of the mourning dove still floats through open windows; the roar of 76,000 voices in Memorial Stadium is no different than the roar of 30,000 when I saw my first football game there in 1931.

My favorite sound today is cubes of ice clinking in a glass of—(you guess)!

The Storm Sewer

By Martha Aitken Greer

Many Lincoln places and things have considerably changed or are here no longer. Every time I drive by the spot where the Turnpike Ballroom stood, it seems to get smaller and smaller, although it used to be a large dance hall where the big bands played, where so many of us danced and drove our parents wild with worry when the country roads were icy and slippery for fast drivers.

Gone is the Capital Beach giant saltwater swimming pool with the attending rides and Kings Ballroom. Lincoln youngsters went out there to splash water at contemporaries, to slide the slide and to float in the heavy salted water. The Ferris wheel was good and when we were older, we danced at Kings.

This photo of Burlington Beach was taken about the time it was sold and reopened as Capital Beach. *Photo courtesy Jack Campbell.*

My collection of "Hair-breath-Harry" events centered around the ponds on the grounds of the Lincoln Country Club on Woodsdale Boulevard, quite accessible by pulling apart two barbed wires and crawling through the fence. Many youngsters ice-skated there; the big boys playing hockey, the little kids scrambling to get out of their way. The Lake Street ice-skating always had more parents in the daytime, so not much mischief went on there. But my favorite time was when the snow melted, then froze, then melted some more, in large chunks, making strange shapes, giant icicles, some safe skating on the frozen surface, some that was quite dangerous. There was always the possibility of falling into the freezing water.

When the ice vanished, one day my sister, Mary Aitken, and I explored the storm sewer going from the large pond and under the corner of 24th and Woodsdale with Harry Meginnis. He was much braver and faster than we. So, he went into the sewer first. We followed close behind, scared to death, of what, we did not know. It seemed endless. We ran with our heads down, so as not to crash into the top of the pipe. We did not even dream of the possibility of rats, raccoons or snakes. It was quite dark. Suddenly, we could see light and we came to the wide open edge of another small lake, on the other side of 24th Street, going east to 25th. Now that second lake is filled with grass. We trusted that Harry would get us out of that sewer, and he did. When I drive over the intersection at 24th and Woodsdale, I wonder what's in that sewer, or if it is quite large enough for three little children to explore.

My sisters and I grew up, surrounded by vacant lots. Nearly every spring, the boys in our neighborhood would burn part of the huge field behind our house so that they could play baseball there. Usually it worked well and they controlled the fire. But one year, the grass was pretty tall and there must have been a strong wind. Suddenly there was a gathering of people around the fire's edge because the burning was going way beyond the baseball's needs. I remember seeing some people trying to kick out the fire with their shoes. The mother of one of the baseball boys was using her coat to beat down the flames. Things had gone too far.

My mother was standing near the edge, beside her precious garden. And my sister, Mary and I were right there, taking it all in. Finally the fire department zoomed in. Soon, there was a black field, still smoking and too hot to walk on, but no longer a threat to the neighborhood. I remember the fire captain coming over to where my sister and I were standing. He said, "These boys over there say that you two girls started this fire. What do you say to that?" You can well imagine what we had to say to THAT.

The Village Becomes a City

By James L. McKee

The village of Lancaster and the first years of Lincoln's growth were built with the help of wagons, horses, and oxen. The settlers arrived in covered wagons pulled primarily by oxen; the lumber was hauled by team from Nebraska City and Garland; mail hauling and personal travel were accomplished by horse or stagecoach. The citizens were well aware, even before the new capital was established that prosperity and progress hinged on the coming of the railroad. Towns that were bypassed more often than not withered, moved, or simply died. The *Nebraska Commonwealth* of November 23, 1867, reported that, at the urging of Elder Young, Lancaster County commissioners had authorized $100,000 in bonds, the principal to be paid to the first railroad to reach Lincoln. The state joined in two years later by offering a two-year premium if the railroad should reach Lincoln by December 1, 1869. The county voters then finally approved the original $100,000 offer with the proviso that the Lincoln terminal be reached by May 13, 1870.

In June 1869 Governor Butler, the capital commission, and a representative of the Burlington Missouri River Railroad met near Salt Creek to break ground for the railroads imminent arrival. After it became obvious that the May 13 deadline was unrealistic, it was hoped that the arrival could be timed for the Fourth of July 1870. On that date the steam engine Wauhoo managed to reach a point northeast of the present site of Havelock. Finally, on July 26, the age of steam arrived. Convinced that Lincoln's growth was now assured, Charles H. Gere, editor of the Lincoln *State Journal,* announced that the weekly publication would hence forth be a daily. The Burlington was quickly followed by the Atchison Nebraska from Atchison, Kansas, the Midland Pacific from Nebraska City, and the Omaha Southwestern from Omaha.

With the recent move of the U.S. Land Office from Nebraska City to Lincoln, the capital city also became a staging point for immigrants. In the spring it was common for 30 to 40 immigrant wagons to camp at Market Square, but by fall the numbers quickly diminished. The Burlington, eager to dispose of its bounty from the state, established an embarkation point in Lincoln and advertised land at low prices, with low interest, minimal down payments, and free or reduced fares to immigrants who bought land at the Immigrant House, north of the present depot, land buyers, who often arrived in a boxcar containing all their possessions, family and livestock, were offered the services of a hotel, restaurant, and laundry facilities while the prepared to move to their newly acquired land.

Although Lincoln was officially incorporated in 1868, the city was not ready to commence business and failed to act on the incorporation. The process was repeated in 1869, and this time a full complement of elected officials, trustees, clerks, and treasurers were duly sworn in. The city prospered: lot sales boomed, buildings sprang up, and the population grew at a geometric rate. In 1867 the village of Lancaster had a population of about 30 and contained only five or six buildings. John H. Ames, an early local historian, reported in the Lincoln *Statesman* in 1870 that the value of real property in the city was assessed at $456,956 and that nine churches, one bank, and two hotels were in operation. The capital commissioners were acknowledged leaders in the community; each built a home to show his confidence in the prairie capital. Governor Butler's mansion was on South 7th Street between Washington and Garfield, Mr. Kennard's home was at 1627 H Street and Mr. Gillespie's house was directly south of Kennard's on G Street. In 1871 growth was proceeding at a rate that allowed Lincoln to organize as a city of the second class and elect it's first mayor, W.F. Chapin.

The south side of O Street between 9th and 10th in the 1870s. On the left is the First National Bank on the southeast corner of 10th and O and in the middle of the photo, in the white three-story building, is Lincoln's City Hall.

Those Were the Days

By Bob Ferguson

I remember the Fourth of Julys ... when I was just old enough to order a box of "works" from the Spencer Fire Works Company in Spencer, Ohio. For five bucks you got a box full of great stuff that lasted all day and all evening. Some of it, my older brother got his hands on and in the intersection of 30th and U Street, we lived on the southwest corner brother Dick and a friend Holmes Congdon used an iron pipe of a diameter that of a Ford Hubcap would just fit over as a cannon. Using a two incher or a cherry bomb, they'd place the pipe so that the fuse stuck out, hold the pipe securely on the concrete surface, light the fuse and keeping heads out of the way then watch the hub cap at zero trajectory, hoping the cap would return someplace in the vicinity for another trip into the blue. Both boys were NU professor's sons which helped to make plans for reaching a non-gravity situation. It never happened ... Goddard was working on it also ... but who thought it up first. I was five working on six.

I remember walking my girl friend home from Lincoln High carrying her books all the way on Sheridan Boulevard to 40th and then south another 4 blocks. I remember standing and admiring the many dance bands that came to the Turnpike. I loved Tex Beneke and Artie Shaw and Glenn Miller. I met a girl who was dating a fellow in college who was among the National Guard men who went to World War II early. He asked me to "take care of his girl friend," I did, and I still am, I am 80.91666 and she is 78.0834 now.

I remember Bishops Hill, Dana X. Bible, Hank Bauer, George Sauer, Louis Brown, Chris Krisinger, Steve Hokoff, Lloyd Cardwell, Charley Brock, Jerry Lanue, Sam & Vike Francis, Freddy Meyer, Butch Luther, Harry "Hippity Pop Hopp," Heavy Day, and all the DU's that went to war and left me behind. Those were really THE DAYS!

Three Points of Memory

By John C. Mason

There is a little unrecorded history in connection with Lincoln High School. Bob Sandberg and I were in high school in the class of '37 and Jack Stewart in the class of '38.

First, there was a boys' Hi-Y club sponsored by the Lincoln YMCA, which occupied a small old house next to the high school campus. They served a buffet lunch every day to their members at a very low cost. They also had an occasional party to which we could bring dates. The significance is that we were still in depression times and many families (mine included) did not have much spare change to give to their kids for lunch money. Many also brought their own lunches and ate them there.

Second, there was also a drug store adjacent to the campus, which was in some way associated with and attached to, as I recall, a florist with a greenhouse. The drug store served sandwiches and cokes, etc., at noon for those who had that much lunch money. My own recollection is that many of the kids who came from South Lincoln, meaning on or south of South Street and Sheridan Boulevard, did have enough lunch money for eating there. They got their food and drinks in the drug store area, as I remember, and then took them in to small tables in the greenhouse to enjoy the ambience of the flowers and plants while having lunch. I had the pleasure of eating lunch there once or twice.

My third item is with respect to Lincoln's place in the civil discrimination issues, which surfaced so prominently in the sixties. In the thirties, Lincoln had very few blacks, and I was unaware of the accommodations discrimination which I now realize affected black musicians, etc. There was no school discrimination evident to me, other than geographic allocation of which schools to attend. There were so few blacks in high school that I do not recall a conscious discrimination, although in retrospect I guess there was no dating across color lines. The white students, were not even conscious of the discrimination taking place in the south.

The class ahead of Sandy and I, the class of '36, included a very good looking black boy who was a good athlete and was on the football team. He had been elected as the senior class president. I remember thinking how nice that was and that I was proud of him and his class for this. In the spring of '37 there was a regional high school student council convention in Sedalia, Missouri. Betty Groth, later Forest Boehm's wife, Dorothy Anderson, later Dorothy Schwartzkopf and I were appointed to attend, representing LHS.

Betty's mother drove us down. During the convention some of the attendees learned about this class presidency from a casual conversation with one or more of us. We were surprised and amazed at how shocked most of the other attendees were, that our "white" school had a black for a class president.

West Lincoln—A Boom Town

By Bob Marhenke

As the business of refining salt from Gregory Basin failed, the area continued to be in demand. At this point in time, Oak Creek wound its way through the basin and emptied into Salt Creek just west of the Haymarket. It was the only fresh water stream to run into the basin. Fresh water was needed for the creation of ice, for the manufacture of brick and for butchering and salt was needed for preserving. Since many of the wells in the area turned salty as the demand increased, the fresh water in Oak Creek played an important role. There are accounts of brick being produced in the basin as early as 1867 and accounts of a packing business as early as 1881. For these reasons I believe the basin area soon to be known as West Lincoln was chosen for development.

In 1884 John Fitzgerald, Lincoln's very first millionaire and a railroad contractor, headed up an investment team called the Nebraska Stock Yards Association. They planned an industrial area along Oak Creek complete with stockyards, packing houses, canning company, railroads, ice manufacturing, a hotel, water system, gas lights and all the trimmings—1,180 acres and $231,000 of improvements.

1885—West Lincoln is a boom town! Investors were transported in for the "Great Lot Sale." One such investor was heard to say as he observed all the hustle-bustle and construction, "could I be standing where Moses once stood, as this looks like the promised land to me." The Nebraska Stockyards Association also platted the village of West Lincoln complete with businesses, post office, their own fire dept., government and a school. Streetcars to bring businessmen and workers from the city were extended into West Lincoln and into the stockyards and packinghouse areas, all of this in a few short months.

The 1889 bird's-eye view shows this was no small operation. Newspaper accounts tell of the procession of 10,000 hogs a day and the production of 60,000 bricks a day as well as a busy canning business all depicted in the bird's-eye. Also seen in the background is the village of West Lincoln. Also visible steeples are the of church's and the school. One of these churches stands today and until recently was used for worship services. This makes it the oldest church in Lincoln. Today's West Lincoln School is on the original school sight and is adjacent to the church. One of the hotels of the era is still standing as an apartment house and Main Street is still called Main Street, the remainder of the original streets have all been renamed. Their original names were: Jersey, Guernsey, Holstein, etc, to reflect the stockyards and packinghouses.

About this same time the adjacent Great Salt Lake was being developed as a Playground, complete with a 50-passenger pleasure boat. A first-class resort, this Playground was first Burlington Beach and later on Capital Beach. In one newspaper clipping, it gives directions as to the best way to get to Burlington Beach. One was to ride the streetcar to Belmont, take the connection to West Lincoln and continue to the stockyards, then board the pleasure boat and cross the lake to the festivities. This route eliminated the crossing of several railroad tracks.

At least two reasons came into play as to the demise of the industry of West Lincoln. The depression of the 1890s coupled with a political struggle over railroad shipping rates made it more economical to ship to the Omaha stockyards and packinghouses so investors abandoned West Lincoln for a more lucrative place to invest.

During the thirty plus years of researching in this area, just about all traces of the stockyards and the packing industry have vanished. Sometimes in the early spring, one can see the cinder trails where railroads once were, the old creek bed is still visible and some remnants of foundations. It takes a little imagination to picture the bustling area of yesteryear. On one trip to the area I did find a gambrel hook and a rail car coupling link, both unquestionably old and definitely used in the packing industry. I was also given a butcher knife once used in the packinghouse. Several years ago while observing a deep excavation I witnessed some of the spoils of the brickyard.

An 1889 bird's-eye view of West Lincoln's packing plants, stockyards, brickworks and canning factory with the village to the right. *Photo courtesy Nebraska State Historical Society.*

What A Good Girl Am I

By Laverne Sconyers

I'm glad to be writing about the distant past as that is a lot easier to remember than yesterday or this morning. I wonder why that is (oh, I forgot—it's my age).

The mid-'20s remind me of monthly visits to the Nebraska Pen to see minstrel shows put on by the inmates for their relatives. No, I did not have a member serving time in the pen. My parents were friends of the warden so we had an invitation to attend these very professional and entertaining performances. After one of the performances, we were taken on a tour of the facility, including the room where the electric chair was located. I guess you might say I am the only person who ever sat in the electric chair and lived. I was very young then and I am not sure if I knew what it eventually would do to people.

In the general direction of the pen was the Turnpike Ballroom. Many famous bands played there, including Guy Lomardo, Russ Morgan, Benny Goodman, etc. And I danced to them all. Kings Ballroom, located at Capital Beach was another favorite dancing spot.

We lived in a house owned by my parents which cost $4,000. During our stay another house located a couple blocks away went on the market for $10,000. Wow, we thought, what a mansion that must be. It was open to the public and, yes, it was a mansion. It was brick and ours was stucco. Shortly after that house sold, the area now known as Woodshire, and the former Lindbergh flying field where Lindbergh learned to fly, became alive with beautiful homes.

Before many of these areas started growing my family and I made many trips to pick strawberries, raspberries, cherries, etc. in the empty fields. Pius High School sits on my favorite asparagus patch.

I lived about 3 miles from Saratoga grade school which is still there. School closings were never heard of. We walked in rain, sleet, snow and cold. I don't think I knew of any family who had more than one car and usually the father drove that car so there was no one at home to drive us to school. We even walked home for lunch. This went on through Junior High also. Irving was just built. I relish my Jr. High days because that is where I met my first boy friend. I had gone to my locker to put in my books before going home for lunch and there I found a package of chocolate candies with a note from a boy—my first love. I was too embarrassed to carry it home so everyone could see it so I stuck it in my notebook and carried both of them. Of course, everyone had to ask, "Why are you taking your notebook home at lunchtime?" No answer. The story ends quickly, as did the romance.

I didn't finish my kindergarten episode. I was sent to the principal's office, the one and only time in my life, yes, that's what I said. I had worn a dress to school this particular day, which was the norm most of the time except when you expected to play on the turning bars. I had forgotten that I wanted to do this and had worn a pretty little dress. Well, I turned on the bars and so did my dress—right over my head and heaven forgive me my little panties showed. That was a No, No, and I mean a big No, No. A teacher spotted me and sent me to the principal's office where I received a severe scolding and made me feel I was a very naughty girl. I guess that's why I am such a good girl today, don't you believe me?

I grew up to 21 or 22 without having much experience in the social world, I didn't even go to parties. I was seated with a few boys and a few girls who were the "cool" people. Well, unfortunately, the waitress came to me first for my drink order. I thought I was really going to show them I was "cool" too so I ordered a cup of coffee as I knew older people drank coffee and had never tasted it. She went to the second person, "beer", the third person, "beer", and so on. By that time, I wanted to crawl under the table. They all laughed at me. That taught me—don't try to be someone you're not, LaVerne.

The memories that bring back the best good times are remembering O Street and Robinsons, Kresge's, Woolworths, W. T. Grant and Hardy's and further to the east the great food my husband and I had at Tony and Luigi's. Well, those were the good old days, right? But I like the present times also. Writing this on a typewriter makes me think I am still old-fashioned. I have never learned the computer, and that's that.

When I Was a Boy

By Jim McKee

In many ways, when I was a boy in the 1940s Lincoln represented what I think of as the "good old days." The population was almost exactly half of today's, there was no TV, a trolley car still rattled down Sheridan Boulevard to College View, there were no cell phones, no credit cards, no sales tax, no road rage, no e-mail, traffic, no cars that rudely honk when locked and no bank account numbers. Everyone knew everyone, there were two policemen cruising after midnight—one south of O Street, the other north, teachers were respected, cars could pretty much be repaired at home, many people didn't lock their homes and there was plenty of time for Boy Scout meetings, summer gardens, going for rides and generally just messin' around.

My world was pretty well geographically defined. My parents built their house on South Cotner Blvd. In 1940, a cluster of three homes surrounded on all sides by fields offering unlimited potential for exploration and sufficient opportunity to become permanently injured to be infinitely interesting. Half a mile east, beyond an interchangeable sea of wheat and corn was the old Taylor farm (now a bagel and record shop) with orchards, melon patches and even horses. This area was annually off limits in the late summer when bands of "gypsies" camped and routinely kidnapped all stray children—or so we were warned. The next habitation east was the Veteran's Hospital so far away it would well have been in the next state. O Street/Highway 34 brought traffic at 60 mph over the hill to a surprise and often missed stop sign—great entertainment. It also brought stray dogs which often ended up at our house where my mother would wash and feed them before they wandered off. Hoboes also occasionally knocked at the back door looking for work but accepting a sandwich before they too wandered off. To the south, 56th Street was a dirt lane, then a few houses in Piedmont. Lincoln was literally another city to the west— beyond even 48th Street which then did not go north from O but sort of sprung up at Vine Street. To get there you had to go north on Cotner and turn west but there was no reason to go there anyway. The trade center was Bethany down Cotner Blvd. with no buildings or houses until you reached Bethany Park and Park Valley Golf Course. Bethany was where I went to church, school, Boy Scouts and there were kids my age. Because Bethany State Bank had closed in the Great Depression, we had to drive "over to Havelock" miles and miles to the north. I still bank in Havelock though they now insist the bank is Pinnacle rather than Vic Anderson's Havelock National.

My father's service station on the southwest corner of Cotner and O was an oasis for farmers, doctors from the VA, attorneys from Piedmont and employees from Northern National Gas whose border station and area headquarters were at 84th and O. Because his was the first business, at the extreme edge of the city, it served variously as a voting place, cream drop, mail pick up, hardware store and, since there was no café, a place where everybody gathered after work, sometimes for a game of cribbage or pitch but often just to find out what had happened that day. Everyone knew Mac and Fleetwing.

When the stucco and board English architecture building was enlarged, the outdoor hoist was brought inside and the old pit covered with six inches of reinforced concrete for an office, a large copper-clad bay window was built looking over the intersection. One of my early jobs in addition to filling the old water-filled zinc-lined Coke machine was to wash the window and put in stimulating displays. The best displays were the seasonal flowers sent up from Del Tyrrell's greenhouse in Bethany. Easter was always good for a lily and at Christmas a huge poinsettia held forth surrounded by a pyramid of Royal Triton, Quaker State, Pennzoil and other esoteric canned oils in weights ranging from 10W to 60W. I clearly remember a Christmas card addressed simply to "the filling station with the poinsettia in the window, Lincoln, Nebr." And it was delivered, not even a zip code!

My WWII memories are centered around isolated pinpoints of war related news, the world map dad kept studded with colored pins, huge stacks of Wings cigarettes, tin can drives, selling the kitchen grease at the Havelock Safeway grocery store, ration coupons, red and blue points, propaganda cartoons and Victory gardens.

By the early 1950s the bus which came down O Street connected me with a huge new world—downtown Lincoln. I was fascinated with the amazing array of goods available from the used bookstores, department stores, Walgreen's and particularly from the three dime stores—everything imaginable from goldfish to photographic darkroom supplies.

Downtown was also where the movies were most accessible, the Joyo was great even then but I never mastered the necessary bus transfers to get there. The Capital at 15th and O was my Saturday morning favorite. There, for the bizarre amount of 9¢ you could get pretty much a whole morning's entertainment from a cartoon, short subject, news reel, feature and one of those great never-ending serials with snippets which left the hero dangling near death every week. A hamburger at the Hotel D' or Acme Chili Parlor and then to the basement of the YMCA at 13th and P or the Carnegie Library for a free film of perhaps a bit more substance than the Capital. A great fun-filled day.

Of course there were the big flossy theaters like the Stuart, Varsity or Lincoln or the slightly less elaborate Nebraska, State or even Colonial/Husker but these were somehow more for evenings when we occasionally popped into the 1940 black Ford with its gasoline-powered Tropic Aire supplemental heater with the whole family. Interestingly the parking lot or garage apparently had yet to be invented but dad always found, perhaps by driving around the block, a diagonal spot on the street.

Were they the good old days? Even without polio vaccine, seat belts, fluoride, air conditioning, power steering, electric garage doors, cable TV and garbage disposals? You bet!

Whitton Carlisle School
By Mrs. Mary E. Poudfit Crabill

Eighty some years ago I didn't think I would be writing an article about "Whitton Carlisle". Whitton Carlisle was a private school in Lincoln situated at 20th and D Streets where First Plymouth Church is located at the present time. I didn't realize the name was spelled Whitton Carlisle until I visited with one of the three former pupils who still survive. I had always spelled Whitton with an "E."

My sister and I, who was three years older than I, started school there. Our classrooms, sometimes consisted of two grade levels and we would listen to the other class instead of doing our own work. There was a large coat closet where, those who misbehaved were sent, fortunately, I don't remember ever being sent there. We kept our books and supplies in large gray boxes about six inches deep.

Every year they had a Maypole Dance that involved all the students, something we all anticipated. There was a well-equipped gym where we took dancing lessons. Miss Whitton or Miss Carlisle rang a large bell when school was starting and closing.

One of my most vivid memories is the lesson we received when we were late returning to school after lunch. We had been to the drug store to buy licorice candy. The teacher put licorice sticks in a glass of water to show us what it was doing to our stomachs.

A number of the students lived at the school. It was closed to make way for First Plymouth Church. I was sent to Cherry Street School, which was later replaced by Prescott School.

Yet Another Perspective
By Nancy Shirey

I remember the Mug that was on the south corner of 33rd and O Street. It had homemade root beer and ice cream. Yummy! Not too far from there was Demma's grocery store.

The Mug was a big hang out for teens. Also the eyes moved on it, the mug that is.

There was a green house and flower store on 33rd north of O Street called Yule's. The Greentree Apartments are there now.

At Wyuka Cemetery the pond, which is still there was a place where you could ice skate in the winter. At Capital Beach the Lincoln Telephone Company would have their annual picnics. The ride I remember most and almost always would ride for hours was the "Bug." So much fun.

Downtown was fun when I was a kid. Kresges was a great place to go for they had a lunch counter and lots of toys. Woolworths and Grants were also stores that we did plenty of shopping at.

Another landmark I remember was the Greenwich where they had the best hot roast beef sandwiches. This was on O Street between 19th and 20th.

Hunting in the '20s on North 27th Street

By James Stuart

There were some ponds on north 27th Street north of the present Highway 80, a mile or two, where I used to hunt ducks with my dad and others. It was an easy time from our house at 1040 Fall Creek Road in Piedmont. I could drive from home and be in the blind in twenty minutes. The duck season opened on or about the 15th of September and went through to the "freeze-up" time. The limits were generous and the shooting was good.

Capital Beach was owned by the Ferguson family and was located in northwest Lincoln. It had all sorts of rides that could be found in a circus, plus a roller coaster, which, I remember, was pretty rickety even in those days—but fun. There was also a swimming beach that attracted many of us in the summer. It was great fun to go to Capital Beach with four our eight nickels to go on the rides.

Streetcars used to run from downtown as far south to the end of the line on Sheridan Boulevard. You could ride on the electric streetcars for a nickel each way, and as you can imagine, it was great sport for those of us who were young enough, and full of fun, to "pull the trolley" which took the power off of the streetcar and brought it to a complete stop—and dark. I don't remember any of us ever getting caught by the conductor.

There was a place in College View that was known as "Peanut Hill" where we would go to get fresh peanut butter. I remember it as a person's home and when we went to the door, the owner would put enough peanuts in a grinder to make the amount of peanut butter that you wanted. I remember it as fresh and yummy.

There was a Yum Yum Hut at 29th and O Street that was something new and different in Lincoln. It was hamburger, steamed, and about the consistency of today's sloppy joe, and put on a bun. All of this for a nickel.

The Hotel d'Hamburger was a place on 14th and P Street where you could buy six hamburgers for a quarter, or a nickel for one. Chocolate pie was 10¢—and good. Bean soup and chili were 10¢.

The Acme Chili Parlor on the northwest corner of 14th and O Street was a great place for chili. As I remember, it was especially good and had at least ¼ inch of grease floating on top of the bowl. I do not remember how much it cost, but it was good. If I remember correctly, it was owned by the Christopolus family.

There were two wonderful beer places in town that were used by college students in the thirties. One was Lebsack's, located in the building at the south end of the street in front of the Burlington Railroad depot. There were two or three Lebsack brothers that ran the operation and if we were someplace away and midnight was quickly coming, we would call Eddie and he would put the beer outside for us and we would come by and pick it up—after hours. We would pay him the following day.

Another great place was Freddies, located on north 14th Street almost to the Cornhusker Highway. It was on the east side of the road. You could get there from the fraternity houses within five minutes. Freddie and Hazel were great friends to all of the fraternity folks. Beer was a nickel a glass and Hazel, Freddie's wife, would keep the beer coming until we told her we had had enough. There was a jukebox in this establishment that had all of the grand records of the day.

The Mug was located at 33rd and O Street on the southwest corner. The Mug was a very large root beer mug. There was room for a dozen automobiles to come by, your waitresses would take your order, bring the mugs of root beer to your car on a tray that hooked on to the window and was braced against the door. A mug of root beer cost a nickel—and—it was delicious. I remember Ralph Beechner being involved with The Mug. Ralph was involved with Lincoln High School, later the University of Nebraska, and was always involved with athletics. A grand person!

Woodsdale Was Part Lake

By Barbara Solomon

Prior to WWII

1920. My grandfather was Edward Walt, who owned Walt's Music Store. In the '20s he and his five brothers had an orchestra that played for all the dance clubs and vaudeville acts that came to town and performed at the Orpheum Theatre located on the northwest corner of 12th & P. One night after a vaudeville show, he phoned my grandmother and told her to get the children up and dressed and to lay out a lunch with cold beer; he was bringing home some friends. His guests were Al Jolson and his manager. They had a musical evening in the living room at 2035 B Street and my mother never forgot it.

1930. My brother and I were four years apart, so that made a baby and a four-year-old. On hot evenings my father would make up two beds in the back seat of the car. There would be a bed behind the driver and a bed behind the passenger. They would run at a right angle to the back seat, being built up by cardboard cartons with a pillow on top. Then my parents would bring a dishpan to the car and we would drive to Valley Ice Co. A chunk of ice would be put into the dishpan and the dishpan would be put on the floor of the front seat between the driver and the passenger. The vent would be open and the air from the vent would come into the car, blow over the ice and voila, air conditioning. That was how my parents got us to go to sleep on nights when often it never got below 90, if that. This was the same era when people who lived in apartment houses close to the capitol would take their blankets and spread them out on the capitol lawn and sleep under the stars. I cannot remember when air conditioning became an everyday thing.

Of course, as a small child but not too small or young to remember there were a few wonderful things and aren't wonderful things frequently associated with food? that we had in Lincoln: The Windmill; The Mug; Acme Chili Parlor (or Acne, as my brother and I called it); and the Yum Yum Hut. Later came Circle Drive-in and Ken Eddy's (where I finally moved a bed and dressing table and took up residence); Bill Merediths Hamburgers, which was later Coatney's Resaurant, and the Beer Garden at 14th and High. As a four- or five-year-old, I particularly remember The Mug and The Windmill on hot summer evenings as part of a ride. Going for a ride was a huge thing—my parents loved getting in the car and driving. In the 30s it was blistering hot. The ride always ended up with a cool root beer at The Mug or The Windmill that was brought to the car window on a tray that hooked on to the rolled-down window. I do not remember a single time when root beer was not spilled by either my brother or me. These haunts were the fast food places I remember.

Stork's Drive-In just east of 13th and High Streets stood with several incarnations until 2000. *Photo courtesy Nebraska State Historical Society.*

If one wanted to go first class, the restaurants were limited. Our family did a lot of cafeterias. One was called the State Farm, which was out on Ag Campus on Holdrege Street. The other was at the YWCA. Both places had food that my parents and their cronies liked and could take the children to. The Pow-Wow and TeePee rooms at the Cornhusker Hotel were always a treat; and the Italian Village and Tony & Luigi's were where you went for steak.

WWII

1940. When I was nine we moved to 2911 South 29th Street. My parents' families said we "moved to the edge of town." The house was previously owned by an executive at the electric company and it had an electric dishwasher. Our new house became a sight seeing spot for all my brother's pals and my pals because whoever heard of an electric dishwasher?

As the 40s approached I became old enough to go to the movies on Saturday or Sunday afternoons with friends. Our parents would take us or sometimes we were allowed to take the bus with friends. This was BIG—we lived quite sheltered lives with stay-at-home mothers and they always knew where we were. At the movies there were a lot of news films like The Eyes and Ears of the World and Pathe News.

The war was going on in Europe and we would see clips of the refugees and/or prisoners leaving their homes and cities with their belongings stacked on wagons or carts being pulled by humans or some farm animal going down dirt roads or over bridges, all very sad and dreamlike for a young girl living a lovely life in a country not at war. When Pearl Harbor was bombed, our family got the news while sitting around our breakfast table in the kitchen, and with the airbase in Lincoln, lots of planes were flying over, nearly 24 hours a day. I asked my father what would happen to us if the Japanese or Germans came to get us and he answered "Don't worry, honey, we'll cross that bridge when we come to it." I of course envisioned what I had seen at the movies and the newsreels and imagined our family with our furniture piled high on carts going over high bridges. I wasn't thrilled.

It was not long after our family moved to 2911 South 29th that I received my first bike. It was like getting a car—total freedom. I could take off and go anywhere, unseen. There were strings attached. I could go on some streets that were paved; 29th Street went from Georgian Court to Calvert but 29th became gravel at Laurel Street. Calvert was gravel from 27th to 40th and anyway the Bishop's home was on Calvert. The long and short of it was no gravel—never go to the Bishop's home! Two blocks on Georgian Court was okay, 29th Street to Jackson Drive was okay, as long as I just went to my cousin's which was on the corner. It boiled down to a total of 3 ? blocks and I could be seen totally.

The Cornhusker

The Cornhusker Hotel was The Place. Everyone loved going there for food, meetings, parties, etc. I still miss it. It was owned and operated by the Schimmel family, which had hotels in other cities, each run by a Schimmel brother: Bernard, Walter, Edward and A. Q. (Abram Quincy).

When I was in Prescott School, I sat alone at a desk-table for two in the front row in Miss Hannigan's first grade room. One day there was a knock at the door and it was the principal with a new girl and her mother. The new girl was put next to me and became my deskmate and immediate dear friend. She was Doris Schimmel, daughter of A. Q. and Marian Schimmel.

Over the years we spent lots of great times at the Cornhusker where she lived and at my house on Woodsdale. Once in second grade Doris invited me to the hotel for an overnight. My parents gave me money for goodies and such and took me to the hotel, where the Schimmel family welcomed me. Doris and I ate lunch in the Tee Pee Room and when I got out my money, she said "We don't need money here" and she signed a ticket. This was my introduction to charging. What a boon! I couldn't wait to get home and inform my parents that we should run, not walk, to the Cornhusker Hotel where we should move, sell the house on Woodsdale and move to the Cornhusker where one did not need money. You could eat, drink, even maybe buy clothes and no money, all you needed was to sign your name to a ticket.

The Schimmel family moved from the hotel about the time we were in Irving Junior High to a lovely home at Sheridan and Van Dorn and a few years later to an even lovelier home on Woodscrest. Doris's parents and my parents were very friendly and we were invited to some fabulous parties at their home.

A.Q. was famous for his Christmas day Eggnog Bash, which started Christmas morning and went all day. Every man in Lincoln I ever knew was invited and by Christmas afternoon and early evening there were literally hundreds of irate wives who had been left alone with the children for most of Christmas day while their husbands partied at what was absolutely a party so great no man in his right mind would ever turn it down no matter how bad things would be at home later for months on end.

Doris and I were always close until she died in her forties. I hated that she was so sick and so young. We could talk about anything. When the Cornhusker Hotel was leveled for the new Cornhusker to be built I mixed a batch of Bloody Marys and watched with friends from atop a parking garage and as the dynamite exploded and the building crumbled we drank a toast to Doris and all the fabulous times we had had together at the Cornhusker. It was not a happy day.

O Street

1940s/1950s. For a town the size of Lincoln, we had some really nice stores: two major department stores, Miller & Paine and Gold & Company; several clothing stores, Ben Simons, Magees, Hovland Swanson. In the fall about homecoming time we had the "Fall Opening" of the stores. They dressed their windows to the nines, wonderfully, extravagantly and beautifully done and people would get dressed up and look at the windows. This was always at night and it was like the Easter Parade at night. The sidewalks would be packed with people and it was exciting and beautiful, one huge style show.

Have you ever noticed how very wide the parkings are on Woodsdale Boulevard between 24th Street and 27th Street? That's because in the early 30s there were lakes where the parkings are now. Two lakes in which swam lovely white swans. The Woodsdale Addition, at the bottom of the Country Club, was brand new at that time and the lakes were quite unique. However, along with the drought and the families with small children who feared a child could drown, the city filled in the lakes by 1936.

2426 Woodsdale, shown beyond one of the ponds in the median.
Photo courtesy Barb Solomon.

My First Night In Town

By Bob Marhenke

I can remember my first trip to the capital city in which I stayed overnight. I can remember approaching Lincoln with my nose pressed to the car window trying to be the first to see the capitol. As we neared the city, first you could see the capitol and then as you topped a ridge, below was the capital city. It was our "Senior Sneak Day" … I can remember we stayed at the Capital Hotel, (now the YMCA) we went to the Varsity Theatre to see the movie "Unconquered," which starred Paulette Goddard, we walked to the Capitol, stopped at the Korn Popper, went to Morrill Hall and we ate at the Grid Café. As I recall though, the outer limits of the city were much more definable then as compared to today. My point is; I remember my "first night in town."

Can you remember your first day in town? Can you remember what you did that very first day, where you went, who you saw? Can you remember what Lincoln looked like? Can you remember your "first night in town?"

Now that I have your imagination working, try to envision if you can, what the same area was like for the very first settler that came here to stay? Try to imagine that person, as he stood on any one of the ridges that surround much of this city, just what he must have seen—just what he must have thought. On his very first night, where would he have stayed? On his first day, what would he have done, who all did he see?

Well fortunately history has recorded this for us. The man was John Gregory. John arrived here, alone, in the fall of 1862. Luckily history has also preserved for us, a speech given by John that gives us a very good look at some answers to these very questions.

Take a listen to some of what John Gregory had to say about his travel and experiences to get here and his "first day in town."

"The early summer of 1862 found me residing in eastern Michigan, possessed of a comfortable bank account, with the ambition for adventure usual to adolescent youth and a government commission as a United States mail agent, a position which enabled me to pass free over the mail routes of the United States, including stage lines. About this time a relative who passed by the salt basins on his return from California called upon us and advised me to take advantage of my opportunities and visit them, which I immediately proceeded to do."

At this point in time it is important to remember that Nebraska west of the Mississippi River to the Missouri river, rail travel was scant and the Civil War was on and a problem for any travel. John explains that being a U.S. mail agent gave him immunity to some of these problems so he made it to St. Joseph, Missouri with minimal problems.

He continues … *"From St. Joseph to Plattsmouth I went by stage. At this point public transportation was at an end, and I hired a horse to ride the rest of the way. From Weeping Water to the Basin I followed and Indian trail …"*

At this point in John Gregory's speech he explains "his first night in town" …

"I reached the present site of Lincoln toward the evening of a warm day in September. No one lived there or had ever lived there previous to that date. Herds of beautiful antelope gamboled over it's surface during the day and coyotes and wolves held possession during the night … About a mile west on Middle creek the smoke was rising from a camp of Otoe Indians and down in the neck of Oak Creek where West Lincoln now stands, was a camp of about 100 Pawnee wigwams. I rode over that night slept upon my blanket by the side of one of them," This is John Gregory's recollection of his first day and his first night. He continues … *"and the next morning went over to the salt basin. The tread of civilization had not marred its surface. Its surface was as smooth as any waxen floor. It was covered with an incrustation of salt about a quarter of an inch deep, white as the driven snow, while the water of the springs was as salt as brine could be"* It was the largest of these springs *"two miles northwest of the present city of Lincoln"* where John Gregory staked his claim.

He returned to Weeping Water, bought supplies, hired men, returned and started a salt business. Soon the area became known as Gregory Basin. This area as we know it today was in the proximity of Oak Lake, Capitol Beach Lake and West Lincoln near the Pfizer Labs complex.

Gregory Basin had the very first post office in the area and John was postmaster. He bought his family here and built the very first frame home (it is this author's opinion that this home is still standing). Willie Gregory, his son, was the first white baby born in the basin. John was the first legislator to be elected from the newly formed Lancaster County. About this time Gregory Basin filled with people ducking the civil war draft.

There are many more firsts one can credit to John Gregory and much more information can be gleaned from memories he left with us. There are many more interesting stories of the 1860s about the area I call West Lincoln but big changes are coming.

Although many more efforts were tried to make the salt industry rewarding, it would never again be profitable. As the land around Lincoln was broken for farming this affected the water table and the salt springs. With the coming of the railroad, salt could be delivered cheaper than it could be extracted locally. This might have spelled doom for most areas.

Page Hamilton's Recollections

By Page Hamilton

I remember going with my grandmother and aunt to Herpolsheimers, which was on the southwest corner of 12th and N Street. I have no memory of what they were buying or looking at but the store had this fascinating system of small cages that sent the money up to the office on visible rail lines above the departments. The store also had a gorgeous curved glass corner window.

We lived at 29th and Ryons and it was the rumor at the time of the unsolved "great bank robbery" that there had been some help from an elected county offical who lived in the general area. That was an interesting area of town. The Cochrans, Jerners, Jearys, Metheneys, Bergquists, Holtzs, Hinzes, Miles, H. Alice Howell, Hollis Linprecht, Knox Jones, McCullas, Cy Sherman, Babsts, O'Connels, and the Locks. As a kid we went to Antelope Park and saw the poor animals all cooped up and walked around the rim of the fishpond which had been in the middle of M Street for watering horses before my time. Now that same enclosure is at the Folsom Zoo. We also, on hot nights during the drought and the depression, went to the "Winkie Man" for root beer. It was The Mug at the corner of 33rd and O Street. The teeth opened up as the service area. Adults ordered a full size mug and the children got the small ones. I also remember getting ice cream cones with more and more dips as the depression deepened. I think it went from three to finally five.

When my buddies and I could get into the movies for a dime, we were taken downtown we walked or rode the trolley and went to the Liberty Theatre where we could explore the entire balcony and back stairs and climb around on the box seats. I do not remember a single movie we saw there. I do remember going with my aunt to some kind of a live performance there and they tossed candy to the audience for some reason. I think that theater may also have been the Oliver. There was a marvelous candy store right in that block and we got real hot cinnamon candy. The Liberty was where the Varsity and NBC building at the southwest corner of 13th and P Street were later located. Just west of the Oliver was the home of the Zerung's. I was in that home only once. It was on the south side of the street and had a beautiful grill on the north windows. Another neat home was the Krause home, it was beautiful and unusual. Too bad we did not have historic preservation then.

When my buddies and I were in junior high, Roy Cochran was the governor and they lived at the old mansion. Mrs. Cochran arranged for the WPA orchestra to play in the ballroom there on Friday nights and any kids were welcome. Since we went to Irving, most of the group was from there. We did not drive so that limited the crowd. My buddies and I did a lot of watching the dancers. We had our first "formal" there. Mary Aileen had wonderful slumber parties and teas. I think that we learned a lot those days because we met interesting people and there was help that waited on us and we behaved. There were times when Mary Aileen and one of us would go through the tunnel to the Capitol and read the funnies in the Governor's private elevator. We would stop it between floors. I have often thought that Mrs. Cochran and Breta Peterson Dow kept us from being juvenile delinquents. Breta used to come to our YWCA cabin in Pioneers Park when we were having an overnight there. It was located in that area where they have the turnaround in the southwest part. We rented the cabin and some family member loaded us out there. We had a great time and Breta would come out later, spend the night and leave in the morning. We wandered the park and talked about all manner of interesting things. I remember lying on the soft green grass and watching the clouds go by as we enjoyed a day of spring vacation. We were a lively group of girls in junior high. We had a newspaper, which we did on a hectograph, took subscriptions and delivered every Sunday. It was the "Teen Times." The front page was real news, by our interpretation, an autograph of any visiting dignitary of the time, a gossip column, a love story, comics, cartoons and advice. One time we got into trouble because we had used the words, belly, belly, belly. It was usually three pages. It kept us so busy because we had to get the copy ready, type it with the hectograph carbon and then print the copies. We had to wait 24 hours before we could print the next page so we really did not have time for other endeavors. I am not going to tell you some of the things we did have time for. There were a number of us in these adventures, and we are all still close friends.

When we were in high school, groups or two girls would band together and have a formal dance or a tea dance at the Cornhusker or the University Club. The funny thing about those parties was, all of the couples were arranged by the hostesses. I think that the band leader was Johnny Cox. This was in the old Cornhusker, and at intermission, we all paraded to the "TP" Tasty Pastry for a coke and shoestring potatoes. We did have fun. We also spent time after a movie on the balcony of Bauers' having milk shakes, which were really thick, it was a gathering place. It was located where Wright's Jewelry is now. We went to the pavilion in Antelope Park after movies. There was an orchestra and we could watch the dancers or dance for 5¢. This was in the summer.

My dad took me down to see the Sower when it arrived on the siding of the capitol grounds in a double flat car, it was beautiful gold and huge. We all enjoyed the progress on the building and it was another place to spend time after church as a family.

When we were in grade school or junior high, they gave spelling tests in the attic of the old McKinley School on Saturday mornings. That building was on its last legs and I was spooked by the atmosphere of the building. My mother's high school class of 1913 was the last one to use the building as a school.

I also remember going with family, to see the baseball team play in the evening at the ballpark, which was located near 1st and West P Street. My uncle was a big baseball fan.

Tap

By Arline Gohde Kraft

The Lincoln City Directory from 1938 listed Hazel Johnson, dance instructor in tap, ballet, acrobatics, toe and ballroom dancing, 1308 O Street. This was upstairs on the northeast corner of 13th and O Street. This was a two story building that housed United Cigar on the first floor corner and Towntalk Bakery and Luncheonette to the east, Hardy Furniture Company and Acme Bakery.

Taking the bus to town was easy and we kids did this at quite an early age. I went downtown for two dance lessons each week. We got off the bus near the Varsity Theatre at 13th and P (southwest corner) bouncing along the sidewalks of Lincoln to Hazel Johnson's studio.

I don't remember much about the United Cigar Company, but we loved Towntalk Bakery and all the pastry in the cases. These tall glass cases at the front window were sloped from narrow at the top to wider at the bottom, with many shelves of sweet and delectable items. Cream Puffs and Mary Anns were our favorites.

To the east of the bakery we entered double wide swinging doors that led to upstairs to the best part of my life, dance class. Halfway up to the second floor was another set of double wide swinging doors. It was like opening up paradise when I opened those doors to run along the long squeaky floored hallway to the very back of the building.

It was probably a typical dance studio, small outer office, changing rooms and a large practice room with a piano. The north side of the practice room was on the alley and had large metal framed nine or twelve paned windows. They had a center section that opened with a long metal push out bar. Opening those windows was the only help for hot days and the music seemed to float out over the alley toward the back of the Stuart Theatre. What a treat—live piano music for rehearsal. To this day I cherish piano music.

One hour on Monday a class lesson and one hour on Thursday was my private lesson. The private lesson wasn't as much fun since dancing with a chorus line is more enjoyable. It was hot and sweaty and great exercise especially if you loved to dance. We got yelled at a lot, "All right kids, ready, 5 6 7 8 begin again." We were such "Tap" snobs back then but we had people like Eleanor Powell, Fred Astaire, Bill "Bojangles" Robinson and Gene Kelly. Not bad for an eight-year-old.

When we left the dance floor the magic was over. Change your workout clothes and tap shoes. Back down the creaking stairs, we exited through the swinging double doors and into the sunlight of O Street.

Outside I walked past the Towntalk Bakery, maybe stopping to get a 4¢ cream puff. One block west to 12th and O Street, the Security Mutual Life Building (now the Anderson Building), was my parents business. There I looked out the corner curved glass window of Room 211 to see Nick, the very rotund cop, directing traffic.

Just a piece of downtown Lincoln and I still love to dance.

A C Grill and a 5 MS

By Jann Loerch

V J Day—We rode on top of a convertible down O Street. Andy Shizas was my heartthrob and we ate a lot at the All American Café just south of 13th Street on O Street. My parents would not let me go across O Street but they let me go as far as the Yum Yum Hut.

We went to St. Mathews for their Junior and Senior High meetings as we got to dance. We all belonged to Westminster and amused ourselves by pulling the trolley off the tracks. My dad tried to teach me to drive just before I was 16 and I drove on the trolley tracks on Sheridan Boulevard.

We all belonged to the Country Club but got our kicks from breaking into the swimming pool after hours. We also listened to Duggie Doyle play and sing his songs in the ballroom.

Marv Haase I started at Randolph School with Maude Rousseau as the principal. She liked the boys better than the girls and had a paddle in her office. I was so skinny I had to have milk lunch. I started kindergarten when I was 4 ? and when they ended the midyear they put me up a grade so I graduated a year before I was supposed to. We lived at 3616 C Street.

My dad was an attorney with Allen, Requartte and Wood and their office was on the 3rd floor of the Woodman Accident Building on the southwest corner of 13th and N Street. Bauer's Russian Mints candy store was on the first floor. When my dad worked late we would go to the YWCA for dinner in the cafeteria. We did our shopping at Rudge and Guenzel and Miller & Paine. Mr. Allen was a brother-in-law of William Jennings Bryan. When the statue of WJB was unveiled on the north steps of the capitol my dad gave the speech. His best friend was Eddie Faulkner. Ed was a staunch Republican and my dad was the head of the Democratic Party. My dad asked Eddie how he was going to like looking out the window of the new Woodman Accident Building and seeing that statue and Eddie replied that he was not going to have any windows on that side.

We moved to 2434 Ryons Street. Jim Ellis and his family and Judge Carter and his family lived across the street from us on Ryons. George Towne lived next door and Jimmy Woodward lived on the corner. The Martin's and Gold's lived around the corner on 24th and South. My dad later went to work for

Farmer's Mutual of Nebraska and the Straub Family lived up on Sheridan Boulevard, a block from the Abel family. My mom shopped at Leon's, which was on South Street and had great chocolate shakes. Spencer's Steak House was at 14th and South Street. We bought our shoes from Nick Guidinger at a shoe store on north 13th Street. I took piano lessons from Alice Rowell and she lived on 20th, about 2 blocks south of D Street and Plymouth Church.

Kids in my class at Irving were Tommy Schlaebitz, Tom Ludwick, Ed Weir and Lefty Leinberer. Jack Moore, Alice Van Berg, Susan Turner, Phyllis Colbert, Jean Walker, Donna Colhapp, Janet Pierce, Betty Guidinger. Colhapp's had a restaurant next to Wagey's at 17th and South Street.

My aunt and uncle lived at 1512 R Street which is now the Historical Society. I was raised by a colored maid Marie Bond, who worked hard so that all of her children could go to college. She was with us until I was nine. Then we moved to Ryons and I went to Prescott School. Our home had radiators and oil heat. I had so many allergies that my parents had to cut down the spirea bushes at the front of the house and the cat had to go. The dog, Cuddles a mutt, got to stay. We would sleep with our heads in the windowsills when it was hot. We had an attic with creaky narrow stairs on Ryons. The house had hardwood floors covered up with carpet and beautiful walnut woods. It had a landing with an office part way to the second floor with French doors. My dad used it for his home office. My parents built a family room onto the house with a first floor bathroom. The house was built in 1926 and looked like it was stucco but was really Portland cement. We were convinced that the ivy held it all together.

Of course I remember going to King's and the Turnpike and hearing the great bands. The roller coaster at Capital Beach was always a favorite. We went to shows at the Stuart Theatre and had burgers and malts at the place next door. I can't remember the name of it, but if you wanted a grilled cheese sandwich and a chocolate malt you ordered an "A C Grill and a 5 MS." The Lincoln and Varsity Theatres were also thriving.

Country Clubs

By Roger Bacon

The group of founding members of The Country Club of Lincoln came together in 1903 and began planning their club. The original property, 43 acres running south from Washington Street and north from 7th Street, was purchased for $22,500.

On September 30, 1905 the members of the club adopted Articles of incorporation, which included the following Article:

"The general nature of the business transacted by said club shall be to buy and own, with the power to improve, mortgage and sell real estate on all or on a portion of which may be erected and maintained a clubhouse, golf links, tennis courts, bowling alleys, dancing pavilions, and the like, for common and friendly intercourse and rational amusements. It shall also have the power to own, mortgage and sell all such personal property as may be necessary to successfully operate a first class country club."

The business of running a club began in earnest. While life was certainly calmer and simpler for Lincolnites at the turn of the century, there was still the occasional crisis, as discussed at a July 19, 1906 Directors Meeting:

"Moved and carried that hereafter chicken be not served at the 50¢ table de hote meals ... Moved and carried that the request of Solomon the chef for a $10 increase in wages be not granted."

Oops!

Two months earlier it was "Moved a carried that the golf professional be instructed to charge 50¢ per lesson." This must lead us to the conclusion that the Directors didn't want to provide golf lessons for the price of a chicken dinner.

The first clubhouse had a restaurant, card rooms, locker rooms for both men and women, tennis courts and bowling alleys. As was the custom for most private clubs of the day, there were also sleeping rooms available for members and their guests.

The club enjoyed steady growth through its first decade, with many of its ongoing traditions being established during that time. The club celebrated the Fourth of July in 1906 with its first fireworks display—at a cost of $50.

After a time, as the club began to outgrow its grounds and clubhouse, its members began to look for a larger piece of property. On July 7, 1917 the club membership approved the lease of 40 acres from the St. Thomas Orphanage and purchase of 65 acres from Woods Bros., and so began the process of developing its present location. There were a series of delays—financing issues, conflicting ideas among the membership, a world war—but construction eventually began in the early 1920s.

At the end of World War I, the "members and sons of members who entered the service of the country for the war" were welcomed back into the club, and Lincoln resident General John J. Pershing was made a life member of the club. Then came the complicated task of planning for the new golf course and clubhouse. Studies of seen and soil, course layout, clubhouse location. Committees were formed, feelings were hurt, members resigned.

Money became an issue when the old club grounds failed to bring the original asking price of $150,000. The property was offered to the City of Lincoln for $100,000, and the city demurred. Then the club approached the Sesostris Temple with a price of $90,000, but the Shriners said "no thanks." In March of 1922 the old property was sold to Woods Bros. For $80,000, leaving the club to do a bit of creative financing.

Fortunately, this was a time of prosperity for the club. New members, many excited by all the work at 27th and High Streets. Fifty-year bonds were issued, and the crisis soon passed. Though the concept of "creative financing" would reappear more than once during the next fifty years.

In September of 1921, with the new course set to open the following spring, the chairman of the grounds committee made the first official mention of that sticky subject which haunts golf pros, women players, and all novices who don't want their good walk spoiled—speed of play!

"I want to recommend some rules that I think we should be more careful in observing. I am perhaps the chief offender in this first recommendation.

Driving into people before they are well out of the way. I will try and reform and ask some of the rest of you to do the same. Second, a few slow foursomes hold up twosomes and faster foursomes ... I think we have had less farming in the rough and mowing down weeds, soiling of clubs in the bunkers, etc., than ever before, but there is still room for improvement. It is surprising how few, even of the older players know the rules."

Things went well during the 1920s, and the club showed ever-increasing activity on the golf course, in the café, around the pool. The club served its purpose as a small, civilized hamlet in a country obsessed by the social changes, which found fertile ground during the roaring twenties. Its members lived well, its employees were well paid and kept busy. The average monthly golf payroll was $175 in 1922. Six years later it increased to $1,200. By 1928 the salaries of the caddy master, lifeguard, dishwasher, and salad girl had doubled, and the club manager was being paid an unheard of $150 per month. It seemed that the club was fulfilling the dreams of its members, and becoming the center of social life among well-heeled Lincolnites.

As the 1929 golf season wound down, Country Club of Lincoln members, along with the rest of the country, suddenly came to understand that when something seems to good to be true, it is, most likely, just that. Nebraska's agrarian economy had been spiraling downward for years as crop and livestock prices dropped from their WWI highs. It was, however, the stock market crash of October, 1929 which marked the beginning of a period of vicious poverty for many Nebraskans, and a frightening period of uncertainty for the club.

In 1928 the Country Club of Lincoln boasted 458 members. During the first several years after the onset of national economic collapse resignations and leaves of absence became so numerous that the club simply quit accepting them except during the month of January. Many members saw their accounts at the club fall behind and were horrified to have their names posted in the clubhouse, as was the custom of the time. This practice added fuel to the fire in terms of members leaving the club.

New member recruitment became a priority and the club manager was given a $10 commission from each new member. Later a salesman was engaged "to solicit new members on a 35% basis." Finally the club came up with a brilliant plan involving "club privilege" memberships.

These memberships involved waiving the initiation fee ($100 plus a $200 deposit) and allowing people to use the club without being full, stockholding members. Anyone who has shopped for Internet or cellular phone service is familiar with this concept—eliminate the large up front cost (cell phone, computer, club membership) and create a steady stream of monthly income.

It worked.

Membership once again began to grow, and the club was able to breathe a cautious sigh of relief.

Cost cutting was an important part of club management during the depression, and creativity was the rule. To save money on chemistry, there was a plan to "permit pumping water direct from our own well to the pool and thus enable the pool to be filled once a week with fresh water."

Fairway fertilization was tricky business in the 1930s, and the Board of Directors debated at length how best to accomplish this vital task during an era of tight budgets. There was a sense of great pride as the manager submitted the actual cost for the year 1938:

Hauling 200 tons of manure @ 75¢ per ton $150.00
Manure 25.00
Labor 31.50
2 pitch forks 3.30
Cost of repair of spreader 1.50
150 gal. Gasoline @ 16¢ 24.00
Oil for tractor 1.50

"... which reflected a savings of $138.20 over the estimate."

The worst fire the club experienced occurred during this time, destroying much of the pro shop, and most of the members' golf equipment stored there. Underinsured, and with few remaining resources the club moved on.

Set against the terrible backdrop of poverty, which had impaled much of the state, these efforts to keep the swimming pool clean, and the fairways green may seem at best inappropriately frivolous, perhaps to many, a shameful waste of time and effort. But the fact is that the club members, in their effort to keep and maintain this organization, which they truly loved, also kept many people working. While they were struggling to pay most of the monthly bills, receiving nasty letters from the bank, and at one point falling dangerously behind on tax payments, the club never missed a payroll. It continued to contribute to the community as an employer, a consumer of a wide variety of locally produced goods, and a symbol that prosperity was still a part of the American dream, even in the midst of its current nightmare.

Almost as quickly as it had engulfed the club, the storm subsided.

Suddenly, beginning in 1940, the crisis seemed to have ended. The club began to make large investments in facility repairs, furniture, fixtures, and all those things that had been neglected during the preceding decade. In August of that year the club decided to "employ an architect to draw up plans and estimate costs for constructing a bar or cocktail lounge and air conditioning the present grill for a dining room, and for any other desirable changes."

Perhaps most significantly, the club was able to purchase the 40 acres it had been leasing from the Catholic Bishop for a sum of $20,000. The Country Club now, finally, owned all 105 acres it had been occupying for the past two decades.

Things at the club in 1941 never looked better. The club was busy, and the parking problems became a topic for discussion among the members. The number of individual liquor lockers—always a reliable measure of country club vitality at the time—was increased to 150. As the year ended the club was ready to act on the decision to make major improvements in the clubhouse and on the golf course.

On November 17th the Board met to discuss the city's proposal to open 20th Street on the west side of the property. They also laid out plans involving "the moving of the pro shop, enlarging of the men's Crying Room, remodeling of the upstairs dining room."

Four weeks later, the members of The Country Club of Lincoln were no longer worried about the seating capacity of the Crying Room.

With memories of the Great Depression and its effect on their beloved club fresh in their minds, the members now faced the reality of another great war. They were worried about their country and their families. The club moved quickly, lowering the dues to $9 per month, and urging its members to remain a part of this little community, which had already weathered several great storms.

But for many, country club life had suddenly lost its importance. Within one month of Pearl Harbor, 3 members resigned. As its members volunteered or were called into service, the club allowed resignations on a monthly basis. In a letter to the membership, the club president expressed anxiety about the club's future:

"Your President and the Board of Directors began the year 1942 in a very pessimistic state of mind. The entrance of our country in the war brought many uncertainties. Resignations at the first of the year were very large in number and the prospects ahead did not look good. Nothing was certain other than that we would in all probability be in for plenty of changes. In this we were not disappointed …

Of the 1943 Prospects for the Country Club of Lincoln, I can only say things looked just as uncertain—perhaps more so—than at the beginning of 1942. With gas rationing a fact, and food rationing an immediate prospect, along with a shortage of sports equipment, it does not give us too bright a picture.

The majority of our members, however, are within easy walking distance of the Club. In this we are particularly fortunate. We will in all probability have our same staff of old timers to prepare such food as is available. At least we will be no worse off in this regard than in our respective homes. We know that what is to be had will be well prepared.

The list of resignations, which is now at hand shows quite a number of members dropping out, who, on the face of it, don't really need to. The club needs their support … It is an asset to the City of Lincoln. Its loss would be a distinct loss to the whole community, and too many resignations can easily bring this about."

During the war, The Country Club of Lincoln became more than ever, that oasis, that carefree place to relax and forget the turbulent world outside the gates. It began to host regular parties for Officers from the Lincoln Air Base, and it was during the war that the club began having large New Year's Eve celebrations.

The shortages of everything from food to golf balls (the government halted the production of all sports equipment during the war) to alcohol, to chlorine for the swimming pool, seems to have been taken in stride, and membership began to rebound. The club offered three different military memberships during the war, including one specifically designed for women—the wives of servicemen. By the end of the war, prospective members were informed "that due to Club facilities being over taxed, we are unable to offer a membership at this time."

The end of World War II brought general economic prosperity to America, and a chance for country clubs to address their deteriorating facilities, neglected during the lean years following the onset of the depression. For more than 17 years, there had been little money, and few resources available to maintain the structural and mechanical systems of the clubhouse, swimming pool and golf course at The Country Club of Lincoln.

While the club began to prosper, it needed additional funds to make necessary repairs and improvements. The membership of this club has been nothing if not creative for most of its existence, and in finding an additional revenue source to fund expansion they created a new pass time for themselves.

Shortly after the war, the club began installing slot machines.

There were problems immediately, as noted in February, 1946:

"… it was moved that the Board of Directors make it a club rule prohibiting the playing of slot machines by all employees and that all jack pot winners be required to count money released by jackpot and sign slip stating same."

The idea of busboys feeding slot machines was enough to prompt the Board to make the first official record of the use of these devices at the club. The were installed and removed regularly to avoid attracting undue attention as noted in 1947:

"As you know, one of the clubs chief sources of revenue has been lost, at least for the present."

But as the golf season was in full swing, the coast apparently became clear for another try at the gaming life:

"… it was moved to increase the jackpots on the quarter machine to $50, on the dime machine to $20, and on the nickel machine to $10. Motion carried."

Money flowed in and out of the club at an unprecedented rate. During this time the club was repaired, remodeled, and expanded. In December, 1948, the club president proudly expanded on the progress club had made, specifically noting many individual purchases, and ending with a prosaic, wink: "and there was money in the bank to pay for it from 'you know where.'"

In 1949, the club considered the purchase of three more slot machines. It also made the tactical error of offering the Governor of Nebraska an honorary membership. By the end of the year, the president included the following announcement in his report to the members"

"You men will also realize that the operations of the club will have to be conservative due to the fact that we no longer have THE OTHER INCOME. However, I am sure that, with your cooperation, the board will be able to operate without any increase of dues."

So ended the four-year "Las Vegas Night" at The Country Club of Lincoln.

Garner and His Boys

By Dick Ryman

Tom Brokow's best seller, *The Greatest Generation,* was released in 1998, I am proud to have grown up during these turbulent years.

I was born in Lincoln in 1925, the son of Pauline Moore Ryman and Dr. Floyd W. Ryman, a well-known dentist and early aviator. My father was killed in a plane crash in 1934 and circumstances necessitated our move to

Rochester, N.Y. We returned to Lincoln in 1940 where I attended Lincoln High School.

Big bands were the rage that memorable summer and they all played at the Turnpike and King's Ballroom. The crowds would form around bandstands twenty or thirty deep and I was always there, in the front row, with my chin on the bandstand. It was that summer that my love for jazz overpowered my good judgment and compelled me to buy a set of used drums for $50.00, the source of which I don't recall.

I practiced for hours each day to the delight of neighbors on Plymouth. Several of my friends and I were hired by Eddie Garner, a local bandleader who, like all other bandleaders, was losing men to the draft. We rehearsed a lot and traveled within a 250-mile radius area of Lincoln. The whole band, except Eddie, was 15 years of age. Often, the band limousine, a 1936 Buick with jump seats, would pick us up at Lincoln High after classes, and we would be off to play for a dance 200 miles away. We would be returned to school about 8:00 a.m., in time for classes. Eddie who was ineligible for the draft would then drive on to Milford where he attended school, learning to be a machinist. Eddie was a great influence on every young man in the band. He was a moral, hardworking, disciplined family man challenged by raising three daughters, learning to be a machinist, and operate and manage a band. He was a wonderful teacher and had a successful band. He also became a journeyman machinist.

In late 1943, Eddie's band of 15-year-olds became 18-year-olds, and we all went to war about the same time. I went to the navy, attended torpedo school, and served aboard the U.S.S. Wilson, a destroyer, in the Pacific. Eddie disbanded the band and worked in a war plant.

After the war, we all returned and persuaded Eddie to reactivate the band. He booked some jobs, and we were at it again. Every member of Eddie's band graduated from the University of Nebraska. Playing music and the GI bill put us all through school and every member of the band has been quite successful. Interestingly, most of us did not have fathers. Eddie was a father figure to all of us.

In March 1990, we had a band reunion in Lincoln. Former Garner alumni came from all over the country. The Lincoln Journal printed the story. Eddie Garner founded Garner Industries in Lincoln and in 1982 was "National Small Businessman of the Year." He retired in the early '90s and passed away December 16, 1998. All of those who were associated with Eddie Garner are deeply indebted to him.

President Roosevelt Visits Lincoln

By Mary Shurtleff Danley

In October of 1936 when I was ten and my brother Bruce was eight, we had the thrill of our lifetimes when we got to meet and shake hands with President Franklin D. Roosevelt and his wife Eleanor. The President had made a speech here, and as they were preparing to get on the train the police let us through as we had a huge bouquet of flowers for them. I will never forget how in awe I felt, and what an added thrill it was to get a letter from Eleanor Roosevelt several days later thanking us. I have her letter framed and on my bedroom wall, and treasure it to this day.

I remember hearing my aunt tell me how my cousin Donna Oehlerking got to sit on the Sower when it was still on the railway cars. Unfortunately they did not own a camera so they were unable to get a pictorial record of it.

Nothing Exciting Anymore

By Burket E. Graf

It was a warm spring morning in 1936, and I, waiting for my nine o'clock French class, stood in the short hall connecting the south entrance and east-west corridor of University Hall. That venerable first building on the campus had by then been reduced to one story and basement, its walls held together near its flat roof with tie rods.

My aunt, knowing that I had my French class there, had told me that I should run for the nearest exit if I ever heard a loud report in that old pile since it was doomed to collapse. Suddenly I heard a sharp noise, but instead of running out the nearby door, curiosity took me to the long corridor. There on the floor lay Dr. Kurz, holding his wrist, shouting, "I'm killed, I'm killed!" He seemed pretty lively to me, and in seconds the doors flew open from all the classrooms, mild bedlam ensued, and within seconds word came that Mr. Weller had shot himself outside the building.

In a few minutes all the nine o'clock students were herded into their class-rooms. My French instructor was too shaken to continue the class, but gave us a written assignment and excused herself.

Before my ten o'clock English class in Andrews, I was telling everyone about being at the scene of the crime, when Miss McPhee entered, tried to shut the open window, because news boys were already on the campus with extras, shouting that Mr. Weller, a French instructor, had shot Dr. Kurz, the Chairman of the Romance Languages Department, and then killed himself. It later came out that Weller had not been rehired for the next year and blamed Kurz for his dismissal. So that morning he excused himself from his eight o'clock class, went into Dr. Kurz's office, told him he was going to kill him and started shooting. Kurz ran into the corridor, and Weller only managed to hit him in one arm. Weller apparently expected to commit suicide since poison was found on his person but things happened too fast, and he ran out the west door, taking better aim on himself.

"Nothing exciting happens at the University any more" said a young friend, to whom I told this tale.

The Dudley Street Bulldogs

By Stanley L. Portsche

I was born in a frame bungalow-style two bedroom house at 2258 Dudley Street on February 25, 1924. My parents were Mike and Fern Portsche. I had two older brothers, Rich and Jack, and a younger brother Kenneth.

Dudley Street was not a main thoroughfare but close to Holdredge Street and not far from a trolley line. Getting to town about two miles away meant either walking, riding the streetcar, or riding in a car or bus. My friends and I used to walk across an old wood bridge at 17th and Holdrege on the hand rail. My brother Rich did it on his hands.

There was a memorable YMCA-sponsored group called the "Dudley Street Bulldogs," which included 11 to 14 years old boys from an area between 22nd and 23rd Streets including a few streets further east and west. We spent one week each summer from 1935 to 1938 at Camp Strader just south of Crete, on the Big Blue River, eight to a screened-in cabin. We had all kinds of activities, canoeing, archery, storytelling by the bonefire, etc. I remember John Dean setting a new record by eating 18 pancakes at one sitting. This association with the YMCA helped all of us boys grow up in the right direction and instilled in us a strong work ethic. We continued activities together away from the camp and have remained life long friends. Original members of the Dudley Street Bulldogs include the Portsche brothers (Stan, Richard, Jack and Kenneth), the Dean Brothers (Clyde, Bob, Guy Jr. and Jim), Leonard Durham, Emery (Warren, Don, Lyle and Norval), Morris Galter, Dean and Leonard Harris, Jr. and Dick Hudkins, Wayne Kingery, Harold Parker, Warren and Les West.

As an example of what jobs were available to us and how hard we worked, when I was 15 years old I worked jobs at Smith's Dairy Drive Inn (33rd and A Street), Robert's Dairy Drive-in and the 20th and N Street Ice Cream Store. I also worked at Ben Simon's Clothing Store in the men's department of the bargain basement. As early as 11 years old I was delivering weekly papers. While I was a senior in high school I worked eight hours at night seven days a week earning $5.00 a week at the University Drug Store, 14th and U Streets on the University Campus. I was only allowed to work every other week delivering orders to the fraternity and sorority houses on my bicycle. This was to have spending money and earn money towards college. After graduating f rom Lincoln High School on June 5, 1942 I took on construction work at the Lincoln Air Base, ten hour days, seven days a week for 60¢ an hour. I hid this money above the ceiling in the attic and only went out a few times during that summer.

Sports were our entertainment. Basketball was played in the alley, football and baseball by the street lights in front of our house. We played against other neighborhood teams at Whittier, Peter Pan Park, Pentzer Park, Muny Ball Park and down at the North Bottoms. Every night in the summer we went to Muny (Municipal) Field to play baseball.

We had makeshift football outfits, old helmets, shoulder pads but no football shoes. Other games played were kick the can, run sheep run, tag and marbles. In the wintertime we rode our bicycles to Oak Lake, took our lunch and skated all day playing hockey. In the summer we went to the State Fair everyday (actually we snuck in) where Dick Hudkins and I would swim in the old fish tank without suits.

Most all of the boys from the "Dudley Street Bulldogs" turned out to be successful in their professions. The Portsche boys, Stan, a Real Estate Broker for 50 years and Nebraska State Senator, from 1957 through 1960, representing Dudley Street and all of Lincoln West of North 27th Street (Old 19th District); Richard, Burlington Northern Railroad; Jack, a carpenter and Kenneth, a pressman and then janitor at Southeast High School. The five Dean brothers (Clyde, Bob, John, Guy Jr. and Jim) in the automobile industry. The Hudkins brothers in the stunt business in Hollywood. The West Brothers, Warren as a chef, which he learned in the Army, at Tony & Luigi's and the Legionnaire Club; and Les as a Postal Service mail truck driver out of Lincoln to small area towns.

As you can see we were successful in our fields, proving it's not where you come from but where you end up and what you want to make of yourself.

I have seen many changes to the city of Lincoln. It has grown from the small town it was when I was young to the small metropolis that it is today. With the university and state government located here Lincoln has maintained a small town feel that I am proud to call home

University Memories

By Wilfred Wignall

I was a student at the University of Nebraska in the fall of 1931. I am now 87 years old and have many memories of Lincoln at that time. I also have five photographs, one taken of the State Capitol when our class visited, Robbers Cave and the state prison back in 1930. The other four were taken from the lookout on top of the capitol looking all four directions. Looking east goes as far as 48th, which was the city limits. Looking west you can see Salt Lake. North at the bottom of the picture is St. Mary's Catholic Church. Just west is the First Baptist Church. On the north is the city of Lincoln and University of Nebraska. To the south on 25th there is a large building. I won't say for sure, but it could be Lincoln General Hospital 25th Street ended there.

I lived with nineteen other students in a large house where we were served home-cooked meals. The room was $10 a month. All thirteen meals, two per day during the week and one large meal at 2:00 p.m. to give students time to be there to eat, ran $4.75 a week. If I remember, enrollment was between 500 and 600. I believe this took in 200 agriculture students, now at east campus.

We couldn't get out much. We were all walking, even the few with cars preferred to walk. Some of the places I remember quite well were Hotel d'Hamburger on 13th & Q which had large hamburgers for 5¢ or six for 25¢. About 9:00 pm we could go through the house to who wanted hamburgers and one person would go and pick them up. Back then everyone had to be in the house at 10:00 p.m. and they were very strict about it. Another place was the Corn Popper on 15th and N Street with large bags for 5¢.

The same lady ran this for years. They sold a little ice cream along with the popcorn.

When we wanted an ice cold Hires Root Beer, we would drive out to 58th at the city limits. As I remember it was a Dutch Mill sitting in a lot by itself. Of course there was Smith's Dairy at 33rd and A. It was sort of a meeting place for college students. Back in 1932 it was just a building to serve out of with lots of young girls to take orders. The Windmill was built a year or two later.

Another place we like to go on weekends for a hot bowl of chili was Acme Chili at 14th and O for 10¢. They also had a bakery where you could get packages of large cinnamon rolls for 25¢.

I was taking fifteen hours, five were labs, and tuition ran $38.00, others with not so many labs ran less than $30.00 a semester. Most books cost $2.00 to $3.00, the most expensive ones were $5.00.

I moved back to Lincoln in 1958. Lincoln hadn't changed a lot sine I was in school in 1931–32. I began working for Miller and Paine hanging draperies. Houses were being built in corn fields, streets went in, and up would go another house. Now look at it.

My Name Was Marie Hermanek

By Marie Hermanek

Wenceslaus grade school in 1919 and from Omaha Central High in 1923. In my early childhood, I was playing jacks and jumping rope and roller skating. At about age 10, I started taking piano lessons and at age 13, I was playing Beethoven Sonatas.

In 1919, I began my high school years at Omaha Central High. In my freshman year, I took penmanship. There were eight semesters of English, six semesters of Latin, eight semesters of gymnastics plus algebra, geometry, etc. In my last semester I received all A's. There was the Omaha Central High student stage show. Henry Fonda was the lead. My transportation was either walking or the streetcar I was born in Omaha, at home, in November 1905. I graduated from the old St. to high school.

I went to the University of Nebraska in 1923 and majored in Physical Education. The gymnasium was the old Grant Memorial Hall, which was located where the Seldon Memorial Art Gallery now stands. When I entered the university in 1923 I had long hair as did all the girls, however, bobbed hair was coming into style. I had a letter from my father warning me that teachers with bobbed hair were not being hired. Before long this was no longer true and bobbed hair and permanents became the style.

At the beginning of my second year at the university, Miss Mabel Lee was hired to head the Department of Physical Education for Women. Miss Lee was a lovely person, and a strong administrator. I think we students felt like we had to mind our manners.

During her second year, Miss Lee changed the gymnasium outfit from middies and bloomers to gymnasium blouses and knickers, but we still had the long black hosiery. Times were changing for the better and in May of 1927, at the outdoor crowning of the May Queen, for of us senior students did a scarf dance before the May Queen. We were in bare feet so the next day's newspaper carried a complaint.

In 1923 I attended my first football game. That year Nebraska won over Notre Dame by a score of 14 to 7. My uncle from Omaha came for the game and I drove back home with him. I don't remember the exact place or town but my uncle said, "from now on we will have a paved road into Omaha." My return trip to Lincoln was by train on Sunday.

As a student I was chosen to become a Tassel, the women's Pep Club. We wore white shirts and red sweaters. In my senior year, I was elected President of the W.A.A., the Women's Athletic Association. I enjoyed a trip to New York to attend the national meeting of the Women's Athletic Association. What an honor. I took a trip to the Statue of Liberty and I walked up the steps inside her to her knees and looked up and down, became afraid and I walked back down.

Our Women's Physical Education Club sold candy at the football games. One year we sold apples but the male students threw the apple cores and that was the end of apple sales.

Early Childhood Memories

By Peg Lemon Maly

Early childhood memories living in the Methodist community of University Place. The street, a brick Warren Avenue, later to be named North 48th Street.

Vivid recollections of fire trucks rolling past, sirens loud, a vibration in our beds as they passed.

Heavy rains brought out make believe boats to float down the street curbs.

Reading the funny papers every Sunday morning in our parents' bed. Paper carriers shouted, "Extra!" to inform us of special events walking down 48th Street.

Sleeping on army cots in the back yard during heat waves, the dog waking us by walking under the cots around 5:00 a.m.

Running inside from window to window with my sister, as mother squirted the hose nozzle against the window panes—spring cleaning.

Mother hurrying to remove red Christmas bulbs in our porch lights after inappropriate remarks in a phone call, no explanation.

Our front porch—a play area for a shoe store, a library "check out" for books, dress-up and even a swing with chains to the ceiling.

Family gatherings on Sunday evenings to listen and laugh at comedian Eddie Cantor on the radio.

As a small child I was a Chautauqua baby. My father George Hartington Lemon's first job as a Nebraska Wesleyan graduate was working as department manager for the Lincoln Standard Chautauqua System in the Lincoln circuit. With no connection to the education system founded at Chautauqua Lake, NY in 1874, the term also refers to traveling groups called Tent Chautauquas. These groups operated in the U.S. from 1903–1930, the movement reaching its zenith in 1924 when Theodore Roosevelt called it the most "American thing in America."

The Chautauqua assemblies reflect the preservation and dissemination of Victorian values. The program took to the road selling "culture under canvas" to 30 million people in 12,000 communities. My father became a Circuit Manager the circuits were largely a rural Midwestern phenomenon. The typical town to sponsor a circuit ranged in size from 500 to 5,000 in population. Without radio, TV or movies to provide the mental stimulation citizens sought, they welcomed the annual Chautauqua week.

The circuit talent—preachers, politicians, performers, authors, and assorted celebrities, liked the extra income during an otherwise unprofitable summer season. The ideal program included one part lecture, two parts music with variety and dramatics. A week's feast of rhetoric and entertainment was served twice daily inside big brown tents. The inspirational lectures were referred to by the managers (off the record) as "Mother, Home and Heaven" members. Our Lincolnite, William Jennings Bryan, the "Silver Tongue Orator," was the most popular lecturer until his last appearance in 1924. It was said Bryan was good for 40 acres of packed fords anywhere he went. Bryan's most popular lecture was "The Prince Of Peace." He often prefaced his religious message with a few thousand firey words about Prohibition which he championed with all his heart and lungs.

Expecting more family, my father enjoyed some of the popular years with Chautauqua, and resigned to start his own business. I made a few trips to tent meetings, and of course appeared on stage informally for the admiration of my parents and history.

Hillcrest History

By Bob Anderson

The game of golf came to Lincoln as early as June, 1900, with the opening of the City's very first course Pleasant View, located at the northwest corner of 27th and A Streets. The course extended west to 24th Street and north to D Street. The game caught on quickly in the capital city, and by the early '20s, golf had become well established in Lincoln with the operation of at least two courses. Pleasant View most likely evolved into the Lincoln Country Club about 1903, near 6th and A Street; and the first city owned course, The Antelope Golf Club, located at the site of today's Chet Ager Junior Golf Course, opened in August 1920. Privately owned Eastridge Country Club at 70th and A Street opened in 1923. The Country Club of Lincoln moved from their previous site near 6th and A Street to their present location in 1923, also. The city closed the Antelope course in 1934 after the 1930 opening of Pioneers Golf Course. City officials felt that Lincoln could only afford to maintain one course, so the Antelope course became an economic casualty after some controversy among local golfers. A sand greens course at Cotner Boulevard and Vine Street called Park Valley Golf Links, also operated in the 1930s. In 1930, Lincoln also had 9 "miniature golf" courses, including the Mauna Loa course at 48th and O Street.

March 31, 1929, at a location 4½ miles east of downtown, Lincoln's third private country club opened for play. Joining the list of Lincoln courses was The Shrine Country Club, which evolved in 1943 into the present-day Hillcrest Country Club. The following is a brief history of the construction and operation of the club and golf course, as best as this writer has been able to discover.

In 1919 a delegation from Lincoln's Sesostris Temple traveled to Philadelphia, PA, and were the guests of soon to be mayor of Philadelphia, Freeland Kendrick, at the Shrine Club of that city. Upon their return they gathered support for the construction of a Shrine Country Club for the capital city. On December 24, 1926, The Shrine Building Association, purchased 320 acres from Harry H. and Emma J. Leavitt for the construction of an eighteen hole, grass greens championship golf course and club house. Plans also called for a picnic and recreation area with shelter house to be constructed west of the golf course. The committee making arrangements for the improvements were: J. Cass Cornell, then Potentate, Charles Stuart, A.C. Lau, Frank DuTeil, and B. A. George.

The golf course was designed by William A. Tucker, Sr., of New York City, son of a "sod roller" at the Wimbledon Commons in England. Mr. tucker also designed the city course at Pioneers Park as well as the Country Club of Lincoln. Mr. Tucker estimated that he designed or remodeled of 120 courses in his career. The clubhouse was designed by the architectural firm of Davis and Wilson and was constructed by Olson Construction Company. The architecture was considered to be of the Spanish-Moorish style. The décor featured parchment colored interior walls, and the Shrine colors of red, green and yellow were used with the Shrine emblems in decorating the beamed ceilings in the larger rooms.

The building was 261 by 144 feet and was topped by a 28-foot square tower. The original arrangement featured a "grille" in what is now the Pro Shop and a very ornate soda fountain adjacent to the grille. The men's locker room and a lounge were in the east wing on the first floor. The second floor also had men's lockers and the manager's apartment and bedrooms for those employed in the clubhouse. In the basement, a large space was prepared for an indoor putting green. The original plan also showed a huge ballroom at the south end of the west wing, nearly twice the size of the present ballroom. This second ballroom was never constructed. The club's swimming pool was completed in 1931 after a successful drive for financial support from Shrine members.

The Sesostris Temple membership at that time was 2,400 and all were automatic members of the country club and granted its use except for the golf course and locker room. There was an extra charge for access to those facilities. The annual fee for use of the golf course was $30.00. About 300 had committed to golf course membership at the time of the opening. C. H. Roper was in charge of golf subscriptions. The playgrounds were intended to be a family picnic type of area, and many sports were included in the design. A pond was built and stocked with fish. A six sided picnic shelter house equipped with four open hearth fireplaces was constructed. The shelter still stands and is visible through the trees from O Street today. It has been used as a residence for many years. A baseball diamond, croquet court, trap shooting range, wading pool, children's playground equipment and outdoor fireplaces were also constructed. The club also purchased a four year option on an additional 80 acres on the west side of the playgrounds but never exercised the option. Future plans were for a third nine holes and eventual expansion to 36 holes.

Five miles of underground water lines were laid to carry water from the 14 inch well to all greens and tee boxes. It was considered to be an automatic watering system by the standards of the era. Virtually unchanged today is the original design of the course. Sand traps and a few newer additional tee box locations have been added through the years. The site as originally purchased was completely void of trees. All those existing on the grounds today are the result of either investment by the club or donations by members and interest non-members. In 1930, J. F. Garvey, who was not a Shriner or even a Mason, donated approximately 300 maple trees. Also in 1930, Emil G Rosewell donated 500 Chinese elms, which were to be planted along the club driveway and other locations. Most of those trees still exist today along with many others planted by the club. March 31, 1929 the course officially opened for play, however some activity may have taken place on the course in the fall of 1928. Wednesday, August 7, 1929, a reception to honor the Imperial Potentate of the Shrine, Leo Youngworth, of Los Angeles, California, was held, and the facility was featured in the Sunday August 4, 1929 edition of the Lincoln *State Journal* in a ten page section containing many and various articles on the club and its construction. Through the early '30s the Shrine held many social events at the club.

Several well known players have played the course since its opening. In October 1929, US Open Champion Walter Hagen and Horton Smith played a match against Shrine Club Pro Charlie Koontz and Lincoln Country Club Pro John Morris. The local golf pros gave a good account of themselves, losing to the internationally prominent Hagen and Smith in a 2 man best ball— match play format, on the last few holes. Hagen and Smith were flown from Kansas to Lincoln in an airplane that landed on the number 9 fairway, prior to the match. In 1963 Arnold Palmer and Gary Player played an exhibition match over the course. Palmer was the winner. Current Hillcrest Golf Pro Charlie Borner, then a young lad, was the caddy for Gary Player. Baseball great Dizzy Dean played the course in 1941 as the guest of then Governor, Dwight Griswold. The Governor mad "Diz" an Admiral in the Nebraska Navy prior to the start of play in the pro-am and after three holes the retired pitcher asked the Governor if Nebraska really had a navy, to which the Governor is reported to have smiled and continued to play. After a few more holes "Diz" asked the Governor if he would like a stick of gum. The Governor replied, "sure thanks." It was only a few moments before the Governor realized that the gum was laced with black pepper! Many state and regional tournaments in the 30s were held on the course including the Midwest Open and the Nebraska Open as well as several city and state championships.

There have been several golf pros at the course over the years including Charlie Koontz, the first pro from late 1928 to 1933, and the most notable William J. "Bunny" Richards from late 1945 to 1979. A plaque on the tee of the

14th hole is dedicated to his memory. Other pros in their order of succession were: Ole Clark 1934–36, Mel Thompson 1937, Les Davies 1938–40, J. Patrick Gianferante 1941, J. G. (Jock) Collins 1942 (Pro and Club manager), Max Pumphrey 1945, W.J. "Bunny" Richards 1945–79, Rich Williams 1980–83, and Charlie Borner 1984 to present. Due to the war years the club was likely without a golf pro in 1943 and 1944. Membership and activity at the club declined to small levels during the war years, but quickly increased to large numbers in the late '40s.

Times were good in most of the country during the '20s and Lincoln evidently shared in profits and optimism; however, the stock market crash and the depression were just around the corner. These two factors, along with what may have been "too much, too quick," proved to be more debt than the club could support, and by 1937 the Shrine had ceased to operate the facility. After opening the club to any Blue Lodge Mason in 1936, the Shrine leased the entire club to a group of local golf enthusiasts who operated the facility as Broadview Country Club from 1937 to 1943. Bond holders forced a foreclosure sale in 1939 and the facility and 175 acres were purchased at a sheriff's foreclosure sale by a group of local investors/golfers, who maintain that ownership today.

Hillcrest Country Club has operated the facility successfully since 1943, over 58 years. Today the course and club are considered by many to be among the area's premier facilities.

Charles Koontz, club professional at the Shrine Country Club (now Hillcrest) is shown sinking a putt on the 9th green in 1933. *Photo courtesy Nebraska State Historical Society.*

A Move to the Big City—Lincoln

By Charles Folden

I remember being about eight years old living on a farm with no electric service, no running water and no indoor plumbing. I came to Lincoln and stayed overnight with relatives who lived near the Randolph streetcar line. The sound of the wheels on the rails, the clanging of the bell as you were about to go to sleep, the lighted Christmas trees made it seem like a different planet.

Then in 1932 we moved to Lincoln. Now I had to live in this big city. New friends had to be made, a new way of living had to be dealt with and I was a shy kid. My folks bought me a season ticket to the Muny pool—the cost, $1.00.

I attended a junior high school on the corner of 26th and O Street that disappeared 65 years ago. In those days there was a streetcar line on O Street that ran to the Wyuka Cemetery, O Street was brick in those days. When they removed the tracks in about 1934 they used blacktop to replace it. Where the railroad crossed O Street at 20th Street there was a crossing flagman to stop traffic when a train was due. The removal of the streetcar tracks was a WPA project. At about this time at the corner of 18th and Q Street there was an office of either the WPA or county relief. One week the paychecks did not arrive and a large number of people went to the Piggly Wiggly store at 18th and O Street and took the food they needed to feed their families. They stopped at the checkout counter and had the groceries checked so they could not be accused of stealing. I do not recall of any charges ever being brought against any one of them.

At about this same time the police stopped an out-of-state car at the corner of 18th and O Street, it turned out to be bank robbers. This was in the days of John Dillinger. The robbers fired at the police and race away east on O Street, the police and the bad guys firing away as they raced. This happened at the noon hour and all of us at the school at 26th and O Street were either in the school yard or on the street going home for lunch. As they pass 24th and O a stray bullet struck a boy in my grade. He died later in the day. I was standing at the corner of 27th when they went by with the guns blazing. They caught the robbers by Prairie Home east of Lincoln when the car overturned.

Those days the milkman used a horse and wagon to deliver his products. Robert's Dairy had a horse barn at 20th and N Street. A man by the name of Tony did the same with his fresh vegetables.

Times were pretty bad during the '30s. I remember needing to have a half-sole put on just one shoe. I found a man who would do it for 30¢ but when I went to pay him I could only find 29¢. He tore off the sole.

The weather was very hot during the dust bowl days. There was no air conditioning and I guess not very many electric fans. The capitol grounds had just been sodded and the area was so crowded with people trying to sleep there that you could not find a place to lie down.

In those days there was no Social Security. Old people had to be supported by their children. I remember an old fellow who had no relative to help him. He finally got a state pension of $25.00 a month. He had to pay rent for a room in a dingy hotel and eat on this amount. About this time he became eligible for $15.00 a month pension from a union he had been in for years. The state then took $15.00 away from his pension.

During this time my mother ran a boarding and rooming house. The charge was $30.00 for everything. She could cram twelve people into a three bedroom, one bath house.

The Liberty Theatre was across the street from the Stuart building. You could take the whole family for $1.00 for vaudeville and a movie. All the boarders we could get into the car were considered family.

There were, as I remember, six theaters on O Street between 14th and 16th Streets.

Checker Cabs in Lincoln—The Beginning

By Lydia Hill Bancroft

The earliest recollection I have concerning Carl Hill took place when I was two or three, and Carl was eighteen or nineteen years old. I was awakened at about 3:00 one morning as mother was in a hushed voice calling Carl to breakfast. I remember the delicious aroma of mother's hot cakes, wishing I could have some then too. I was still very dark outside, and mother was urging Carl to eat well for the long hard day he had ahead of him in his work at the icehouse.

Near to that time I recall mother and dad encouraging Carl to find other work; they were fearful of injury to his health that prolonged work at the icehouse would bring.

Soon thereafter I remember Dad and Carl standing, talking next to the range in the kitchen. Carl had found a way he could get into the taxi business if he could get money enough to buy a car. He and dad were arranging that dad would lend him the money to pay for the car. It was a beautiful car a rare and exciting vehicle in the early years of the second decade of this century. With purchase of the car, Carl was also taught to drive it, and then he immediately took our family all for a ride—a ride that seemed like a beautiful floating sensation to me. So Carl was ushered into the taxi business, with at that time the only evidence of the car being used as a taxi consisting of a sign "Taxi" which he placed on the windshield while working.

Carl did extremely well in the taxi business, and very soon urged Al to also quit his work at the icehouse and join him in the taxi business. The boys located another car to buy; dad lent the money, and then both boys were in the taxi business.

Radio Days In Old Lincoln

By Jack Hitchcock

I started work at the two stations, which shared studios off the lobby of the Lincoln Hotel. I was a junior at Havelock High School in 1937, and remained at the stations while I got my education at the University of Nebraska, graduating in 1943. The stations in Lincoln proved to be a great learning place to prepare me for my 50 years in broadcasting.

Commercial radio stations slowly emerged all over America in the mid-'20s. KFAB was one of the first around 1927. Because of its power and frequency on the dial, it covered a big circle, including Nebraska, Iowa, Kansas, upper Missouri and lower South Dakota. It was housed in the Nebraska Buick Building in the hopes it would promote the sale of Buick cars. I think it was the Sidles family that interested other investors in applying for a station license. It became one of the first stations in the state and the most powerful, with 10,000 watts of power. My dad built one of the first radios in Havelock, and the neighbors would come in to hear KFAB, KDKA in Pittsburgh, and several other stations on the air then. They all looked at that big "speaker horn" in complete enchantment.

A few years later KFOR settled in Lincoln after being in several other locations. The Lincoln newspapers bought and combined the two stations and moved to the Lincoln Hotel. Later, KOIL in Omaha joined the group and Central States Broadcasting was formed.

A first in the nation was Foster May's "Man on the Street" talk show conducted on the sidewalk in downtown Lincoln and broadcast on KFOR.

Another first about that time was KFAB's recreation of baseball games in the afternoon from a studio. Wire reports would come in from the site of the game and telegrapher Don Combs, would hand them to Harry's wife "Tuffy" who would give them to Harry and keep the scoreboard on a big blackboard in front of him. A sound effects man also played records of crowd noises and cheering in the background to complete the picture being created by Harry. In the off season, Wheaties, one of the sponsors, sent Harry around the country to conduct schools for training Wheaties sports announcers to do the games in their station locations.

KFAB was a basic CBS station, KOIL was the basic NBC Blue Network affiliate, and KFOR had the unique position of taking the Mutual Network's offerings, plus the option of carrying CBS or NBC Blue programming not carried by KFAB or KOIL. This arrangement gave KFOR access to three networks which carried nightly broadcasts of big bands form ballrooms, night clubs, and hotels from coast to coast in the 1940s. Many of those bands came to the Turnpike during their yearly tours. Someone at KFOR came up with the idea of creating a two hour parade of those big bands from 10 to midnight each week night and until 1:00 am on Saturday. The parade was sold to Magee's clothing store and took the name Magee's Dance Parade." I conducted the parade until I graduated in 1943 and left Lincoln. By using earphones to listen to the introduction of the band over its opening theme song, I got so I could use practically the same words and it sounded like I had a direct line to all of those locations. Three nights a week at 11:00 pm we covered the five minute network newscast with news from the Nebraska campus provided by reporters from the Daily Nebraskan. Margaret Crouse did the gossip programs and Charlotte Bierbower, the Sports Editor, covered N.U. sports. Because of the Big Band era at that time, we probably had nearly 100% of the radio listeners.

A program for kids in New York was headed by "Uncle Don." We had an hour of network programs from four to five each day, such as "Hop Harrigan," "Superman," etc., and a segment filled with kids' songs (records), their letters, etc., and the whole hour was pulled together by me and was known as "Uncle Jack's Adventure Hour."

Uncle Jack's popularity quickly spread to children and young adult couples, as my responsibilities grew to be the one who read the funnies every Sunday morning at an early hour giving the young parents at least an extra hour in bed.

In the mid-'30s, KFAB had its own locally written and produced soap opera. It was called "The Jangles" and it was written by Jettabee Ann Hopkins. I believe Gretchen Lee, the grand old lady of the stations, and commercial writer, also had a hand in writing the daily "soap." She had been an actress on Broadway and later taught writing courses in an exclusive girls school back east before coming back to Lincoln where she was a member of a distinguished family that I believe was one of the founders of KFAB. Most of the performers were station personnel, including a sound effects man. Children were selected as needed from a junior acting school at the station. Jettabee went on to New York to be part of a writing team for one of the daily soap operas produced by CBS.

Capital Beach instituted dancethons and walkathons and the 4H arena at the fair grounds followed suit during the depression. Dan Fogarty, a former Havelock athlete, became a featured performer and later joined a sort of touring group that participated in contests all over the country. The participants sang songs requested by their fans, and Dan used to sing "Danny Boy." KFOR broadcast several times a day from the contests particularly describing the "elimination" races that were designed to reduce the number of contestants still on their feet. One couple decided to get married during the contest at the fair grounds and arrangements were made to transport them in a truck to a department store in downtown Lincoln to select wedding clothes, etc. Naturally they had to keep walking through all of this, including the wedding at the walkathon. We broadcast all the featured events. The couple dropped out soon after the wedding.

Many readers will remember the daily organ broadcasts from the Lincoln Theatre. Mylan Lambert played the "mighty Wurlitzer" organ and Lyle DeMoss announced and sang. The early morning program was called "Time in Tunes." At noon on a more lighthearted note, the program from 12:00 to 1:00 was called "The Squirrel Dodgers," with announcer Bob Moon and Mylan at the organ.

Barney Oldfield was surely one of the first persons to have a daily radio program (on KFOR) reporting on movies and other entertainment news from around the world. He also had a daily column in the papers, and was a national correspondent for Variety, Billboard, and Radio Daily. Many of the stories came from his personal interviews with the Big Band leaders who came to the Turnpike and other entertainment figures who made Lincoln one of the Midwestern stops. Also, he had many reports on the doings of former Nebraskans. When Barney went to war, his wife, Bulah, carried on in his place until she, too, joined a branch of the service.

Lyell Bresmer began play by play broadcasting of the Cornhuskers football games in 1942. I was his color man that year and again in 1945 and 1946 when I returned to Lincoln.

LINCOLN
WARTIME

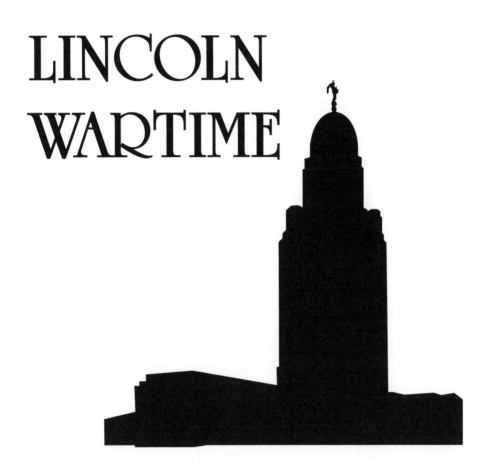

At 29th and O Streets

By Ron Doan

The year 1936 was the first year for the Cushman Scooter in Lincoln. You could rent one for an hour at the Phillip Gas Station at 29th and O Street. Only requirement was that you had 25¢. No age restriction, no driver's license, no questions. Of course, in order to get your money's worth, you and your close friends ran it wide open for exactly 59½ minutes. Later, the station was taken over by Mr. Al Trumble and it became a well-monitored hangout for teens with cars. Al was always there for good counseling, a small loan for an honorable cause, etc. Back of the station was the Yum Yum Hut, one of Lincoln's first drive-in's. Two ladies ran it with an iron hand. Parking on the premises was strictly monitored; no backing into stalls, no obstreperous behavior, no spinning of tires, EVER. If you behaved over an extended period of time, you eventually attained the "inner group" status, which occasionally resulted in slightly more filling in your Yum Yum (a special sandwich), or a dip of ice cream in your hot chocolate.

It goes on, doesn't it?

Let's You and Him Fight

By Dale McCracken

Remember that one? Roll back to December 1942. Stop at the last day before Christmas vacation ... the word spread through the halls of Lincoln High that there was going to be a big one right after school. "Who's fighting?" "Mickey McDermott and Marv Epp." Whoa, two guys who are teammates on the football team, friends of most every one but different as night and day. Mickey is Allstate Bad Boy (just opposite of brother Jimmy) and proud of it. Marv is Allstate Nice Guy (just like brother Mil). "What's it about?" Everyone wonders. "Who knows ... but it should be a good one."

Sure enough, right after last bell the two combatants and a goodly crowd (well over a hundred) gathered on the old St. Mary's football field a block west of the Oval (apartments are there now). Talk about organization, the two participants had even agreed upon having a referee, Bobby Glen, perfect. Bobby was Mr. Football that year, every ones buddy (still is) and tough as they come ... you knew he could handle either one of the two at hand.

Nobody heard the ref's instructions ... I think Bobby just said fight and they did, serious back alley style. Trouble was there was about two inches of snow on the field so the mayhem was muffled a bit by a lot of slippin' and slidin'. Someone soon spotted an old garage open off to the side with a dry dirt floor, so the bout, really kind of floundering now and ready for a breather, was moved inside. The dry flooring proved to be good for the fight but bad for the garage. In no time at all it seemed there was a huge crash and out through a side wall came the two fighters all asses and elbows. This was pure Hollywood stuff.

Then, as if on cue, the call came from somewhere in the outer reaches of the crowd "The police are coming."

Referee Bobby grabbed both Mickey and Marv, shook some sense into them and ordered them to take off running. He then stepped to the center of the crowd, raising his arms for their attention and by the time the patrolmen arrived on foot the assembled multitude was slowly and piously singing Silent Night, Holy Night ... God, even the police loved it.

I don't remember how or if ever the conflict between McDermott and Epp got settled. They both got in enough good licks to soothe their pride or even claim victory; but even though they were the main attraction in this event, I do remember it was Bobby Glenn who stole the show.

Life's Memories

By William D. Schlaebitz

The following is a memory trip through the life of William D. Schlaebitz, born in Lincoln, Nebraska, April 9, 1924, at the St. Elizabeth Hospital, Eleventh and South Street. With the exception of three years in the Air Force, 1943 to 1945 and 1946 to 1958, in an architectural partnership with a friend of Downers Grove, Illinois, I have spent my entire life in Lincoln, as did my father who was born in 1900.

When I was attending Elliot grade school in the early '30s, there was a daring bank robbery at the First National Bank, 10th & O Street. The robbers sped away down O Street heading east with the police in pursuit. They were captured, as I recall, in the country at 70th & O after a gun battle en route. I found several pieces of glass on the street at 29th and O on my way home from school the day after the robbery that I was sure in my own mind, came from the back window of the robbers car. The pieces of glass became one of the treasures in my collection box, which since has disappeared with time.

The excitement of Christmas during my early years was heightened by the visit to The Rudge and Guenzel toy department at 13th and N Street, to ride the ponies and to see the clown perform at Gold's Department Store. Another memory was of the visits to Gold's was the sales my mother attended. She was always first in line as I remember, and before the bell would ring and the rope removed to open the sales, there would be Mr. Nate Gold giving my mother a greeting, "Nice to see you, again Mrs. Schlaebitz." My arm is still sore from my mother dragging me through the aisles for those sales.

In my teen years, the Capital Beach Amusement Park became a great place to have fun with friends. The roller coaster built with wood frame construction was a thrilling ride magnified by the fact that it should have been classified as structurally unsafe. The electric bumper car ride, and the fun house were also favorites. The fun house had this wooden slide where you used gunny sack for the conveyor of the ride. A walk through the large revolving barrel provided many laughs for those trying to get from one end to the other. The swimming pool with its salt water and sun tanning area was a great attraction during the summer season. The manager was the great Lincoln High School Football coach, Ralph Beechner, lifeguard Bert Amgwert, and clothes hanger girl Irene Hansen Thompson provided the beauty of a high school classmate. Speaking of swimming pools, the Muny Pool was also a great hang out during my junior and senior high school days. The concession stand supplied those wonderful Power House candy bars for 5¢. Les Oldfield was lifeguard, Bun Galloway Northeast High School coach was manager and Chelis Mattley was in charge of checking and hanging the clothes. I passed my Red Cross lifesaving course and spent some time on busy days as an assistant lifeguard. No one drowned when I was life guarding, and that may have been one of my shining hours.

There were two great gathering places for dancing. The Turnpike Ballroom located seven miles south on 14th Street and Kings Ballroom at Capital Beach. My lifetime high school sweetheart and wife, Shirley Brigham, taught me to dance and we went to every big name band that would come to Lincoln. Bands such as Glen Miller, Benny Goodman, Tommy and Jimmy Dorsey, Vaughn Monroe, Charlie Barnett, Woody Heman, Xavier Cugat, to name a few. After the dance we would head for the Cornhusker and have a milkshake and curly ques. The other great place to go was the early McDonalds known as the Yum Yum Hut, located at 29th and O Street. The Root Beer Mug at 33rd and O Street, owned by Jack Nebelsick's father, was extremely popular, as was the Windmill at Cotner and O, and the Lighthouse at Normal and South Streets.

While at Lincoln High School, I was on the Lincoln High School swim team and lettered in diving for two years. I was fortunate to have had as my coach, Mr. Harry Kuklin. He taught us more than competitive swimming, he taught us how to be a good person and citizen. Perry Branch carried us through two State Championships with his swimming skills as did Bill Fenton and Roger Ellis.

I started a pursuit of an architectural degree upon graduation from high school at the University of Nebraska. As a member and active of the Phi Delt Fraternity, I recall one event that took place that was to help out the war effort in 1942. All the fraternities and sororities took on the project of seeing who could collect the most scrap iron in a short period of time. The Phi Delts thought they would be winners until they had to return some of the items they had collected to their owners. A couple of such items were a windmill, and part of the Wyuka Cemetery fence. The loyalty to our country would never be questioned, but our approach for helping was lacking some careful, intelligent thinking. All of us in the Class of '42 ended up in the service of our country, and I was among those that enlisted in the Army Air Force.

I believe I might have been an Aviation Cadet the longest of anyone in the service of the Air Force. I was called into service February 12, 1943, and received my wings as a navigator, July 24, 1945. As the war progressed, the need for flying positions changed. I was originally classified as a pilot and when partially into the program, they changed my classification to bombardier, and then finally to navigation. Along the way, I experienced some health problems with ear infections, put in military hospitals for a period of time, which reverted me back from my original class. I realize that I was extremely lucky, because many of my service friends gave the supreme sacrifice with their lives.

Upon being honorably discharged from the service, I returned to the University of Nebraska Architectural College, and received in 1949, two degrees—one in architecture and the other a B.A. in French.

During my schooling, I worked part time, for the architectural firm of Clark and Enersen and after graduation, I joined the firm full time, eventually becoming a principal partner and owner. My specialty was school and bank design. As a project architect, I was involved with school districts as far west as Scottsbluff. The firm designed over 60 schools in the state. I was also the project architect for the city offices in the County-City Building in Lincoln, among others.

Since my retirement, I have been to Europe nine times and teaching in rural schools as an artist in residence for the Nebraska Arts Council. I am also a paid mentor for gifted students in the Lincoln Public Schools, which has been a great experience for me. All my students have been blessed with great drawing skills and unique personalities.

I lost my wife to cancer after 53 years of marriage, and I have one son, a forester, three daughters, one is a teacher in Lincoln going on her 26th year. I have nine grandchildren. One, a granddaughter is pursuing an architectural degree so as to follow in grandpa's footsteps.

My life has been wonderful! I have served on many boards and received numerous honors. The ones that were especially meaningful were from my high school and university. For a kid from the wrong side of the tracks, Lincoln has been a wonderful place to live and raise a family.

Randolph at 27th

By Jacqueline Sittner Meister

It was in the late '30s when we moved to the big cement/stone house on the southeast corner of 27th and Randolph. As two little girls, we were excited to be able to each have our own room. After living on a quiet street we weren't used to all the traffic and were instructed to watch out for the cars. I remember getting up early and watching all the traffic go by. The streetcar ran on Randolph Street and then up 27th. Kids had a big time pulling the line off the cable, which meant the conductor had to get out and put it back on.

Our father fixed radios part-time and started a repair business in part of the house. The war started soon after and people needed their radios to keep up with the news of the war—checking on their sons and husbands involved. The repair business grew. Because of the war there was a great need for radios so he soon started to sell them. As the business took more time, this became his full-time work. Soon he decided to build a store and our beloved house was demolished and we moved to the house next door. This was the beginning of Sittner Hardware and Gifts, which was in business on that corner for thirty years.

When we first moved to that corner there was a drug store that had a soda fountain across the street. The drug store was open Sunday mornings a few hours so doctors could call in their prescriptions, otherwise it was closed on Sundays. Handy System Store was on that side of the street, too. They were open late on Saturday evening but closed on Sunday. This continued until Kushners bought the grocery store and their hours included Sundays.

On our side of the street there were a few houses and one old house/shop where shoe repair was done. The older couple that ran the shop lived in the back and had a large garden and a few chickens. Gates garage was next door and is still there.

27th and Randolph is now an all business area. It is fun to remember when it wasn't.

The City That Was Gold's

By Ron Doan

From the summer of 1941 until 1942 and after I returned from service from 1944 to 1949 I was employed by Gold's in the display department and served as display director. Here are the reasons I remember Gold's as a city.

Gold's was alive, vibrant, exciting. It offered most products and services available in moderate sized cities all under one roof. They had departments for clothing and shoes for men, ladies, and children. It also had a grocery store, a pharmacy, a lunchroom, foot care, optical store, millinery, furniture, white goods, fabrics, sewing needs, appliances, carpets, stationery, and books (including a rental library), candy, cosmetics, paper/office supplies, business machines, leather goods, luggage, cameras, and photo finishing, toys and gifts. Household goods, and snack bar were offered and such services as free gift-wrapping and free delivery. They also provided personal shoppers and Santa Claus during the holiday season, and a redemption center for savers of S&H Green Stamps. The list goes on with many I've forgotten.

There was a behind the scene intrigue. Nate Gold's 6'6" talent for calling a before opening meeting on the main floor inspiring the troops (co-workers) to greet the milling throng waiting at the entrances after the minute of silence observed every morning.

Some of the departments and services were leased, but all adhered strictly to the Gold's policies. There was competition, and politics among the managers. Each department was a store within the "city." Behind the scenes were settings for furniture repair, advertising department, display sign shop, personnel, stock rooms, paint shop, carpenter shop, and delivery. There was a large room on the 6th floor that was devoted to salvage and paper bailing.

I wonder if the basement under the basement is still in the Gold's Building. Few knew, but it too had a purpose. Gold's was, if not the first, early with complete air conditioning and escalators.

In those days, merchants were encouraged to buy large blocks of football tickets. Gold's as I recall bought two hundred. However, if any employee was caught at a Saturday afternoon Nebraska game they were subject to immediate dismissal. Nate would always parade through the main floor during the first quarter. Nate Gold drove a modest Oldsmobile to work. There was a Buick Limited limo in his garage.

About the "O Street Gang" I dunno, but things surely got done downtown. Does anyone remember fall opening, or the beginning of the holiday season?

I'm not certain, but it seemed that every small town within driving distance was represented with at least one employee somewhere in the store. Saturday was the big day. Customers usually sought out employees from their hometowns whether in sales, or stockroom. It was like old home week. This welcoming was encouraged by the store. The visiting families would usually split up for shopping through the store. With little need to go outside of Gold's, they would meet in the lounge, a large area on one of the upper floors, adjacent to the lunchroom, which was convenient (by design).

American flags lined the curbs for patriotic holidays and other special days, always distributed and taken in with proper protocol.

Remember the beacon—another story.

During WWII many display windows were devoted to the war effort, bond sales, etc. as scarce products started to emerge after WWII great effort was made to distribute them fairly. Women's nylon stockings and the first ball-point pen made by Reynolds from surplus aluminum created long lines of waiting customers. There were also long lines for war production bikes. Employees waited for the same lists and the same lines as our customers.

That was the "city", and that's the way it was.

In January of 1933 Gold's Department Store sponsored this rhythm band. *Photo courtesy Virginia Sharpnack Dzerk and Bob Sharpnack Hall.*

Lee's—'A Small Beer Joint'

By Alice Franks

In the summer of 1945, Lee Franks, daughter Mary Clee, and I moved to Lincoln from Houston, Texas, and, in October we bought a small "beer joint" from Pete and Dorothy Dreith. It was located on the corner of West Van Dorn and Burlington Avenue (later renamed South Coddington Avenue) both gravel roads at the time. This location was considered a long way from town. A vendor once referred to it as being on the other side of the world. The old building seated 16 but Pete and Dorothy had started an addition, which would seat about 40. The old building had three booths, seating a total of 16 plus four bar stools. A wood-burning stove heated the structure and we hauled water from Lee's parents home in Lincoln. Lee and his brother, Bill Franks, soon hand-dug a 22-foot-deep well outside the old structure on the west side of the building. The toilet facility was a tiny outdoor building on the east side of the business. Dorothy remarked that Lee and I would never make it in the business because "Alice didn't even know how to cook a hamburger," which was about the only item they offered for sale, other than beer and soft drinks. But I learned. Early on, I somehow came into possession of a huge black book named the Wenzel Menu Maker, which quickly became my constant companion and Bible. Everything I know I learned from the Wenzel Menu Maker.

Our transportation in those early days was a 1928 Chevrolet. We had sold our 1941 Dodge after moving to Lincoln, in order to raise money to buy the business and the few household items we needed. Our living space was a small lean-to behind the business.

The first item I remember adding to the menu was hardboiled eggs. Then we added french fries. There were no fast food chain restaurants in Lincoln at that time and very few, if any, places where one could buy fresh deep-fried foods. We were selling quite a few packages of potato chips, which yielded only a few cents profit. So I bought a pot and fryer basket, and some peanut oil and potatoes. I hand peeled and cut the potatoes then fried them from raw to done as they were ordered. The potato business boomed! Soon the pot could not keep up so I bought a small Fryalator for $5.00 down and $5.00 a week. The Fryalator held about 5 gallons of oil and had an automatic thermostat, which made it a marvelous tool. I also bought a device to cut the potatoes into nice even strips. Marvelous! I was using peanut oil because that was what I had been using in Houston for frying foods. It was expensive and not easy to find here, but I liked it because it had a high smoke point and did not gum up the cooker. I didn't know then that it was also heart-healthy (I continued to use peanut oil until I left the business in 1969).

The fried potato business was good but did not fully utilize the equipment, so we decided to offer fried chicken. Lee and I had raised the chickens and rabbits for meat during World War II and we used to invite friends to share meals with us. They would say, "Wow this is good, I bet you could sell it." So I started cooking fried chicken in Lincoln, Nebraska, like we had cooked and served to our friends in Houston. The next problem we encountered was a source for fresh chicken. It was not available in stores at all times. So we started buying entire flocks from farmers and keeping them in a yard behind the business. Then we could kill and dress them as needed. Yes, it is true that on one occasion, I killed, dressed, and cooked a chicken for a customer while he waited, but that was not our usual practice. However, once we put in an item on the menu, we simply did not like to tell a customer we were out of that item. This was our policy as long as we owned the restaurant. Another strict policy had to do with posted hours. Our hours were from 4pm to midnight, Monday through Saturday. We were closed on Sunday. Even if we did not have a customer for hours, we remained open during posted hours. Lee said that if anyone made the effort to drive all the way to Lee's, they had a right to find us open for business during posted hours. Of course, it was easier to do this in the early years, since we had no employees, and we lived on the premises.

There is a picture of Lee's taken in the spring of 1946, after the first addition was finished. It was still heated with a wood stove. We added on to the building a total of 13 different times. We kept the business open during our regular business hours—just swept up the sawdust and kept going. We used to think people kept coming out mainly to see what was going to happen next. We still had no indoor plumbing. You can see the outhouse to the right of the building. The auto is the 1928 Chevrolet we bought when we sold our 1941 Dodge.

At one period we had picnic tables located in the area that is now the parking lot. It was a very popular gathering place in the summer. Jim Fras, composer of Beautiful Nebraska would play his accordion in the picnic area and Lee later bought a piano and organ, and hired Jim to play in the restaurant.

In the early years we closed the restaurant during the worst of the winter and traveled (I tell young folks they should travel when they are young and can't afford it because it isn't the same when you are old, for one thing you have a life time of memories). One of our most memorable trips was planned by Van Duling Travel Agency in 1955. We went island hopping in the Caribbean Sea, flying from one island to another. We visited Cuba, as well as most of the major islands in the Caribbean. It was a wonderful trip. I suspect Van Duling was a customer of Lee's because Lee was a great believer in patronizing people who patronized his business. He called it "scratching each other's back."

Although I worked at every position in and outside of the restaurant in the early days, my main contribution to the business was in the kitchen and office (when we later had an office). I think that one of the reasons Jan and Ozzie were able to keep the business going so well when they took over was that I had written instructions prepared for all the food items and procedures. Even so, I find it amazing that they have been able to be successful for so long at such a highly competitive and difficult business. They have been truly wonderful and skillful.

Authors Jerry Mapes (L) and Van Duling (R) are shown in front of Lee's Restaurant July 2001 after the original building had its 7th or 8th addition.

Spencer's
By Gail Gade

In the year 1946, Spencer's Steak House located at 14th and South was about the only restaurant in Lincoln where you could get a steak dinner, due to the shortage of meat caused by World War II.

Jack and Fred Spencer were the owners and they were good friends of the Nebraska football team, who visited the restaurant quite frequently.

It is recalled upon entering the café, Hoagy Carmicheal could be heard singing from the juke box the popular song at that time, "Old Buttermilk Sky."

Muny Integrated '46
By Dale Harp

Several summers I was employed as a lifeguard at the Lincoln Municipal Swimming Pool, commonly called Muny Pool in those days.

The day Lincoln City Fathers allowed Negroes to integrate Muny Pool was in the summer of 1946. Prior to this day the pool was white only.

We had observed three or four Black airmen swimming at Muny Pool, during the hours the pool was isolated for troops stationed at Lincoln Air force Base. Therefore we were certain the sky would not fall.

I recall very vividly the day several Negro teenagers emerged from the locker rooms, several were classmates of mine attending Lincoln High School.

Most of the regular Muny swimmers stepped out on the concrete and stood silent, as one particularly muscular, very athletic class mate waded out waist deep and proceeded to baptize his arm pits with Muny water.

The crowd laughed as Muny was integrated very ceremoniously, on that day.

Northeast High School—A Dream Come True

By Nola Jean Chore Newsham

In 1941, Northeast High School became a reality. This school had been a dream of the northeast community for nearly a decade. Jackson High School, the school in the University Place area, was so over-crowded the students could not pass in the halls without maneuvering and then going up the stairs, their combined weight would cause the steps to sway beneath their feet. The building had been condemned for the number of students it served, but the ruling was not enforced. Havelock High School was crowded too, and badly in need of repair. Bethany High School's enrollment was down, and this building was also in need of repair. To build a new school that could accommodate all three student bodies, and incidentally unite the northeast community seemed the perfect answer.

The adults who initiated and worked so hard to see this dream of a new high school come true were equally determined to see it succeed. To this end, they tried to take every precaution to alleviate the problems and controversies they feared would materialize. This was certainly understandable since these three schools that would unite had been enemies in sports and other competitions for years, even though Jackson was a Class A school and Havelock and Bethany were in Class B. The Class A city rivals of the earlier years were Jackson and Lincoln High. Now in 1941, these three northeast enemies were expected to unite and as a result be the new foe in the Class A rivalry with Lincoln High.

It happened as envisioned. This Class A rivalry exploded into its first controversy following the 1942–43 basketball season with Northeast and Lincoln High competing in the state regional finals. Lincoln, the eventual Class A Champ, won the regionals 34–33. The aftermath of this event required apologies to the city and the mayor from both schools. An administrator and two students from each school performed this duty. Robert Wilcox ('43) and Phyllis Teagarden Coonley ('43) were the Northeast student representatives, and they have vivid memories of this responsibility.

The classroom memories we have of those first three years differ by reason of individual experience, but all are interwoven with the unforgettable feeling of community that came to us as we faced this huge, new school together. We knew the excitement and a bit of the fear of this adventure, but it did not take us, the students, long to get acquainted and forge new loyalties and friendships as we enthusiastically responded to this challenging educational happening.

We have varied memories of the ground-breaking ceremonies for the school, but we are of one accord in remembering the rain, the mud, and the temporary, wide, wooden walk that graced the front entrance to the school that very first September. There were no sidewalks to the building and the streets coming from the north and the east had yet to be paved when school started. And, it continued to rain and rain.

Those who chose to enter the back of the school by cutting diagonally across the field that bounded the school, found themselves forced to assist their boots with alternating tugs or lose them in the clayey mud. Those who chose to enter the front of the school were greeted by the wooden walk. It stretched as wide as the opening expanse of the school doors and extended nearly to the street. Once muddy boots met wet wood, a particular physical balance was required. To assist a friend who was slipping or had fallen was fatal to remaining upright yourself. We cannot imagine there was any student who did not crawl up that wooden walk, at least once, during those first, rainy, September days!

Most students wore boots. Some did not. Others wore boots, but did not remove them until they got to their lockers. Those who removed their boots before entering the school and placed them on newspaper received the undying gratitude of the janitor, Carl Lamborn. Generally, the halls were a mess those first few weeks of the new Northeast High School beginnings.

The first year it seemed to us that there were adults intent upon making lines of demarcation between the three student bodies they wanted to unite. The tabulated the student leadership for equal participation in all opportunities. When the adult pressure became too much, the student vocal objections became vociferous.

Selection of the School Logo—We remember how the rocket symbol was chosen. The Board of Education allowed us a number of choices from which they would aid us in our final selection. We were in an assembly when Jeanne Westmoreland Elliott ('43) suggested the rocket as the Northeast symbol. Jeanne was partial to a rocket symbol as the skating group her boyfriend (later her husband) was a part of used a rocket symbol. We were all aware that other groups had chosen such a symbol, but most of us were delighted when the rocket symbol was approved by the school board. It appealed to us as a symbol of our soaring into competition, a force to be reckoned with, and it gave us a feeling of being in touch with our then modern world as the introduction of the liquid fuel German V-2 long-range rocket was new on our horizons. Max Long ('42) designed our rocket logo, but we had to wait patiently for a copy to be built and placed near the front entrance of the school. The rocket symbol became even more appropriate for the current times as December 7, 1941 dawned and the United States was at war.

Selection of School Colors—We remember we were allowed to submit our suggestions for the school colors, but our choices were limited to any color that had not been a school color of Havelock, Bethany or Jackson. So, at the suggestion of the art teacher, Miriam McGrew we opted for the temporary, neutral colors of Black and White. The School Board approved and 51 years later, those temporary colors still wave!

Choosing a School Name—We do not recall any controversy about the naming of the school. It had been known as the school for the northeast community, and Northeast High School seemed most appropriate. It was not until some twenty years later when it came time to name the school being built in the southeast area of the city that a location as a name was challenged. This challenge was resolved by calling the new school Lincoln Southeast High School, changing Northeast to Lincoln Northeast High School and Lincoln High to Lincoln Central High School. In 1968 when a school was opened in the direct east area of the city, it was named Lincoln East High School. The public seemed to agree with adding Lincoln to the new schools, but never did accept the change to the established Lincoln High School.

Choosing a Newspaper Name—We do not recall any controversy about the decision to name the school paper the Northeastern. We all remember it just sounded right.

Naming the Student Body and Pep Club—Once the rocket symbol had been chosen, the student body automatically became The Rockets. It took a Pep Club meeting to receive the vote to call this group the Rockettes. Roscoe Shields ('43) designed the logo for the Pep Club sweaters.

Choosing a Yearbook Name—There was controversy and a flurry of student objections to calling the 1942 Yearbook the TRI/HI. Amid a chorus of student approvals, the 1943 Yearbook was established as the Rocket.

We share these memories of our beginnings with pride and ownership. We are pleased that many of our choices have lasted for more than fifty years. We have been gratified to watch Northeast grow and remain strong in academics, the arts and athletics. Those adults who wished to build a school that would unite and serve the community certainly succeeded.

Northeast Becomes a Reality

By Georgia Lemon Duling

University Place, Huntington Grade School and Jackson Junior High School, all a part of a closely-knit community is where I grew up prior to September 1942. Elementary schools offered mid year enrollment, so I was enrolled in January and then pushed ahead a semester in third grade. Home was two blocks from the school; we always walked and went home at noon for lunch.

September 1942 changed my life! Now the new high school was two miles from home and walking into the rough unfinished grounds of the new Northeast School produced some skinned knees! Some of us rode city busses; none of us had autos.

Meeting students from Bethany, Havelock and the Ag College area, learning to accept their good ideas and work with them was a pleasant time. There were many new faculty to meet also. Some familiar faculty who moved with us from Jackson somehow became even dearer friends such as Ann Munson and Myrtle Clark. Helen Miller and Julius Humann became new faculty friends.

The new building offered facilities for new and expanded programs: swimming, theater and set designs, musicals in the new auditorium, new science lab facilities. School dances in the new gym were fun as was jitterbug dancing after school to records provided by students. A new cafeteria was a place you could bring your own lunch which I recall doing. After walking home from school we often gathered at Yanney's Restaurant in Uni Place operated by Jim Yanney's parents.

There were large challenges: a new principal, a new journalism advisor for the school newspaper, school colors to choose (black and white seemed to conflict the least) and naming the school newspaper Northeastern. Tri-Hi was the title given to the first yearbook, which was later changed by a vote to the Rocket. We worked hard because we really wanted to succeed, but everything was so new for us and we were the pioneers. Our strong sports programs probably did more toward building school spirit than anything else. School activities such as our musical shows directed by Margaret Crone were tremendous fun! Girl Reserves was a service organization offering a city wide council which provided further opportunities to expand our acquaintances. During our junior and senior years many classmates left for the military service and several boys from my class joined the V-12 and V-5 programs.

Our love of ballroom dancing carried on into the summer months. Open air dances at Kings Ballroom at Capital Beach Amusement Park or featured dance bands in the Turnpike Ballroom were considered very special occasions with a date.

May 1944 our senior class of 148 represented the first three year class to graduate from Northeast High School.

The Havelock Businessmen's Organization December 31, 1940. Victor Anderson, later Lincoln's mayor and Nebraska's governor, is shown in the back row at far right. *Photo courtesy Nebraska State Historical Society.*

War Time Alarm Clock
By Chris Lyberis

Oak Creek Lake north of Lincoln offered an opportunity during the war to catch a few fish.

1943 was the year my bicycle riding friends and I invented the "24 foot string alarm clock" designed to get an early start for the ride north of Lincoln to our carp fishing resort (Oak Creek Lake).

My family did not have an alarm clock available to me, so my friends Tony Bassen and Dale Harp rigged up a sure fire alarm. My bedroom was on the second floor, so a 24 foot string was tied to my big toe closest to the window, the string dropped down the side of the house. Several jerks on the string worked every time.

The Original Gridiron Club
By Jerry Mapes

Now that I've gotten the editorializing out of my system via the title of this article, I wanted to acquaint some of you lucky enough to be in your twenties, thirties and forties how the Gridiron show used to operate.

In trying to research the genesis of the club I have fallen short. Probably sometime in the 1940s The Gridiron show was limited to male members of the University Club and the two shows on Friday and Saturday were limited to male members only. In those days the language and antics were not fit for the ears and eyes of the gentler sex. Occasionally, however, one of the female employees of the club would sneak a peak from some vantage point and report to the rest. Of course, now since there are no more obscenities that are tasteless or situations that are only for the eyes of the male species, all bets are off. The result: It's a much better produced, choreographed and directed show and a helluva lot more fun.

We began preparing for the show, which was usually in April, by meeting every Saturday noon and kicking around ideas and reading scripts, etc. Of course, all this good work was done only after sufficient alcohol induction. Many preplanned Saturday night husband and wife outings were sometimes put on hold so a late Saturday afternoon nap could cure the damage done at lunch.

After three months "horseplay" and a lot of strained relationships, the dress rehearsal was imminent. All the lines that had been learned, the stage direction that had been mastered and the songs that had been memorized all went up in smoke at the dress rehearsal because of that ever present catalyst of "demon rum" (plus demon vodka, demon scotch and demon bourbon).

Actually, this was a blessing in disguise because all cast members were so hung over the night of the show (the next night) that out of contrition for their sins, they had really learned their lines. Of course, there were always a few of the old guard that you could count on to be in a catatonic state for all three nights. They shall remain anonymous but their memories will be preserved forever (in alcohol).

Footnote: This is in no way an affirmation of the "way it used to be" but I remember also that on Gridiron night, the reigning police chief notified all his street officers to be a little gentle with poor souls as the wended their way to their respective homes. That could possibly account for the fact that when a local businessman was pushing a local physician down O Street in a wheelchair at a high rate of speed, neither was arrested. They were given rides home.

One of the University Club Gridiron skits is shown here with Jerry Mapes at center being held vertical by two "supporting" cast members in the 1970s.

Trumpet Blues
By Van C. Duling

The Great War was raging in 1944. It was difficult for nearly every industry to recruit qualified people ... the music industry certainly being no exception.

I was a young 17-year-old kid who had been trying my hand at playing drums with various local dance orchestras when out of the blue I received a call from radio station KFAB in Lincoln, located in the old Lincoln Hotel, to audition for their studio orchestra.

The position would require me to play with a small jazz orchestra for a noon show from

12:15 to 12:45 five days a week ... returning in the afternoon for a one hour Polka Show in the late afternoonn— the music provided by, coincidentally the same orchestra. The only difference was the noon show was entitled KFAB Studio Orchestra the afternoon show the KFAB Polka Band.

I could work it in beautifully with my schedule at the University of Nebraska where I had just enrolled. It was the perfect part time job.

I was well acquainted with the musicians having played with them often before ... The absolute delight was meeting and providing music for the featured performer at radio station KFAB—none other than Texas Mary on the noon show.

Many will remember Texas Mary as the premiere country female vocalist certainly of the middle west—if not the entire nation. She was not only a great entertainer playing super guitar and singing those cowboy songs like crazy ... but she was a wonderful human being. Daily the Fan Mail arrived for Mary. It amounted to hundreds of postcards for requests. To our sponsor Hybrid Seed Corn Company, needless to say she was worth her weight in gold.

Speaking of Mary—she had problems with one of her legs and periodically she would commit to the Mayo Clinic in Rochester Minnesota. On one occasion we were told, she received the largest amount of fan mail any entertainer had ever received up to that time— eclipsing even Clark Gable who had been a patient there. Her fans were legendary. They truly loved this lady, as we all did.

Just one little aside that I am reminded of ... some of the musicians were older men and were musicians by profession. In other words this is all they did. Like many musicians they had plenty of time on their hands to shoot pool during the afternoon and quaff some serious or not so serious libations along the way.

Well, as luck would have it one of our trumpet players showed up one afternoon stiffer than a new broom before the afternoon broadcast. He stood up to take a solo and blow toward the microphone when he lost his balance, passed out, and fell forward with the bell of his trumpet catching the string connecting the chimes, the sound of which was our trademark as we went on and off the air. The string on the chimes was broken. All of the chimes fell on to the floor ... and trust me when I tell you that it sounded like the start of World War Three.

The announcer started laughing uncontrollably and there was so much racket and confusion that the engineer took us off the air until we could compose ourselves.

No sooner having done that than in through the door burst Jiggs Miller the station manager who's face was as red as a beet ... .he fired us on the spot. This would have been very bad news except that Jiggs was rather volatile and had been known to fire us before for even less serious offenses.

We went to bed knowing that night that we should report for work the next day because he would rehire us—and sure enough he did. Just another day in the life of the musicians!

Thank You Emily Whoever You Are

By Virginia Guenzel

In November, 1943, I managed to turn my life topsy-turvy in just ten days. I felt that I was living inside a kaleidoscope during that time, with the pieces of my life tumbling about and rearranging themselves every few days into a whole new set of circumstances. On a Thursday, my fiancé, Bob, returned to our home town with gleaming new lieutenant's bars on his brand new uniform. On Saturday night there was a wedding in which I turned out to be the bride. Four honeymoon days in Chicago preceded our return home to spend Thanksgiving with our parents, and two days later, I found myself in Lawton, Oklahoma, breathless, bewildered, homeless but happy.

Lawton is a very small town bordering on the mammoth, sprawling complex that is called Fort Sill where the United States Army trains its Field Artillery units. The war awakened this sleepy town and by 1943, it was bursting its seams with the soldiers and their families who were stationed there. The housing of all these newcomers posed a problem and the natives' efforts of turning everything from garages to outsized chicken coops into apartments did little to alleviate it. I started bravely out on a quest to find our first home.

Someone advised me to go to the Traveler's Aid Bureau where a woman would help us with any vacant accommodations. My rosy glow of innocent hope faded quickly as I saw her add our name as 125th on the waiting list. I knew if we lived long enough to achieve first place, we would surely have long since left Lawton in the dust behind us.

My next gem of advice worked out a little better. Many people, someone told me, would go to the newspaper office when the day's edition came out so that if there was an ad, you could race to the address and apply. That is how I found our first "home," one room in a small house in which we shared the bath with others and were granted what they called "kitchen privileges." While this was an improvement over the hotel in which we had been staying, I was determined to find something better.

Very soon, I did find our second "home." Located at the edge of town, we now had a huge bedroom, a small bath, and a kitchenette, although the refrigerator was down the hall in the owner's kitchen. I could have put up with that, but I soon found we weren't the only residents of this apartment. We were sharing it with the most enormous colony of cockroaches it has ever been my misfortune to see. They were everywhere, skittering through drawers and adorning walls. Bob was very understanding, never once asking me if I'd caught even a quick glimpse of the place before I rented it. I believe he had never seen me cry before, and the avalanche of tears that flowed down my cheeks probably came close to breaking his newly married heart. Hugging me, he said we would spend just one week here, and if we didn't find anything else, we'd move back to the hotel and start all over again.

A few days later, Bob came home with the marvelous news that a friend at the fort had told him of a house that was soon to be rented. We raced to the telephone and got an interview that very evening. I dressed as carefully as a contestant about to enter the Miss America Pageant. Not too dressy, I told myself, but certainly not slacks. We rang the bell at the nicest house I'd seen since I left home. I knew at once we had to have this home. The woman who answered the door was nice looking with a friendly smile. Actually she looked a little like an angel from heaven to me. Sitting in her well-furnished living room, the three if us talked for at least an hour. I could tell Bob was trying to be as charming as I hoped I was being. She said she expected her home to be kept very clean, and I didn't even blush when I told her that I really enjoyed dusting and sweeping. When she told us we could rent the house and could move in the very next day, we thanked her profusely. Just as I was promising myself that I would clean this house right down to its roots, I heard her add, "I knew if Emily liked you so much that I would like you too." Bob and I glanced quickly at each other, but neither one of us seemed to be able to say, "Who is Emily?" We left as quickly as possible after that, fearful she might discover we were not the couple someone had recommended to her. "After all," I said to Bob on our way home, "all's fair in love and war and there's a little of both in this case."

We moved in. I cleaned her house with fervor all the time we were there. And every night, and sometimes in the daytime too, I would stop a moment and say with honest gratitude, "Thank you, Emily, whoever you are."

'Well, It Looks Like We're At War'

By Midge Van Pelt Irvin

Is it *David Copperfield* that begins, "I was born?" Well so was I. On June 18, 1931, I was born to Robert and Mildred Van Pelt.

I lived in one house throughout my entire childhood and growing up years (my mother lived there for 66 years) so my memories are all of one neighborhood. Our house was at 2323 Woodcrest, just up the street from Irving School. Across the street were the Ira Beynons, next door to the west was Dr. Clyde Davis, who founded the University of Nebraska Dental School, next door to the east were, as we called them, "The Aitken Ladies," Grace and Gertrude, spinster aunts of Bill and Phil Aitken.

In my early years, there were few fears of children being in danger when on their own. The first time I was allowed to go downtown on the bus, (Irving school bus, of course) was when I was four years old, accompanied by Esther Beynon and Bob Bryan, who lived next door to the Beynons, both of whom were seven. Bus rides were a nickel and movies were 10¢, so with a quarter, you could go down town, see a movie, have a nickel to buy a treat, and get home again.

I remember learning of Jean Harlow's death sitting on the Beynon's front steps. Esther Beynon, three years older than I, could read and I couldn't, so she read me the article out of the paper. Jean Harlow was the glamour girl of the 30s and her untimely death shocked the nation.

We kids were free to wander around the neighborhood and Irving school was a magnet. With no TV for evening entertainment, we often attended whatever was going on at Irving. It could be a dance recital or a Boy Scout Court of Honor. All such things were free and we would just walk down the street and go in, whether we knew anybody there or not.

We all remember where we were on Sunday, December 7th, 1941. I was at Sarah Fulton's 11th birthday party (Sarah is now Mrs. William Ginn of Omaha). I still remember my father's words when he picked me up after the party. He said, "Well, it looks like we're at war."

I remember practice blackouts. We would turn out all lights and wait till instructed to turn them on again. Our neighborhood blackout warden was Joe Fenton, who lived at 22nd and Harrison. He was the manager of Kresge's store at the corner of 12th and O. Joe was a friend of my Dad's and when he got to our house, they would visit. Joe was allowed a flashlight as he made his rounds.

A practice our family followed throughout the war was inviting servicemen from the airbase to Sunday and holiday dinners. Every Sunday the airmen would gather in the back of First Plymouth Church and families would approach them and invite several home for dinner. They would stay at our house for the rest of the day and my father would always drive them back to the base at night. On Christmas and Thanksgiving we would go down to the USO (located in the Rudge and Guenzel building at 13th and N) and find servicemen there. My brother, Sam and I always felt especially lucky if one of them played the piano, because then we were treated to something no one in our family could do. My father always got the names and addresses of each man and I think he kept in touch with some of them for many years. I recall one fellow, when asked for his name and address, saying he would like to write them himself as he had just learned to write in the service. He was from Arkansas and was very proud of what he could now do.

I am five years older than my brother and his reactions to the war were different from mine. One day he said to me, "If I tell you something, will you promise not to tell Mother and Daddy?" I promised. He then said, "I hope the Italish win."

In the late spring of 1944, we all knew that D-day was coming, but we didn't know when. It had been announced that when it happened, all the church bells in Lincoln would ring and signal the beginning. My mother, an avid gardener, woke up early on June mornings, so she could be in the garden before it got hot. On the morning of June 6, as she awakened she heard bells chiming from all directions. Then she realized it was "the invasion," as we called it, and she turned on the radio, awakened us and we all listened. The local broadcaster announced that the churches in Lincoln would be open so citizens could go to their churches and pray for the success of our troops.

I remember when KFAB was in Lincoln and Texas Mary was their star. I also remember Jimmy the Chimp at the zoo. During the war, his routine was to be handed an array of flags, from which he would always pick the Stars and Stripes, wave it over his head, and the audience would cheer.

The continuity and stability of families is one of the great things about Lincoln. Today, my grandchildren live exactly two blocks from where I grew up. They attend the same Prescott and Irving schools that I attended, play kick the can on the same streets, and Irving school is also a magnet in their lives. It is through them that I know that you can go home again.

My Memories of the Depression, World War II and Post–World War II

By E. H. (Al) Kauffman

Having been born in 1921, I was too young to realize the seriousness of the Great Depression and the hardships thrust upon the American people. All I knew growing up was that we always had a place to live and food on the table. My father worked for the CB&Q Railroad and made a decent living. As a matter of fact, my two uncles also worked for the CB&Q, but were laid off during the Depression. Fortunately, my dad kept his job and ended up supporting my two uncles and their families for a considerable length of time on two hundred dollars a month. That was quite a feat.

I always found a lot of things to have fun with that didn't cost money. I had a dog, a car made out of an orange crate with wheels, chickens and a pet rabbit. We had a lot of chickens to eat because our outhouse was in the chicken yard and sometimes when I would go there, the roosters would chase me. My mother would get mad, catch the rooster, wring its neck and we would eat it for supper.

Looking back, I was never jealous of my playmates because we were all in the same boat—little or no money to buy toys, candy or any of the things kids have now days. I remember my cousin, Larry Price, who was more like a brother, and I would get 25¢ a week allowance. On Saturdays we would go to town, eat at the Hotel-D-Hamburger where you could get six hamburgers for a quarter, go to the show for 10¢ each and have a nickel left over for a big bag of popcorn.

I didn't realize it at the time, but later found out my dad lost his life savings ($10,000) in a savings and loan that failed. I guess that's why he was reluctant to put his money in the bank so he kept it under the mattress. Ha!

Although we moved a lot while I was growing up due to my dad getting transferred in his railroad job, I always managed to return to Lincoln to spend the summer with Larry Price. We did many things together, like run an icehouse, deliver newspapers, collect garbage, etc. I'll never forget the time Larry was gone and left me in charge of the icehouse. We had built a little hamburger operation on the ice house and every day the city bus driver would stop and order one or two hamburgers. Then he would drive north on Cotner Boulevard in Bethany and by the time he made his turn-around, the hamburgers would be ready. The day I was left in charge, the bus driver, as usual, stopped and ordered two hamburgers. I went to prepare them and noticed the stove needed fuel. I filled the tank with coal oil and some must have spilled on the buns. Anyway, the next day the driver stopped the bus, came over to Larry to tell him the hamburgers tasted funny. Larry looked at me and I had to confess that I must have spilled the coal oil on the buns. The driver laughed and said it was a good thing that he didn't smoke.

For inexpensive fun, Larry made some wooden rifles and helmets out of Model-T headlight covers. He would drill us and we would go on maneuvers like we were in the Army. As a result, I took a liking to this sort of thing and later made the Army a career, which spanned thirty years. I was the ROTC Cadet Colonel in high school. I attended the CMTC where I won a scholarship to the Wentworth Military Academy and entered the Army in 1942. I served in three wars—World War II, Korea and Vietnam. I rose to the rank of Colonel and was awarded every combat decoration except the Medal of Honor.

Between the Depression years and the end of World War II, there were so many technological accomplishments, so many advances in creature comforts and uniting of the United States of America. Like it or not, we were thrust into the role of world leader.

After my retirement from the Army, I returned to Lincoln in 1970 to join Larry Price in his famous King's Food Host operation and have lived here ever since. I have been around the world, but I must say unequivocally that Lincoln, Nebraska, is the best place to live.

The Ending: My Recollection of the Last Attack Flight of the PUDDLE JUMPER II

By Dr. Bob Hayes, 1st Lt. Navigator

It is May, 1945 and the European partners in the axis powers have been beaten and their surrender has been accepted by the allies under the command of General Eisenhower. The armed forces of Europe can now look toward the probable rotation back to their home within the near future following the final clearing of the war debris. There will be, to be sure, some of the newer arrivals that will stay and monitor the return of the European countries to some sort of peaceful rebuilding and to the reestablishment of organized governments. Germany is in veritable collapse with no organized leadership and with the sting of having to be the losers in their attempt to be the rulers of the world under the Nazi regime. The war criminals of the axis powers will be hunted and sent to trial before a war crimes tribunal composed of the members of the allied nations with the United States, Britain, and Russia generally leading the charges.

Now there is the continuing war in the Pacific with the third member of the axis powers to contend with even though there seems to be some light in the successes in that theater. The Japanese have shown no sign of quitting the war and so the advances of the United States and the British, French, and Australian forces continue toward the homeland. Island after island is either taken with surrender or is bypassed by some of the tactical maneuvers of General MacAurthur. Wake Island, a fairly large atoll, held a large contingent of the Japanese Marines that were to hold that island if and when the allies planned to make the jump from Enewetok before the next island group, the Marianas. The allies bypassed Wake and continued to Saipan, Tinian and Guam.

From Guam, many sorties toward Japan and the southern islands of the Ryukyu group were made by the B-29s and the B-24 squadrons. During this period, Okinawa was attacked and after many costly ground battles, was occupied and secured which made it possible for the U.S. Air Force to move to the various fields built by the Seebees and Engineers. The Yontan field became the principle home of the 11th Bomb Group composed of the 26th, 98th, 50th, and 431st heavy bombardment squadrons. The attack on the Japanese homeland was increased from this vantage point and many large and small raids were made during the next few weeks.

Our Squadron, the 431st Heavy Bombardment Unit now had the opportunity to make raids on the lower island of Japan both in group flights or singly to some of the lesser targets. I was the navigator on one of the lead B-24s when we flew formation raids. We also made night raids to the area between China and Japan where there was an illicit trade between Chinese junks and some of the Japanese submarines. By this time, the effectiveness of the homeland raids by the various air force squadrons had reduced the Japanese fuel supply to extremely low amounts and their defensive air cover was reduced to zero. On only one raid of our squadron did we encounter any aircraft of the Zero type and those dispersed promptly as we closed formation for the attack.

Now there was a tactical change in the attack campaign toward the Japanese islands. Instead of formation bombing by our 11th Bomb Group, the idea of "snooper" missions was conceived. This plan consisted of one plane departing each hour of the day and night and seeking a different target for each plane. In this manner, this constant hitting of various targets had the effect of demoralizing the populace of Japan and causing their military to let down their guard as to which attack was to be the major attack. Nearly all of these attacks were carried out by the B-24s and B-29s from Guam and Okinawa.

On August 3, 1945, our crew had the target of Sasebo on the western coast of Kyushu for our daylight snooper mission and we proceeded to that area only to find that there was a heavy cloud undercover and our bombardier was unable to visually see the ground. With that event, we then elected to bomb off the navigator's LORAN terminal.

This enabled us to at least see an outline of the target area with this capability, we made our run, released our bomb load and circled to leave the target area when we saw a huge black cloud arising from the target. This meant that we had hit some oil depot and further subtracted from Japan's low fuel reserve.

The trip back to Yontan was as routine as you could imagine until we turned on our IFF radio identification at the 300 mile contact site. We could not understand the confusion and excitement that came over the radio when they announced that the U.S. Air Force had dropped the BIG BOMB on Hiroshima! We were stunned when they estimated the BIG BOMB at 40 tons of TNT when we only carried 500 pound proximity fused bomb loads. As we landed on Yontan, the field was in uproar with the likelihood that the war may be over the celebrations were everywhere. As we returned to the operations tent, there was a poster on the bulletin board that described the first atomic bomb that Hiroshima was the target on this day. That poster had been in our CO's office for three weeks and there was no leak about what was to come. However, the Japanese military refused to surrender and the snooper missions continued as before. On August 6, 1945, only 3 days later, we were back in the air for our mission to Kure where one of their battleships had been sunk early in the war, but the deck guns were awash and they continued to act as an anti-aircraft gun emplacement. As we cruised at an altitude of 14,000 feet, the air was full of small particle debris from the Hiroshima blast. Little did we know that we were flying in a cloud of radioactive dust and debris. We made our bomb run and we dropped 12 of the 500 pound bombs, our usual load. As we finally turned off the target and dropped down over the south inland sea between Hokkaido and Kyushu, we looked to the west and there was the rising plume of the Nagasaki Atomic Bomb drop. This was probably the most poignant moment our crew ever experienced since we realized that we were a diversionary flight for the last major air force attack on Japan.

The last leg of this mission was nothing short of pandemonium on our plane, The Puddle Jumper II. Now we knew that the Japanese would certainly surrender and we would soon be heading to our various homes in the United States.

U of N—'A Girls' School'

By Sally Stebbins Knudsen

It was Sunday June 4, 1944 and the Lincoln High School graduating class was having their baccalaureate service at St. Paul's Methodist Church. Two days later the invasion of Europe began at Normandy. For some time before this all men 18 years old were called to service for the armed forces as soon as they graduated.

As a girl I was privileged to stay home and, lucky me, go to the University of Nebraska that fall. However, the University in 1944 was virtually a girl's school. Only a few dental students remained on campus. The classes were all women, the activities and sports all involved women and weekends were spent going to movies and playing bridge with women. All but one of the fraternity houses were closed-empty and there was hardly a car on campus. Gasoline was rationed—3 gallons a week!

There was a sign up sheet in the sorority house where you could help with the war effort by rolling bandages for the Red Cross, gather scrap metal and working for the USO (United Service Organization). The USO was located at 14th & P, close to the campus. We would go there to be a hostess, playing cards, conversation with the service men and serving food. There were dances with the men stationed at nearby bases: Fairbury, Fairmont and Lincoln Airbase. The USO bus would take us for the evening to one of the bases. All very well chaperoned, I might say.

In November our sorority had scheduled a fall Formal Dance. As it happened, another sorority had chosen the same date for their dance. Within a few days it became apparent that there were simply not enough men to go around. As a result both houses canceled their parties.

By January of 1946 all that changed and there were men everywhere. The fraternities were open, the classes were full and a few old cars appeared on campus. Most of the men were returning to University of Nebraska on the G.I. Bill. The drought was over—so was the war.

A Special Team

By George E. Howard

The 1941 Lincoln High football team was indeed special. We were undefeated and untied. The line up was Mickey Allen and Jerry Regelean at the ends, Gordon Hall and Neil McPherson at the tackles, George Howard and Bob Keller at guards and John Blumer at center. In the backfield was Ed Hall at quarterback, Bob Glenn and Leslie "Crook" West at halfback, and Ray Boehmer at fullback. The first game was at the old Oval on the dirt field. We played Lincoln Northeast in their first football game as the school just opened that fall. We won 14–0.

In another memorable game, we played Omaha Tech on their field in Omaha. There was about four inches of water and mud on the field. After the first play there were no numbers on uniforms that were legible. We won 7–0 on a pass to Jerry Regelean. Another game was played at Omaha Benson. There was about a foot of snow on the field. Coach Ralph Beechner suggested that we clear it off, but Benson officials did not want to damage their new grass turf. It was the only field at that time with grass. We won that game also 7–0 on a pass, again to Jerry Regelean.

The last game of the season was against Grand Island. They had beaten us the two previous years and Coach Beechner wanted to beat them in the worst way. We were ahead 35–0 at the half, so they reduced the third and fourth quarters by two minutes each. After the game Coach Beechner came down to the players locker room. Usually he and the other coaches went directly to their own. He congratulated us, took off his baseball cap which he always wore an slammed it to the floor and said, "We should have beaten them 100–0." The final score was 58–0.

We had a great year, but later that fall on December 7th was the bombing of Pearl Harbor and the beginning of World War II for the United States.

Lincoln Remembers

By Barc Bayley

I remember the start of WWII (when Germany invaded Poland on September 1, 1939) as a newspaper carrier going down the street in front of our house and yelling "Extra! Extra! Germany invades Poland!" I bummed some money from my folks and bought one of the papers (I still have it). This started a collection of WWII papers that have cluttered the walls in my home ever since.

I remember December 7, 1941 when the Japanese attacked Pearl Harbor. It was a Sunday and all the "old folks" usually had the radio going while the kids were outside goofing around. It was early afternoon when somebody came out and told us to come in and listen to the radio because something important had happened. We listened but we didn't have the foggiest idea what Pearl Harbor was, where it was, or what all this meant to us. I was just 12 years old at the time.

We quickly found out some of the things that it meant. All of a sudden you couldn't buy a new car, even if you were one of the few who could afford it. Next came the rationing of shoes, sugar, meat and butter. Imported food like bananas became scarce as hens' teeth. Like all loyal Americans, we quickly figured out ways to get stuff without the required ration stamps. Ten years after the war some of this hoarded stuff was still on shelves in the basement.

One of the early big changes the war brought to Lincoln was the hurry-up construction of an Air Base where Lincoln's airport was (and still is). The base was one of a string built throughout Nebraska. The reason for this was supposed to be because the state had a lot of good flying weather and cheap land. Lincoln soon was home to 20,000 soldiers who lived in tarpaper barracks at the base. In what seemed like a short time, the sky seemed to always have Air Corps planes criss-crossing. As an airplane nut, I thought this was great.

The aircrews were still in training and a many of them were new to planes so we had our share of crashes to be concerned about. The pilots looked like old guys to us but were mostly in their very early 20s. Today, I'm sure I would refer to them as kids.

I remember how Dick Joyce from Lincoln, one of the 1942 Tokyo raid pilots, spoke to us at a jam-packed assembly in Irving Junior High. We were all blown away by the fact that one of the hero-fliers was actually from Lincoln. At that time no one would admit the bombers flew from an aircraft carrier, they just kept saying they were from "Shangrila."

In those days ninth-grade girls didn't do much to make themselves look older at school, even though they were at an age were they looked and acted older than most boys. But when you had 20,000 young men suddenly in town and looking for dates, these girls had quite a different look. When you saw them with some soldier, they were all dolled up trying to pass for at least 18. When their classmates saw them "faking it," the girls were given a heavy dose of ribbing.

I remember that one of the big weekend entertainment items were the movies. As I recall we could have quite a time for 25¢. Here's the break down: College View streetcar, a nickel each way; double feature movie (usually including the latest episode of a serial) for a dime; and the other nickel went for something to eat.

Speaking of cheap entertainment, school kids then could get a "knothole ticket" to Nebraska football games for a dime. You were supposed to sit on end zone bleachers but when the game started we usually could take seats in the main stadium because the crowd was pretty small and nobody minded our "invasion."

Since parents couldn't and wouldn't waste precious gas hauling you around—even on those few days when the family car wasn't taken to work, kids usually had to rely on bikes for transportation. Boys, at least, rode them anywhere in town without a thought to any place being "off limits" or dangerous. Often we went in twos and threes, but sometimes there'd be a whole pack traveling together. I can just imagine how popular we were with car driving adults.

I remember an afternoon when several of us rode our bikes down by the statehouse when all of a sudden some Dutch pilots, training at the Lincoln Air Base, decided it would be a lot of fun to fly their light bombers around the capitol tower and drop little sacks of flour on the place. Of course, everybody down below had a fit but I'm sure the pilots laughed all the way back to Amsterdam and of course were never given worse than half-hearted reprimand for the stunt.

When I was 14 I got a school permit to work as a soda jerk at Terminal Drug at 10th and O. It turns out that spot was a major bus stop for soldiers going to and from the Air Base. It was great for the soda business but you sure heard every fast line that bored GIs could think of. I learned about double-talk, big city lingo and just about everything else a kid my age would think was really "in" stuff.

I remember that we had War Savings Time, which moved the clock two hours ahead all year long. This meant that in the dead of winter you went to school long before sunrise. In junior high it was sometimes second period before the sun came up. I can't remember what the benefit of this was supposed to be.

When the Japanese surrender was announced around supper time on August 15, 1945, everybody who could get there went downtown. Nobody said do it—it was just that everybody had the same idea. This included all the guys stationed at the Base. It was wild, packed with people on O Street from 9th to at least 16th and on all the side streets. People were kissing, swapping ties with soldiers, yelling and laughing, drinking anything that remotely resembled booze, and just generally going nuts in celebration.

Lincoln had never seen anything like that night and probably never will. Football celebrations can't hold a candle to the scene. I was just 16 but I vividly remember the last day of The War In Lincoln.

'But It Takes One To Know One'

By Bob Sawdon

When I was about 18 years old I lived with my mother and brother at the Manor Apartments, 501 South 13th Street. My wife (then Helen Newman) lived near 32nd and Randolph. I had no money or car so I either walked or rode the street car—on the back.

The streetcar made a very slow turn from 18th Street to go east on K Street. I walked from home to 18th and K and when the streetcar made its turn, I would grab onto a thin metal rail across the back and ride out to 32nd Street. There were no other riders at that time, about 7:00 p.m.

When we reached or approached 32nd Street, I had to stop the streetcar, and did so by pulling the trolley off the cable (a long rod with a wheel on top). The streetcar would stop and I got off in a hurry and went to my girl-friend's house.

The motorman, an old Irish man named Mr. Heelan, came out cussing and "renamed" me, replaced the trolley and went on his way.

If I left Helen's house before the streetcar stopped for the night, I rode back the same way, but at 18th Street the turn was so slow I did not have to pull the trolley, I would get off and walk home to 13th and K Street.

Probably a bad habit but I had to resort to ingenuity rather than walk. This may not reflect too well for a later career police officer, who rose to the rank of Assistant Chief of Police (Chief of Detectives). "But it takes one to know one."

At last, Motorcycle Officer Lavern Campbell—who you will remember for the football deal from Lincoln General was the most hated cop in Lincoln.

Lincoln's Police Department in 1938. During the 1930s the LPD provided specialized instruction for its officers in such areas as law, fingerprinting and traffic accidents, leading the state in training standards. Note Joe Carroll, later long-time police chief, is second from the right in the second row. *Photo courtesy Officer Thurber, LPD.*

The Soda 'Jerk'

By Jerry Mapes

When my brother Jack went off to the Navy in 1941 during World War Two, I was thirteen years of age. Jack left behind his pride and joy, a beautiful Packard convertible. The instructions were: "Don't touch!" Jack was fiercely proud, and rightly so, of this fine car which he had bought with years of toiling.

When I became sixteen and got my first job at the Donley Stahl Co. working for Claude Donley, I commandeered Jack's Packard to make drug deliveries to the various doctor's offices. Most boys would either walk or deliver on bicycle since there was not much distance between doctor's offices in those days. It was quite a sight to see a young kid driving that car around town making 25¢ an hour, which just about broke me even with the gas expense.

The economics of the situation finally dawned on me so I took a job with Gulley Drug in the old Cornhusker Hotel. Mel Gulley hired me but my real boss was "Curly" Hershberger who had been employed at the store since he was about seventeen. Gulley's was a very small store but we managed to have a small soda fountain and everything a drug store should stock in addition to a full line of auto bombs, stink bombs, itching powder, exploding matches, fake vomit and dog droppings.

The airbase had been activated and we also had a full line of wings for flight officers and all the bars and leafs that signify rank on an officers epaulets. We also carried silver and brass belt buckles that some enterprising person had cast for the well dressed officer albeit non regulation. We sold hundreds at $2.50 each when you could buy a pack of Camels for 20¢.

Due to the air base and associated activities tied to the Cornhusker, we also had about a dozen brands of condoms which most of the servicemen would not order from me ... they waited for Curly to help them. Nowadays, the condoms are sitting out in the open in a multitude of colors, flavors, enhancers, etc ... and the cigarettes are hidden under the counter.

Mel Gulley had a heart attack and died in the store, I believe, and Mrs. Gulley came on board. I remember every one bemoaning the death of Mr. Gully and I couldn't understand why. After all, the man was in his forties.

The other big plus from working at Gulley's (I was now up to 35¢ per hour) was the daily trips through the kitchen of the Tee Pee room of the hotel. As I would walk through twice daily to mix up "simple syrup" and procure fountain supplies, I could usually find time to filch two or three brownies just as the a la mode portion was placed on them. Occasionally, a steak burger in the basket with curly fries would also fall prey to my marauding. It was a wonderful time of my life (pimples and all) because I also had first grabs on items that were severely rationed during the war, like Hershey Bars, etc.

The Cornhusker Hotel was then, and remained for many years, the focal point of social functions in Lincoln. Mr. A. Q. Schimmel ran a good hotel. He was a very colorful character to say the least and many of the town's civic leaders enjoyed some special privileges offered in the spirit of good fun. These privileges, of course, will go unspecified.

The Tee Pee Room was on the M Street side of the building and featured the famous "steak burger in a basket" which I think was priced at about 35¢. It came with curly fried potatoes, which no one had ever heard of before. The Tee Pee collected a lot of late night diners and particularly, revelers, coming out of the ballrooms and other functions taking place at the Cornhusker. Needless to say, the atmosphere was usually festive depending on the hour of the day. The Tee Pee also had a "to die for" glass pastry counter selling incredibly delicious pumpernickel, white and whole wheat breads as well as other offerings.

The Landmark Room on the 13th Street side was a much more sedate restaurant open for breakfast, lunch, and dinner. It was here that perhaps the town's oldest coffee klatch had it's beginning. This will be disputed by other coffee groups, as far as date of conception.

Maybe progress is a wonderful thing, but in the case of the Cornhusker Hotel, nothing will ever duplicate or take the place of the venerable Cornhusker of old.

Memories of World War II

By Irene Hansen Thompson

The Japanese bombed Pearl Harbor on December 7, 1941. What a shock! I was a senior at Lincoln High planning to enter the University of Nebraska in the fall.

The whole tone of the University was affected by our entering the war. The new Love Library was turned into a barracks for servicemen. The ROTC was the first to be billeted there until they left for officers training. The campus emptied of men who left for the service. A somber note prevailed. There were no more formal dances. For an hour dance at a sorority young men from maybe five fraternities would be invited.

Soon Love Library was filled with air cadets. They marched in formation to classes. It was my pleasure to date several of these men who come from all parts of the USA.

The air base in Lincoln also trained many soldiers and sororities would go to the base and put on shows. We also went to USO dances in downtown Lincoln. I remember folding bandages and of course our food and gas were rationed.

The last soldiers to come to Love Library were the ASTP. They were an extremely bright group and it was my understanding that they were hurriedly shipped out as they needed soldiers for the front lines.

The war years were filled with a true sense of patriotism for our great country. They were also filled with sadness as we learned of many friends who gave their lives for our country.

A handsome first lieutenant in his Eisenhower jacket and paratroopers boots stole my heart in my senior year. He was wounded at Bastogne (the Battle of the Bulge) and spent lots of time in army hospitals—but he was very happy to be alive and to have survived this decisive battle.

We married two weeks after my graduation and he was able to go to medical school on the G.I. Bill.

Looking Back

By Ron Gibson

Because of World War II, our neighborhood was served by Lincoln's last trolley for a few years after it was to have been discontinued. We lived on South 30th between Randolph and J Street. We walked a block to Randolph, then rode the trolley east on Randolph, north on 27th and east on J Street. There the track divided and became double for a little more than the length of the trolley. Then the two tracks merged into one. The outbound trolley and the inbound trolley met at this point, passing on the double track. The car that arrived first waited for the other, and I don't recall ever having to wait long.

At the end of the line, the driver got out to reverse the pole carrying the current to the car. He walked to the other end, where there was a second steering wheel and second fare box. The seat back could be reversed so passengers would not have to ride backward, but sometimes we did that anyway for the novelty. I remember fondly watching the rails roll back behind me. If you never look back on the path you have traveled, what good are golden memories? That's the reason for this book.

The Milk Lady and the Horse

One other survivor of earlier times was the delivery of milk by horse-drawn wagon. The horse, Bob, had been scheduled for retirement. World War II made every form of transportation that didn't require gasoline look like a good idea as gas was rationed. So, Bob delivered out milk for Meadow Gold, one of Lincoln's two large dairies.

The war took many Lincoln men away to the armed forces, so women stepped up to do the jobs. Our driver was a woman, Mrs. Crawford. The Milk Lady and my mother became good friends, coffee break friends. Mrs. Crawford usually arrived about mid morning. Mom had the coffee on, served with cream from Meadow Gold, naturally.

More than once, Mrs. Crawford walked out on our porch to discover that her impatient horse had gone on without her. Bob knew the route and he new how long a delivery stop should take, so away he went, although not very far, and she always caught up.

Think of that. Delicious fresh milk brought to your door with no air pollution from gasoline. I suppose the street cleaners had some extra sweeping to do.

Summer Days, Places to Hang Out

I knew about wonderful Antelope Park from the time I was three. My dad, Russ Gibson was a professional musician and in the middle 1930s, during the Depression, he played cornet while fronting the big band at Antelope Dance Pavilion.

On some summer nights, mom would drive me to the pavilion to hear dad play. He would let me choose one song for the band to play, and play it they did, even though it might be Row, Row Your Boat. I thought it a very fine thing to have a daddy who wore a tuxedo and led the band and could have them play any song I requested. Dancers didn't seem to object to this interruption, perhaps because they thought that a guy who would do that for his child must be an especially kind father. And he was.

I think it cost 10¢ to come in and dance all night. Many couples who danced to the music of the Leo Beck, Eddy Jungbluth band made lifetime commitments. I have often met Lincoln married couples who remember Russ playing for them. He had a wonderful ability to remember just what songs individuals wanted to hear. Fifty years later, he used to go to Lincoln retirement homes and play the same songs for the same people. He and his listeners like the music and each other.

Looking back along the rails, I see the Great Depression, but in the dance hall no one was depressed. Many of our pleasures had been swept away, but in that sweet long ago God enlarged the smaller pleasures, so we had enough.

Antelope Park and the Old Zoo

My 30th Street friends and I used to visit the old zoo, not the wonderful Children's Zoo, which Arnott Folsom brought to life much later, but our limited zoo at 27th and A Street. There were bear cages, sometimes a wolf or two, maybe a fox. A monkey house provided cages for little simians, who behaved abominably toward visitors. "Oh, look at that cute little rascal holding onto the cage bars so he can ... Jeez, Harold, he's peeing all over me! He's grabbing something to throw ... "

We learned to watch the monkeys briefly from a safe distance, then head for the cage where the big alligator lolled in a pool. He rarely moved, but he behaved.

Antelope was a destination for summer adventures in childhood. Mom was the den mother for perhaps the liveliest Cub Scout den in the city. We built things, won all sorts of competitions, did handcrafts, collected 29,000 pounds of scrap paper in a war drive, and had dandy summer special events. On one day she divided our 10 cubs into teams of two boys, gave each team a page of code symbols, and challenged each of the teams to be the first to find our secret destination. There was a treasure chest at the end of the trail if we could find it. Each team was led to the destination by a different route, which you could only follow by looking at chalk code symbols on utility poles, trees and sidewalks.

Of course the destination was at the Antelope Park picnic area, where we found a treasure chest, all arriving at the same time, thanks to mom's skillful planning. In the treasure chest were frankfurters, buns, condiments, weenie forks, paper plates, and Kool Aid, all of which we cheerfully finished off. Why have just a weenie roast when you can throw in hidden trails, a secret destination and treasure chest?

We had good times growing up in Lincoln. During our years in Cub Scout Den 1, Pack 5, the times were magnificent, rollicking and unforgettable.

One year, a member of our den contracted rheumatic fever a week before Elliott School let out for Christmas vacation. The sick boy's doctor advised parents to take their perfectly healthy Cubs out of school a week early, because close contact with the sick child might spread the disease.

Gosh, we thought, we're going to sacrifice a week of school, so ... dress for snow, boys, grab your sled and hit that reservoir in Antelope Park. Thus began a week of joyous romps on the carefully graded slopes of the big reservoir, which we had to ourselves. In the end, our sick buddy recovered.

Where the Goodies Were

Many of the joys of Lincoln in the 1930s, 40s and 50s were good eating, child style and growing up style. The list below includes our favorites. Caution: A whole lotta cholesterol is in these childhood memories, but who knew?

Doughnuts from Kresge's. We rode the bus to Kresge's five and dime store on the southwest corner of 12th and O Street. Just inside the 12th Street entrance stood a doughnut fryer. It was rarely idle because the smell of frying doughnuts draws shoppers. As a boy I watched the unending march from dough to hot, scrumptious doughnuts, waiting patiently for the 12th one to slide gently from the machine. You could buy a dozen fresh.

The machine dropped one circle of dough into a round pan of hot oil. The pan slowly made half a revolution, and then an automatic spatula flips the half-cooked doughnut so that the done side was up. The rotating pan finished the 360 degree journey and gently slid the freshly finished dainty into a pan. There it was joined by others, one arrived every ten seconds or so.

The operator thrusted what looked like a short, blunt sword through the holes of twelve of these morsels and put them in a box to take home. You could get powdered sugar or granulated sugar on them for no extra charge.

The allure of hot fresh doughnuts overpowered my desire to take them home. Several disappeared on the bus ride.

The Mug. A huge root beer mug invited thirsty Lincolnites on summer evenings. The unpaved parking lot on the southwest corner of 33rd and O Street would fill with cars. As I recall, the mug stood three stories tall and looked exactly like a mug filled with root beer, foamy head included. From the rear jutted a handle built to scale.

The front was made to look like a human face. A big nose stuck out below a pair of eyes framed by blue neon lights, and under the nose stretched a row of white teeth, when the place was closed. When customers were being served, the big mug opened his mouth into a wide grin. Through the open mouth came ice cream, hamburgers and root beer. Carhops then brought your order to you on a tray that balanced on your open car window. In the years before air conditioning, there was no happier, cooler spot that The Mug.

In the 1940s we acquired new neighbors from New England. Their two little girls loved to go to The Mug, but weren't allowed to call it that. Their mother's Bostonian ideas on vulgar language dictated that the girls must call it "The Face." I guess mom never saw the handle in the back and the foam on top.

Perhaps the most frequently mentioned Lincoln landmark was the Mug on the southwest corner of 33rd and O Streets, shown here in 1931. *Photo courtesy of Nebraska State Historical Society.*

Sunnbrooke. This sunny restaurant at 12th and H Street lured people from all parts of town, including the University, with its superb cream pies—coconut cream, banana cream, chocolate cream. The "Brooke" was only about a block form the old Kappa Sigma fraternity at 11th and H Street. We Kappa Sigs frequented it for nighttime desserts. My parents had been taking the family there since I was very young and we never tired of it.

The Hotel d' Hamburger. The "Hotel D," as it was known to regular customers, stood on the west side of 12th Street between P and Q. It was the epitome of the greasy spoon restaurant. Good, juicy hamburgers and chili. Short on décor, long on atmosphere, which was smoky and smelled of grease. During the Depression, the excellent hamburgers went at six for a quarter, my father said, adding that it wasn't easy to get a quarter. The D was there through my college freshman year, 1951–52.

Spencer's Steak House. Sad to say, this great hangout never reopened after a damaging fire in the 1950s. The popular café on South Street had three great attractions for me. First, was good steaks, Spencer's had a delicious swiss steak, a dish that many restaurants do not do well. Second, it was a popular gathering spot for the sports fraternity: sportswriters, coaches, baseball players, football players and others. It was exciting to go there with my folks because you might see a famous Cornhusker or one of the Lincoln Athletics minor league baseball team. The third attraction was the presence of juke box controls in each booth. You didn't have to walk to the Wurlitzer to play a hit song—just pop a coin in the selection box in your booth. To me it meant we had entered a new American age of technical marvels. What other wonders were about to march over the horizon?

Yum Yums and Tastee Burgers. These loose-meat sandwiches were alike but also quite different from each other. Both restaurants served wonderfully flavored ground meat on a bun. Tastees were spiced with a red sauce, and Yum Yums with something yellow, mustard perhaps? We never learned the secret, which was carefully guarded. You couldn't deny that a Yum Yum was yummy and a Tastee was tasty.

The Original Runza Hut. A tiny hut the size of a small home kitchen stood beside Park Drive on the way from South Street to Sherman Field, the baseball park. In the Hut a woman prepared the epitome of Lincoln food specialties, the Runza. A Runza is a large roll, stuffed with cooked cabbage, hamburger and flavorings. In later years, she sold the business, including her fabulous recipe, to a company that turned it into a successful food chain.

For many decades, Lincoln residents who had emigrated from Russia had prepared the Runzas for church suppers and bazaars. They were undescribably delicious, especially when accompanied by a root beer or a real one. Service was in the cramped parking lot only, what a fine way to prepare to watch a baseball game at Sherman, or top off a date.

The Greenwich. On the south side of O Street just west of the Rock Island railroad stood the unpretentious but inviting Greenwich Village restaurant. Best onion rings for miles around. The cook apparently had brought great skill and some genius to the preparing of the batter. An order of these was very large. I used to order a double portion and make a meal of it along with one of the fine chef's salads and a bottle of Michelob. Good, good, good;

best served with lively table talk about important subjects like jazz, poetry and baseball.

The Korn Popper. Cities do not always succeed in locating sites of cultural significance so they can be preserved. But, Lincoln got it just right when it came time to spare the popular Korn Popper on N Street between 14th and 15th. No one anywhere ever made better popcorn. Mr. Redenbacher was a distant second. You could buy and still can, plain corn with or without salt. The menu included cheese corn (it is to die for), caramel corn, ice cream and soft drinks.

In the mid 1950s college days had come to an end and we got down to the serious business of life: the all night poker game. No business could be conducted unless we had the extremely large bag of Japanese white hull-less from the Popper. The top of the bag was at table height when it stood on the floor and did not last past dawn. Neither did the poker players.

Tony & Luigi's. Tony Alesio was a congenial restaurateur, born to be a host. He made Tony & Luigi's the place to go for an excellent steak, fine service and an inviting atmosphere. Ideally situated on O Street not far from Cotner Boulevard, Tony's was a mecca for steak lovers, be they Lincolnites or visitors.

Remember the delicious French onion dip, into which we thrust fresh green onions for appetizers? Remember the impeccable service from waiters and waitresses who worked for Tony year after year and became like members of your family? Remember the delicious club steaks, T-bones and filets mignon? The succulent Italian dishes?

Lincoln was dry in the 1950s, so Tony's provided set-ups to customers who brought a brown bag. At special celebrations, a bottle of good wine might appear without advance notice, courtesy of the host. Everyone went home happy.

In 1962, I was visiting my parents' house when dad received a phone call from his Doane College buddy, Hollywood actor Robert Taylor. He had flown to Lincoln to look up his old friend Russ. Taylor told Russ that he was going to Tony & Luigi's for a steak. Could we meet him there? You bet we could.

When we arrived, Tony was in a state of euphoria. He said a waitress had run to his office to tell him that Robert Taylor was in the restaurant. In those years, KOLN-TV had a very popular weatherman named Bob Taylor. So Tony said to the waitress, "Yeah, Bob comes in all the time. What a nice guy!" "No," she answered. "I mean the one from Hollywood." Tony confirmed the identification and went all out to give the star a big welcome home. The movie star got a great steak, a warm welcome from fans and an impromptu piano recital from his old pal Russ. Dad played "Back Home Again in Indiana," blowing out the jams as he so loved to do. Great night for all.

My First Look at Lincoln

By Charles Thone

On a Sunday in August of 1940, I was a hitchhiker dropped off at 15th and O Streets, 16 years old and a recent graduate of Hartington High School. I had never before been to big Lincoln and I knew I wanted to be a lawyer. What a dream!

In my pockets I had $70 from the sale of some hogs that dad had given me and had carefully fattened and I carried a beat up cardboard suitcase with my other belongings. I knew that there could no be further financial help from home.

I asked someone where the university was and they pointed to the north so I headed that way and finally found a rooming house at 1029 R Street. It was run by a caring Mrs. Kleinschmidt who had moved to Lincoln a couple years earlier from Grafton, Nebraska, and she kind of looked after me for the next three years.

A couple of days after arriving I got a job in a café that was on the same block where I had been left off. The job paid three meals a day and required me to be there at five o'clock in the morning to scrub the floors and wash the windows and evening dishes and do the dusting. I ate breakfast before I left every morning and then came back for lunch and supper.

A week or so later I enrolled at the university from which I received my law degree ten years later. The reason it took so long is that I was out of school from 1943 through 1946 saving the world for democracy as a U.S. infantry officer.

Lincoln was a very friendly place for students from outstate Nebraska because everywhere you went you ran into students from Polk, Uehling, Grand Island, Sidney, Valentine, you name it. You must also remember that 1940 was the beginning of the end of the Great Depression so everyone was pretty much in the same boat, and nearly everyone worked two or three jobs to get along.

Shortly after getting started at the university, I was hired to be the janitor for Pharmacy Hall for the magnificent sum of 25¢ an hour. My next big job was at the University Club where I stayed for three years, getting lunch and dinner *and* 25¢ an hour. After getting some experience my big break came when I was assigned to wait on the businessman's Roughneck Table which was frequented daily by Lincoln notables such as Nate Gold, Bob Ferguson, Joe W. Seacrest, Elmer Magee, R.E. Campbell, Al DuTeau and others. I memorized all of their likes and dislikes and quite often got a dollar tip apiece which was pretty big stuff those days.

It was in these years that I got firmly and totally hooked on Lincoln. I never wanted to live anywhere else and promptly came back to Lincoln after a couple of tours of duty later on in Washington, D. C. Several of my good friends urged me to consider good Omaha jobs, but Lincoln was always home to me.

In 1943 World War II was boiling over and I enlisted in the army before an inevitable draft call. All of our friends and acquaintances were going into the military service, and it was the place to go. You might call it patriotism, but nearly all of us truly wanted to go into the service. After what was a second education in responsibility and traveling around the world courtesy of the U.S. government, I headed back the University of Nebraska Law School in 1946.

The financial situation this time around was profoundly different, mostly because of the GI Bill of Rights. In addition I was elected president of the Phi Gams and received a free house bill. I also had a rinky-dink with the laundry company that served the fraternity, so finances were no longer that much of an issue. I was in law school, involved in campus politics and having a merry time and spent Friday afternoons and some weekends at the Diamond Bar and Grill. It was a high old time for all concerned. The only problem was eventual graduation and the cold cruel world at hand.

I first worked as Deputy Secretary of State and an Assistant Attorney General and continued to live in a "penthouse" apartment on the fifth floor of the old Lincoln Hotel, which was our senior year of law school lodging. Some of the roommates who shared this crazy time were Don "Fox" Bryant, UNL sports publicist deluxe for 50 years, Norrie Andersen, *World Herald* reporter and now retired *World Herald* publisher, Carter Kokjer and George Abbott, both now retired lawyers of note.

I never wanted to be a farmer, where I thought it was always too dusty or too muddy and I could never forget how terribly tough things were in those Dirty Thirties when I grew up. I've thought many times of just how I ever ended up going to the university when this just wasn't at all the thing young people in Cedar County did in those days. It was mostly because of the strong insistence of my mother and the push of two high school teachers that I ended up on O Street in Lincoln that August Sunday afternoon.

Lincoln is home and still most friendly. There's just nothing like a football Saturday or, for that matter, remembering those first days that I came here with all my impossible youthful dreams.

In 1914 Hiett-Carey & Trombla, the first Ford agency in University Place, offered free automobile rides to people 80 years or older. Those taking part in the venture are pictured in front of the agency at 2714 N. 48th Street. Also in the picture is C. L. Trombla, who owned the building, which is still standing. *Photo and information courtesy Geraldine Trombla.*

LINCOLN
POSTWAR

A Bonding Experience

By Dale Tinstman

April 1, 1960, I opened a one-man investment firm called Tinstman & Co. in one room in the Stuart Building. About as foolish an idea as April Fool Day is fun. This event however, in mid 1961, led to merging with the Investment Department of the First Trust Company under the name of First Nebraska, Inc. On September 11, 1961, this firm joined the New York Stock Exchange as Nebraska's first and at that time only Nebraska based firm to have a membership in the NYSE. Joe W. and Fred Seacrest requested the privilege of making the first trade, and it was granted. The original partners were Dale Tinstman, E. M. "Bud" Hunt, Jerry Druliner, Gene Tallman and Charles "Chuck" Burnmeister.

In 1964, Tipy Dye, Athletic Director, and Joe Soshnik, Vice Chancellor of Finance at the University of Nebraska came to First Nebraska and said Memorial Stadium had to be expanded. Along with Frank Williams and Warren "Bud" Johnson as board counsel a method was devised—a tax-free municipal bond issue of Stadium Revenue Bonds in the amount of $375,000. To our knowledge this was the first of its kind in the United States, however, millions have been sold since that time. The only security was 50¢ per seat per game which was pledged to pay the interest and principal of the bonds. The bonds were not easy to sell, but they paid off long before maturity.

An interesting side line was when Bud Hunt called Tommy Wake at Seward and said, "You just bought $25,000 UNL Stadium Revenue Bonds," the response was, "The hell I did. I bought $25,000 a month ago and have already charged them off."

These funds built the first section on the south end of stadium. The program was so successful that a second issue was completed two years later to fund the north middle section—remember how people said it moved and swayed—it is still there with no complaints. The third issue funded the corners to take the seating to 76,000.

First Nebraska became First Mid America, Inc. (FMA) in 1969 and developed 15 offices in the midwest dedicated to financing ag-related businesses. During the '60s and '70s they handled all the financing for IBP, Inc., now the world's largest meat packing company. FMA was sold in 1986 and ceased to exist.

A Reporter's Eye View of Lincoln

By Bill Dobler

My wife, Nancy and I arrived in Lincoln shortly after our marriage in 1948, in our hometown of St. Joseph, Missouri. It was not long before I finished my last two years at the University of Nebraska with a major in journalism and a reporter's job with the Lincoln Star. James Lawrence was the editor and a man of admirable accomplishment. City government was my daily assignment and it led to many adventures. Mayor Clark Jeary was a reporter's dream. He believed in an open approach to government and kept the press completely informed of government matters.

Mr. Jeary also loved his outside farm life. I remember his explaining how his cattle would be given food and drink before being sold on the market so their weight would bring the highest price, a common practice among cattlemen.

Many good and competent men and women have given Lincoln the foundation for doubling its population in approximately 50 years. I look back at those years and realize that Lincoln is an unusual city. The growth of its commercial business, its educational advantage and its limited amount of serious criminal life has served us very well.

But Lincoln is not alone. It is a capital city but Omaha is the largest city. Omaha's commerce, its population and its many medical, educational and entertainment facilities are another major asset. Thus Lincoln is not a place alone, but rather a mix of statewide growth and strong leadership. As one looks back through the years, the vision is one of people with a multitude of foresight, a dedication to success and concern for their fellow man. Lincoln in those days prohibited the public sale of alcoholic beverages. But with the return of so many World War II veterans, the law was mostly ignored.

At the University of Nebraska, academic and athletic programs fostered an array of war-proven students in a range of levels, mostly in their early to late twenties. This period, I believe, welcomed and contributed a high level of determination and its ultimate positive results.

Lincoln's history could hardly be completed without remembrance of its single most startling crime—the 1958 Charles Starkweather murder of 11 victims. Before he was captured, many, many citizens armed themselves with loaded guns. People locked their doors and near panic prevailed for the two or three days before capture and ultimate electrocution.

In the world of commerce, city downtowns found themselves faced with an upstart known as the Mall. The formation of this retailing and its diversity of services introduced an entirely new approach. Names such as Miller & Paine, Brandeis, J. C. Penney and others either moved to a mall or went out of business. Another generation of Lincoln leadership now prevails among those who joined the malls.

The years of growth expansion and opportunity are the product of good leadership and citizenship.

A Tribute to Nathan J. Gold

By Marilyn J. Oestmann

The most memorable secretarial position I held during 45 years in the business world in three states, Nebraska, Arizona and California, was that of personal secretary for Nathan J. Gold, Chairman of the Board of Gold and Co. from 1959 to 1963. While he was a man of imposing stature, over 6 foot tall, with a deep voice, he had a kind and gentle heart, always concerned with the youth and their future. He supported the FFA (Future Farmers of America) and the Nebraska Resources Department.

The retail industry recognized him, electing him the President of the NRMA (National Retail Merchants Association). Long time employees told of how his father, Wm. Gold I, taught him the trade from the bottom to the top. Starting in Shipping and Receiving Dept., Maintenance, Stock Boy, Marketing, Sales then to the top in his walnut paneled office in the northeast corner of 3rd floor and Chairman of the Board. He made it a point to know each employee and make him or her feel important.

The University of Nebraska also recognized him by presenting him an Honorary Doctor of Humanity. While he did not attend the University, he did, as I recall, attend some courses at a business college. One day he came up with the word "ostentatious" while dictating to me. I asked him where he came up with that word and he pulled out a pocket size thesaurus that he carried in his pocket. I ultimately ended up with a full size one at my desk that his son, William Gold II (Bill), had used in college.

I replaced the only secretary he had ever had for 27 years, so I was Miss Wilson for several months. The only reason that happened was because she turned 65 and retired before he turned 65, so I had big shoes to fill. At this point many of his friends were passing away, so he would say to me, "Mrs. Oestmann, please be patient with me, these things disturb me."

He was a person of means and yet humble. He drove a 1957 Chevrolet, which people wanted to buy, but he told me he really loved that car and didn't want to sell it. One day he told me to write a check to a Cadillac dealer and I had written one a few weeks earlier for a new Cadillac. When I mentioned that fact, he replied, "I couldn't wear my hat in it without hitting the top of the car." He referred to Mrs. Gold (Evelyn) as his "better seven-eighths." He was always respectful to others regardless of their level in society or race.

My mom always said she thought if Mr. Gold told me to jump off the building, I would probably do it because I always spoke of him in such high regard. I always said it was unfortunate that the mold he came from couldn't be duplicated. Also, if one had a prejudice because he was Jewish, while being associated with him you forgot that fact.

'Bang, Bang, Bang Went the Trolley; Clang, Clang, Clang Went the Bell'

By George Hancock

Lincoln used to have a fairly extensive streetcar system. Among others, lines went from downtown to Bethany or Normal and I especially recall the line that went through my neighborhood on it's way to College View.

I have a card signifying that I actually rode on the last run in 1945. The card is signed by Emmitt Junge, Director of Public Health and Safety, who must have been Lincoln's most honest public servant. When he retired he publicly advised the Mayor and Council not to replace him as the job was unnecessary.

When re-packing some boxes that had perhaps not been opened since we last moved in 1973, I found this card and was reminded of great times on Sheridan/South Street trolley line. Downtown was the center of everything then, of course, and the streetcar, 10¢ I think, was our access to the movies, the "Y," Brick's malts, sports events, our fathers businesses, the Hotel d' Hamburger, etc.

Our group of boys rode regularly. Sometimes our girlfriends would also board, but God forbid we ever sat together.

The cars were powered through a spring-loaded boom on top of the car to an overhead electric line. A light rope ran down from the boom and was fastened to the back of the car. The driver used this to guide the boom back onto the power cable should it bounce off.

This rope was simply too much for red-blooded thirteen-year-olds to resist. We learned from our older friends and brothers how to "pull the trolley." Finding some substantial bushes fairly near the track we would run out, pull the rope disengaging the boom from the electric line and watch delightedly as the car rolled to a stop and the operator got out, walked to the back and reconnected to power. We even learned how to do this from a bicycle.

It may, or may not, have been our group who refined this stupid, dangerous and illegal game to its ultimate level of sophistication. Carefully estimating speed and distance we calculated just where to pull the trolley so that the car would stop right in the middle of Sheridan Boulevard Bridge just west of 33rd Street. The bridge was so narrow that the driver could not get out the regular side door, but had to open the front window, climb out, walk across the bridge, back on the other bridge to the rear of the car, put the trolley on, walk all the way around and climb back in the front window—all of which took several minutes. We learned some new words from the drivers. A few times when the driver was particularly responsive, we waited for him to climb back in the window and then ran out and pulled off the trolley again.

I'm not proud of having done this although there is a certain (warped?) satisfaction from having figured it all out and pulled it off.

Buying a Bicycle from Billy Wolf

By Bill Orr

When our son John was 6 or 7, we wanted to buy him a bike. At that time (1967) bikes were pretty simple. They came in small, medium and full size. There were no racing bikes, very few with more than three gears and all were made in the USA. Billy Wolf was THE place to buy. His store was on O Street and Billy manned the store all the time. I went there and found the right bike for John.

When it came time to get the price from Billy, I thought I was driving a pretty shrewd bargain—offered less than he was asking. When it came time to write the check, I know I was paying more than Billy expected me to pay. How did I know that? He kept giving me accessories—bicycle-clips, padlocks and reflectors. Two years later, buying a bike for our daughter found me offering even less. I am still not sure, but I think I must have arrived at a better deal—there were no bonuses this time.

David Doyle

Excerpted from *Magazine of the Midlands*, March 3, 1979

By Gary Johansen

So who is David Doyle? My professional work mates weren't so sure but their interests perked when I mentioned girls. The publicity person at KETV, Omaha's ABC affiliate, surprisingly failed to recognize the name.

The only TV trivia expert I know (a neighbor who watched the tube from "Today" through "Tomorrow") refused any hints and finally confessed the only Doyle she knew was a boy she dated in high school in Denver but his first name was Eddie.

There are probably millions who watched "Angels" and didn't know that David Doyle portrays Bosley, a smiling, raspy-voiced steadying influence on three of the prettiest sleuths ever conceived by a scriptwriter. Doyle didn't mind the semi-anonymity one bit as long as "Angels" and Bosley continue to stand strong in the ratings.

There was a certain mystique—and envy—about watching an actor perform with Kate Jackson, Jaclyn Smith and Cheryl Ladd weekly and Farrah Fawcett-Majors when she made one of her infrequent guest appearances. "Working with angels is very good duty," said Doyle by phone from his home in Encino, California, "but it's nothing like the fantasy that the male viewer imagines." Sure, sure. We know. "Really, there's a tremendous amount of work involved in producing an hour-long show," he said. "We are busy eight months out of the year; my contact with Aaron Spelling calls for 24 episodes and each requires at least a week." "We have to get up early some mornings to take advantage of the certain weather conditions. We even spent three weeks recently at Aspen, Colorado, to shoot a segment." Hmmm, that does sound rough.

Getting back to his three angels, an interesting area to return to, Doyle said that each is an individual and a pleasure to know. They don't pretend to be the world's greatest actresses, and they maintain a sense of humor on the set that helps to pass the time quickly and enjoyably. So what else is he doing? "Whatever comes along that I like. Guest spots on other serials, talk shows, and game shows. Right now, I'm sitting on my back porch, relaxing. We worked early this morning. The weather isn't shirtsleeve, but it is tolerable," he said. "I heard the nasty report back home (Lincoln) and I can honestly say I don't miss the snow and cold."

"I haven't been in Nebraska for a couple of years and I do miss seeing some old friends and family. One of my closest childhood chums was Jerry

Mapes, who still lives in Lincoln and owns Mapes Industries (manufacturers of porcelain panels for storefronts and buildings and aluminum awnings). "Without Jerry, I would have missed a lot more classes at the University of Nebraska. My sister Mary and I were always late and Jerry would pick us up and drive us there as fast as possible." Even with Jerry's help Doyle didn't graduate. He started with every intention of becoming a lawyer like his older brother and his daddy and his daddy's daddy. (It does seem to run in the family). However after two and a fraction years at NU, the call of the theater burst from his chest in 1950 and he packed his bags and took off for New York City.

Speaking of the clan, John "Dugie" Doyle, that "other Bosley," enjoys talking about David, their dad and the fact all three were pretty fair football players.

"The family has been around Lincoln for a long time. My great grandfather, John Fitzgerald was a railroad contractor. He settled here long before the turn of the century and my mother was his granddaughter. John came over from Ireland as a small boy and worked on canals or railroads in upstate New York," John Doyle explained.

"His first exposure to Nebraska was helping build the Burlington Railroad. He was a dynamo—took the pledge in Ireland and never drank—came out west and figured rather quickly that you could work out on a regular basis and be very successful.

"On my father's side, we're a string of lawyers—my son, me, my father and his father. Grandfather T. J. Doyle set out from Tennessee for the Great Northwest and got as far as Greeley, Nebraska, a big Irish settlement. He hung out his shingle and it wasn't long before he was coming down to Lincoln. He was counsel for International Harvester Co., which wanted him to move to Chicago, but he decided to stay in Nebraska so we number five generations on my mother's side."

John's Sharp Building office in Lincoln is small and crowded—maybe systemically cluttered is a better description. The bottom of the drawers still contain some of his stuff I haven't been through yet.

Nebraska football is displayed all over typified by a photograph of the all-victorious 1914 team coached by Jumbo Stiehm. "There's father," said John, proudly pointing him out (the glass was smudgy there, like previous pointings had been made). Dad was a good football player. He lettered three years at full back and did all the punting. On road trips he roomed with Guy Chamberlin (a Cornhusker legend).

"David and I went to Cathedral Grade School ... across the alley there," John said, pointing out the window toward a carpark garage. "Dad was on the fifteenth floor of this building at the time and he would look out the window and watch us on the playground." That limited our activities a bit. "David was a good athlete. He played football and did something in track, but I can't remember what it was. As a smaller child, in grade school, he had a companion who was in trouble all the time ... I think every active person has a friend like that."

"One day my mother couldn't stand it any longer and asked David point blank, 'What in the world do you see in so-and-so?' David's eyes glazed over and he looked up and said, 'Mom, he'll do anything.'"

"David was five years younger than me, which is a lifetime when you're a kid, so we didn't pal around. He sometimes would tag along, play the little brother role and embarrass me. He and our sister, Mary, were about the same age and they were thicker than thieves."

Knights Plumbing

By Bill Orr

One of the most unusual establishments in Lincoln is Knights Plumbing. The inventory includes parts for plumbing fixtures such as faucets, toilet mechanisms, etc., some of which were manufactured years ago. My first trip there found me taking the entire inside from an old toilet. I figured I would buy the whole thing, which might cost more than $20. One of the owners examined my item and said, "We can fix that in a few minutes." They did and charged 75¢!

Lincoln Reminiscings

By Ken TenHulzen

Do you remember the smell of leaves burning while listening to Lyle Bremser's call of a Nebraska away game; the heavy iron rakes that we used.

The great shakes and malts at Brick's on the east side of 13th Street just south of Love Library on UNL's downtown campus.

The old Cornhusker Hotel where I worked as a busboy and my good friend Red Worster was a bellman.

Movies were a dime at the State and Capital Theatres then and the Lincoln Theatre was on the south side of N Street between 12th and 13th streets.

The Varsity Theatre was right across the street from the Stuart Theatre. It was next to the Grid Coffee Shop where theater manager, Walt Janke could be found most days enjoying a cigar and chatting with other Lincoln businessmen. This was when NBC was the bank situated on O Street between Hovland—Swanson's, on the west 13th Street on the east and the Grid to the north.

The Missouri Pacific Railroad had a one-car train that ran between Lincoln and Union. It was called the "Eaglet." It went through Wabash, Elmwood, Weeping Water and Nehawka as it jostled along from Lincoln to the Missouri River's edge and back. There was a place for the engineer at each end of the car, so it never turned around. He just walked to the other end of the one-car train and sent it back the other way.

I always thought this would have been a neat addition for Lincoln commuters living along the abandoned Rock Island tracks that ran from the Knolls to downtown.

I grew up along those tracks on south 33rd Street about two blocks north of Sheridan Boulevard. Memorial Park runs all the way along 33rd Street from Sheridan Boulevard and "Penny Bridge" to the Lincoln Zoo and Sunken Gardens just south of Ideal Grocery. It was there that I enjoyed countless hours of football, baseball, hide and seek and smoking cigarettes behind the bushes and trees when I was growing up.

Do you remember in the early 1950s, when one of the local radio stations would hide "The Golden Egg" around town? The value would go up each week for the lucky person who found it. While in high school, I worked nights and weekends at Sheridan Conoco at 33rd and Sheridan. One night I heard the clues given while I was at work. I told Jim Dill who worked there with me that I thought I knew where the egg was hidden. He and his pal Harlan Mook, who were about four years older than I, went to the small stone bridge located in the park where Van Dorn Street would cross if it were a through street. Sure enough, under the bridge was the Golden Egg, just like I said it would be. They got all the glory and I got ten bucks. A lesson was learned, however.

In the early 1950s I went to College View School. It was a kindergarten through 12th grade facility that is now Calvert Elementary School. One of my best friends was Dick Cheney. Yes, the same Dick Cheney that took the oath of office as the Vice President of the United States in 2001.

Dick and I played a lot of baseball, basketball and other games together. Many afternoons after school we would stop at his house on south 44th Street because it was on my way home. Dick's family moved to Wyoming when Dick was in the 8th grade.

Two days after his being selected as the Republican Vice Presidential candidate, I got a call from Kate Storm at CNN headquarters in New York. She said, "I understand you and Dick Cheney were childhood friends." I said, "Yes, but how did you know that?" She made some vague reference to someone in Omaha having said something. I never did know how she found out and it was disconcerting to think that anyone could learn so much so quickly. Especially about me.

She asked if I could relate any stories, about when we were kids, so I did. I told her that Dick was a good third baseman. I also said that if he had been an architect or a truck driver I would not remember this, but I recalled that when we went inside for a peanut butter sandwich after school, the McCarthy hearings were on TV. She asked if Dick was interested in politics at that early age? I said, "Not at all." He was interested in the peanut butter sandwiches his mom had made for us, but when someone is yelling, "Are you a Communist," at someone else, you tend to notice it. Dick has managed to do pretty well since that time.

College View High School closed its doors in 1955. That was the year Lincoln Southeast High School was born. I was fortunate enough to serve on the original Student Council. The Knight mascot won instant approval, the choosing of the new school's colors was a totally different story.

College View High School had purple and gold as its colors. Since nearly all of the juniors and seniors at Southeast had come from College View, it seemed logical to them that the same colors should apply to their new school. However, many of the younger students went to Irving Junior High and would have gone to Lincoln High School, with all its tradition, had LSE not opened its doors. These people did not want purple and gold as the school colors. At a meeting of the student council, we suggested that a compromise might be reached. Lincoln High's colors were black and red. Lincoln Northeast had black and white. What if Southeast used black and gold? This incorporated the black used by all the existing high schools and the use of the gold color satisfied the College View students. Everyone agreed and the rest is history.

Growing up in Lincoln was exciting and fun when Rock and Roll, Elvis and all the famous 1950s groups were changing the music we listened to forever. Bobby socks, blue jeans, letter jackets, hot rod cars, drive-in movies and restaurants were the rage. Cars were hotter and more powerful, but gasoline was less than 20¢ a gallon.

Lincoln has grown so much over the last 50 years. Back then the pavement on 33rd street ended at Hillside Street two blocks south of Sheridan Boulevard. I learned to drive in a field south of Highway 2 where today, Payless Lumber and the Lincoln Water Park are located. We hunted pheasants where Maude Rousseau School now sits.

Lincoln, through all its changes, still remains one of the nicest cities in America. It is a perfect place to make life-long friends, raise a family and call home.

Lincoln Tennis

By Sandy Hilsabeck

A number of Lincoln tennis enthusiasts started the Woods Tennis Corporation, a list of which is located on the wall at Woods Tennis Center. This group constructed the "bubble" providing year-round public tennis in Lincoln and a new tennis clubhouse with locker room facilities. This new clubhouse has since been donated to the city of Lincoln. Previously, an old wooden building not much larger than an outhouse was the home of Lincoln Tennis. Today the Woods Park Tennis Corporation runs the tennis activity at Woods Park from October to April and the city assumes operations for the balance of the year.

In 1987 John Wilson said it was time to create a viable organization for which tennis could grow in Lincoln. As a result, the Lincoln Tennis Association (LTA) was formed and I was elected its first president and served for two years. There was no bank account and no record of members. During those two years we accumulated over 400 members, printed a membership book, collected dues and started a formal system of committees and payments for tournament directors and umpires. Today we have record for 800 regular players.

Lincoln resident Joy Rodenburg had previously become a tennis umpire at the national level and had set up a good training program providing umpires for collegiate matches. Around 1985 she succeeded in getting John McEnroe to play an exhibition match at Pershing Auditorium while he was ranked number one in the world. I was either very fortunate or very unafraid as I volunteered to learn umpiring so I could be a line caller for his match. Unfortunately, he picked on Bill Woito, the umpire standing next to me and I never got to give him the smile I prepared to respond to his antics.

With an organization and great volunteers we soon had the NTRP (National Tennis Rating Program) being used in our local tournaments. It was a system, which can be compared to the handicap system in golfing. It allows the players to have a rating number, which is recognized, by all players. When entering a tournament, they can sign up at a level, which gives them good competition. New players can see their improvement by seeing an increase in their NTRP rating.

A most remarkable thing has happened in the past couple of years for the tennis community of Lincoln. Because of recent presidents Tom Tipton, Margaret Donlan, Kile Johnson, Rick Boucher, Leslie Campbell, John Keller and Deb Hartman, the LTA is now a solid financial organization. It as sponsored the "Park It at Woods" Capital Campaign, headed by Margaret Donlan and Sandra Hilsabeck, to complete the Master Plan for Woods Park. With the help of many contributors, large and small, $1,100,000 has been raised, showing the Lincoln community support for a better Woods Park. Construction is planned for a new clubhouse, a sculpture garden, an interactive water fountain and a pathway with extensive landscaping throughout the park. Because of the efforts of the LTA, we truly will see a great gift to Lincoln.

Lincoln's Been Good To Us

By Vance D. Rogers

Our introduction to Lincoln came from two O Street businessmen: Ernest Smith from Magee's Clothing Store and Tom O'Donnell from Gold's Department Store, both in downtown Lincoln.

My wife, daughters, and I had been very happily located at the Methodist Church in Brookfield, Illinois since 1946. However, in 1953, Ernest Smith and Tom O'Donnell asked me to join them for lunch at the Palmer House Hotel in Chicago. I was surprised to learn that their mission was to persuade my family and I to come to Lincoln, Nebraska and become the minister of their church, Trinity Methodist. What could we lose? A trip to Lincoln via United Airlines, a stay at the Cornhusker Hotel and a meeting with the Committee from Trinity Church. So, we came. We had a wonderful dinner at the University Club with Tom O'Donnell, Dean Roy Green and Grey Jewett. After looking everything over very closely and meeting with the church committee, my wife Barbara and I said, "yes." We moved to Lincoln in 1953 and served Trinity for four years.

My next professional experience in Lincoln came in 1957. The chairman of the board at Nebraska Wesleyan called me to tell me they were having a meeting and I was going to be named president. I told him that I had no interest in the job at all. Bishop H. Bascom Watts then met with me and said that he was going to appoint me to the position of President of Nebraska Wesleyan effective August 1, 1957. I agreed and stayed there for twenty years.

During those twenty years I raised money by approaching foundations and local businesses which enabled us to build a new campus center, library, dormitories, Olin Science Hall, Smith-Curtis Administration Building, Rogers Center for Fine Arts and Elder Theatre. We also had several distinguished visitors on campus such as President John F. Kennedy, Madame Chaing Kai Chek, Senator Barry Goldwater, Jesse Jackson and the ambassadors from Great Britain, Australia and Japan. Our enrollment increased from 700 students in 1957 to 1200 in 1977.

As the campus grew, so did other problems. I welcomed student protests as long as they didn't get out of control or destructive. When a band of protesters threatened to take over my office in the late 1960s, I said, "fine, but tomorrow morning at eight o'clock classes resume as usual and I will be in my office." I remember a radio announcer came to me and said, "What are you going to do?" I said, "I'm tired and I'm going home to bed. And if the students want to take over my office, fine. This will be a really good experience for them." I went home and went to bed and they took over my office. Some of the faculty members brought them cookies, candy and coffee. In the morning, at eight o'clock when I showed up, they had left, had gone back to their classroom activities and everything was near normal. No damage was done ... they had a good experience and frankly, I had a good experience too.

In 1977, I decided to retire and enter a new phase of my life. Some people remember that I had a brief run in the 1978 gubernatorial primary. Since politics weren't meant for me, I then served on the board of directors at NBC Bank, was interim President of the Lincoln Foundation and Chairman of the Board of ETV Commissions. I have to conclude that I have been richly blessed in being able to do so many different things. I have never gotten away from the idea of ministry. I have felt that I have been serving God and man in all of the activities with which I have been identified.

My ministry to my country began when I enlisted in the Navy in 1943. As a Navy Chaplain stationed in the South Pacific, I consoled the wounded and mourned the dead. The weekly presentation of Purple Hearts was always a highlight of the terrible yet galvanizing experience of wartime. My military service from 1943 to 1946 earned me medals and a letter of commendation from Fleet Admiral Chester Nimitz.

We continue to live and enjoy Lincoln, Nebraska. Lincoln had been very good to our family. We shall always be indebted to the friends we have made and the privilege of calling Lincoln our home. Our sincere wish and prayer is that Lincoln may always be the "best city" in America.

Location from Hell

By Diana Warner

How pleased we were when the Boar's Head opened in the early '70s. The steaks were great, the salad bar included super-chilled plates retrieved one by one from an ice cream freezer. Life was good. Then, for reasons unexplained, the place closed.

The next occupant was The Rose ... an Irish-themed restaurant with a lace-curtain décor. Pleasant enough, I guess, but without enough identity to keep it going.

Next came something whose name I don't remember ... a safari-type theme. I do recall giraffes on the wall. 'Nuff said.

Enter Sherry's Dining, Dancing and Romancing. Same show every night but reasonably popular. Popular enough that they moved to Cornhusker Highway's old Satellite Club, previously closed because of a fire and vacant for a few years until Sherry's renovated it.

Now comes Lone Star. It appears that since the first manager was replaced, it may be here to stay. And then again ... originally, a bucket of peanuts in the shell appeared at every booth, and customers were encouraged to toss the empty shells on the floor. A very slippery situation, and the place always looked a mess. With that corrected, their saving grace is their baked sweet potatoes.

Who is next?

Lump and Bump

By Bill Orr

A few years ago, a few Lincolnites got together and decided it would dress up the corner of 10th and O Street if the northwest corner had a small sculpture garden. That block had the old Federal Building and another historic building, which are not being fully used. The project received approval of the city and other officials subject to funds being raised and an artist to sculpt an appropriate object.

This resulted in an artist drawing two objects, which appeared to be large boulders similar to those one might find in the Black Hills. The drawing was presented along with a request for funds to businesses, including Woodmen Accident and Life where I was a member of the Executive Committee. The Committee met to discuss whether or not we should help fund the project.

A member of the Committee, retired CEO and Chairman, E.J. Faulkner whom Woodie Varner called "The Big Eight Champion of the Verbal Bench-press," was seldom without a word or two. When he viewed the proposed project, he said "Humph, looks like two Pterodactyl Turds to me!" Despite that comment, we did support the project. It has been called by various names, the most often heard—"Lump and Bump."

Memories of the Thin Man

By Bus Whitehead

I didn't become a Lincolnite until the fall of 1945. Up until that time, I had lived in Scottsbluff. My only experience with Lincoln was going to the Minnesota/Nebraska football game in about 1939 which Nebraska won and a couple of trips to the state basketball tournament.

In 1945, I was a tall, skinny, naïve kid who had thoughts of playing basketball. The Great War had just ended; I pledged sigma chi. There were 12 actives and 13 pledges, the largest pledge class in six years. Nobody had a car at the house, walking was the main form of transportation.

By the fall of 1946, the veterans had returned; we had 48 pledges and about 80 actives. Living in the house was by seniority of which I had none. My first room was over the Uni Drug next to Dirty Earl's. From there, I moved to a room above the Owl Drugstore, I seemed to be big on drugstrores. In 1947, Dr. Dees the athletic trainer, let me move into his attic. I usually got to campus by walking—once in a while by bus and I was eating my meals at the fraternity house.

By 1948, I was back rooming at the fraternity house. I still didn't have a car, never did have one, but my good friend Henry Cech let me use his. He seemed to spend a lot of time studying. Actually, life was good to me. After years, I graduated from Teachers College having failed Engineering College.

In 1953, I returned to Lincoln for a three-year stay and in 1959 returned for good. I have raised my family here and wouldn't trade Lincoln for any place.

Parker's Steak House

By Jim Haberlan

Rumor has it Carl Parker's apron is ready to be picked up at the cleaners. It's been there for a few years and no one is claming it. Well, I want it and I'm going to go get it. I want to own the apron worn by the guy that may have cooked more steaks in his lifetime than anyone before or since.

But to think the apron is clean changes a lot of the character and atmosphere of Parker's Steak house in Denton, just west of Lincoln. Any one over the age of fifty doesn't need to be told where Parker's was; they have all been there, many times.

Like a picture that never changes, there is Carl, Carol Parker, owner, chef, janitor, interior designer, butcher and bartender, standing at the end of the bar, his apron covered with steak blood, grease and anything else that might stick to it. Carl was a little short guy with a big stomach, bald on top and a deep gruff voice. He had very few words to say to anyone except a close friend. On occasion he would use his apron to wipe his face that was always sweaty from cooking steaks on the grill in the kitchen. He would come out of the kitchen from time to time, stand at the end of the bar, and look over the crowd and his waitresses and then he would return to the kitchen to turn the steaks. They always were served just the way you ordered them. How that happened I'll never understand because many times there would be maybe 80 steaks on the grill at one time. During these times Carl would still come out to look over the crowd, wipe his face with the apron and then back to the kitchen.

If Carl could see the steaks that are now being served in Lincoln, he would die. Carl's steaks were one of a kind. He butchered his own steaks, cut the way he wanted them cut, and not always according to the standard cuts. The clubs, rib eye's etc, may not have looked like the standard cuts, but the T-bone, New York and Sirloins were his specialty. If you thought yourself to be a big steak eater, you ordered the larger sirloin. It covered the entire plate and even hung over the end. Carl didn't fuss with cutting the fat off his steaks, that gave the steaks the flavor, according to Carl, and besides there was plenty of meat after you cut away the fat.

The hash browns were the best for miles around, because they were fried in the fat left over from grilling the steaks. No, sir, there was no peanut oil in Carl's kitchen, nor had he ever heard of the stuff, or in his famous voice, "Who would cook anything in that stuff?"

Another story, maybe true and maybe not, one night a two foot square piece of ceiling tile fell on the table below while a couple was eating dinner. It caused quite a stir, not from the mess the tile made when it hit the table, or the dust and dirt that was on the tile, but because a live cat was standing on top of the tile when it hit the table. It might have never happened if the cat had not been so heavy. Carl always had a lot of cats, out back by the kitchen door, where he fed them scraps from the dirty plates. Carl's cats were always fat and heavy.

On another evening a farmer customer was dining at Carl's, all dressed up in his bib overalls and smoking a large cigar. Smoking was allowed anywhere in Parkers. The poor fellow had to use the restroom when he was about halfway through his T-bone steak. The restroom was located next to the dining room, the door opened directly on to the dining room floor. The toilet was placed looking out of the door and because of the cold weather, Carl had placed a propane heater next to the toilet, it made it nice and warm. When the customer lowered his bibs to sit down he took the cigar out of his mouth with his left hand and let his arm drop down between the toilet and the propane heater. You guessed it; the propane heater blew up and knocked the fellow out through the door onto the dining room floor, pants down. It caused a hell of a stir and Carl said he was sorry but the farmer filed a lawsuit against Carl and won. The lawsuit was only for $2500. It was rumored around that the fellow still had trouble trying to sit himself down on a toilet.

When Carl wasn't busy cooking and cutting up his steaks, he was busy with his other business venture. He raised about fifty fighting cocks out in the back yard of the steakhouse. Carl's partner in the cock fighting business was Ed Taber. Ed had been a big league pitcher in baseball and was still one of the best handball players at the Lincoln Y.M.C.A. One of Ed's roles as a partner, was to work out the chickens every day, usually accompanied by one or all of his three sons, Matt, Tim and Ed Jr. The chickens were kept in separate cages, naturally, and each one had to be taken out each day and ran back and forth on a six wide board about for feet long. The chickens were held with both hands and ran back and forth on this board. I guess it would be called, road-work, by the chickens. It kept the chickens in shape and ready for the next fight. Chickens fight in weight brackets and so the trainers try to keep the chickens weight the same for each fight.

Sure, cock fighting is illegal but it is an event that everyone should attend, at least once. They were held, at least the one that my attorney friend and I, with wives attended, in a barn in the back of a farm house somewhere in the hills around Louisville, Nebraska. The atmosphere was perfect, a light snow was falling, the directions, given to us by Carl and Ed, were perfect and the farmyard was packed with cars from as far as four states away.

The inside of the barn had been remodeled into an octagon fighting ring about twelve feet across. A two by eight, on edge was the wall of the ring. The spectators set around the octagon ring, similar to a cattle auction ring. If you wanted to bet, say, $10 on one of the cocks, you yelled out, "ten dollars on the red cock" and if some one wanted to cover your bet they would yell back, "got it covered." The loser had to go around and pay the winner. God, what an experience, and to make things even better, at this illegal event, the county sheriff stood guard over the ladies selling admission tickets.

The ladies, probably the wives of the cock owners, served pie, hamburgers, and beer. No, no chicken dinners, but there were plenty of dead chickens that could have been used. I don't have an interest in going to another cockfight, but my life is fuller by having gone to my first one, and on the expert advice from Carl and Ed, I won $40 that night. The next day Carl was back in the kitchen cooking steaks and the customers probably thought he had spent the evening at home watching T.V.

Parker's Steakhouse and Carl are now gone. After Carl died, the building was torn down to build a filling station. Believe me, there will never be any memories come out of the filling station to match the ones of Carl and Parker's Steakhouse. Tonight, I will go out and pay $18 for a half-inch thick steak, with no taste, frozen hash browns and a dry cold roll.

Things just ain't like they used to be, and what a loss.

Reminiscences

By Addis T. Ward

My family joined Holy Trinity Church shortly after leaving the University. In January of 1954 a terrible fire reduced the church building on J Street to a hollow shell. We had just finished a fund drive for a new wing. The vestry studied and planned for the new building to be built at 61st and A Street. A number of the parish members insisted that the church should remain at the original location. When I was elected to the vestry a year or so later I found myself party to a lawsuit, as did every new vestry person elected for the next 15 or so years. The suit was eventually dismissed, but it took years to heal some of the hurt.

When I first arrived at Miller & Paine there were no advertisements for 'cocktail dresses' and it seemed that there were no parties with alcohol served. We all had to bring our own bottles when we went out. This brings to mind two big surprises announced by John Campbell at store meetings, first that we would begin to be open on Thursday evenings, second that our customers were asking us to be open on Sundays. What a change and now we even have retailers open 24 hours a day. The cooperative spirit of The O Street Gang did work and was a great benefit to the city. These were days when businessmen served as mayor as part of their civic duty. The same cooperative effort seems to be missing today.

Roundball in the '40s

By Bill Wenke

Our family moved from Stanton to Lincoln in January, 1943 (9th grade for me) and I left for California in June, 1952, upon graduation from law school. This was 9½ years of a great city and lots of basketball.

My first friendships were made shooting baskets at Jack Campbell's, homeroom games (B-114) at noon in Irving Jr. High's boy's gym (Ken James, Jack Defenbaugh, Bill White and Bob Burns) and the First Plymouth Congregational team in the church league on Saturday mornings at the YMCA (Al Cesare, Bud Wendeli, et al).

Street cars were the mode of transportation to the "Y" in the a.m. and back to the theater—Lincoln, Stuart or Varsity in the p.m. with your date.

Then it was on to Lincoln High and it was awesome! Our sophomore basketball team, under Coach Max Pumphrey (Johnny Wilson, Bob Evans et al) was undefeated. Next year our reserve team (Bob Pierce, Duane Grady, Jack Defenbaugh et al) under Coach Charlie Worrall lost one game to Greenwood when "Chief" Grady, our star, was sick. Then the Varsity, in our senior year, (Bob Pierce, Bruce Bergquist, Grady, Defenbaugh, et al) was undefeated, State Champions, 26–0 under the great Coach Lyle Weyand—a wonderful man.

Then it was on to the University of Nebraska. It was the wrong time for a 17-year-old to start college if he was thinking about basketball. The veterans were back and they were older and better. As I recall, 145 were involved in the tryouts and the game was changing. In high school, defense was featured, in our 26–0 season, no team scored more than 30 points against us. At the U of N, Harry Good was pushing the "run and gun." The late Claude Retherford, my fraternity father, led the way. I made the freshman team but at the start of my sophomore year knee surgery put a temporary halt to my basketball career. The good news was that it saved me the embarrassment of not making the cut on what I believe was called the "B" team. The game (offense) had passed me by..

In my law school years, I put together a law school team in the intramurals with the great Don MacArthur and the late Bud Gerlach, a team in the City League sponsored by Lincoln Caterpillar (Bruce Bergquist's father) and also a town team featuring MacArthur, Jack Campbell and Fran Nagle (who drew crowds). Eagle, Murdock and the likes were not the scenes of great basketball but they all had a tavern.

Did I ever get it out of my system? No way! A bad neck condition stopped my full court, fast break basketball at age 65. But I can still go to the taverns.

Shopping Trips to Lincoln
By Mort Novak

I became a resident of Lincoln when I enrolled in the University in 1948. My introduction to the city occurred several years earlier at the onset of what became an annual pilgrimage to the city by a group of high school boys from Brainard, Nebraska.

I was born and reared in Brainard, which is a little village about 50 miles northwest of Lincoln. The 1940 population was 444 the current population is 270. We were and are a village. There were about 36 boys in high school at the time our pilgrimages began and about half of them participated each year.

It all began in the early forties when one of the smarter guys came up with the idea of making a Christmas shopping trip to Lincoln on one of the first Saturdays in December. The Union Pacific had a two-car diesel-powered train that we called the "Motor," which came from the Grand Island area and stopped in Brainard at 8:00 each morning and returned from Lincoln arriving in Brainard about 4:45 in the afternoon. It took about an hour to get to Lincoln and about an hour and a quarter to get to Brainard from Lincoln since it was uphill all the way back. When the Motor was nearing the town of Loma on the way back, we used to jump out of the train and walk along beside it until the conductor caught us.

The first car of the Motor was the engine with a mail room where postal employees sorted mail during the trip. There was also an area for freight such as cans of milk and cartons of eggs and return merchandise being sent back to the Sears Roebuck catalogue department or to the John Deere parts department. The second car was strictly for passengers and usually had an almost capacity crowd.

When we arrived in Lincoln, one of the first stops was the F. W. Woolworth Five and Ten Cent Store at 12th and O Street. We could usually get most of our Christmas presents at the five and dime store, which was fortunate considering the amount of cash we had. But my favorite memory of that store was the beautiful lady that played the piano in the sheet music department. She couldn't play as well as Jerry Solomon, but she surely was a lot easier to look at.

From there we would go down O Street to Miller & Paine to ride the escalators until we were asked to leave the store. This was usually lunchtime, which meant a trip to 14th and O to the Acme Chili Parlor. That was the best chili ever made. It must have been the half-inch of grease that was floating on top of the beans and the teaspoonful of meat that made it taste so good.

The remainder of the afternoon was spent wandering up and down O Street in and out of stores like Lawlors and Gold's, Magees, and Ben Simons. One year as we were ambling along there was a teenage girl approaching us and she winked at me, I about wet my pants. Girls never wink at me anymore. But I don't wet my pants as much, either.

Speakedda Greek

By Greg Kallos

Hello to the curious ...

How do you start a journey of one's happenings, when you started with three strikes against you? Where do you find the Alpha, the Genesis, the Origin?

Three strikes ... when you meet your kindergarten teacher at a 50-year high school reunion and she calls you by name ... what gives? Miss Hanna informed me, "Gregory, how could I forget you, having taught for over fifty years, you were the only student whose mother came to school with her child, because he couldn't speak English. I hurried for over four weeks to get you current with the class. My only fears were, if I couldn't teach you quick enough, I was afraid that you would have the whole school speaking Greek."

I managed to get to high school on time, and became an athlete of sorts; my glory was making the football team my sophomore year. Yes, not many students. Falls City 0, Creighton Prep 55, the fourth quarter was almost over. Coach Tolly had lost most of his backfield, and I was seated last on the bench, praying that he had forgotten me. He started walking down the bench, and spotted me, trying to hide behind a lineman. Problem was, he wasn't much bigger than me. I, in full uniform, shoes and all, couldn't reach 120 lbs.! You guessed it, first play to Kallos up the middle to Subby Sollnero—390 lbs. The last thing I remember was his shouting, "where the hell do you think you are going?" A fulfilling career!

I started the University of Nebraska—it almost ended before we had a good start. I got involved with the Awgawan campus magazine. Johnny Carson's future wife Jodie Walcott was on the staff as an artist. I wrote articles under the name of Gerg Sollak. One of the issues was deemed to be of a porno nature. Meeting with Dean Thompson. His first words to the four of us staff people were, "give me one reason why I shouldn't kick the four of you out of school?" We immediately were informed, no more Awgawan.

A fraternity person ... capers galore ... breaking up the walk of some of the other houses, under the pretense that the alums wanted it repaired before rush week. We broke it up and left it for the rushe's to fall over! The sorority house, whose take-up carpet in the main area needed to be cleaned ... the days before carpets were placed permanently picked it up and stored it until after rush week then suddenly appearing on the lawn after the activity. One of our brothers decided we needed to cop the homecoming Jayhawk and hang it over our door so we called the row and dared them to come get it the rest you can imagine. Wearing dresses to sneak into an all women's function ... and getting caught! Listening to Carson between acts of the Kosmet Klub. Panty raids on sorority row.

The Acme Chili Parlor ... Greeks galore ... late night haunt, when you needed to get your act together ... sober up after partying.

The Diamond Grill ... owner, the myth of our times ... Jerry Mapes. Where friendly beers and charming damsels could be seen with shuffle board games a plenty.

The Tee Pee room at the Cornhusker Hotel ah those steak burgers in the basket with the big sundaes with Indian names ... brownies with thick chocolate overlay all hits with the ladies, a great way to impress your lovely of the night.

The student union dances ... Stan Kenton the first time he played his Artistry in Rhythm tunes then he asked everyone to sit down on the floor ... go out and get anyone you can find to come in and listen. I was on the committee to get him to come to Lincoln. His singer was June Christy we hosted her at the Sigma Chi house for lunch before the concert.

The Turnpike days ... all the name bands played there, and dancing was a pleasant thing then.

The Capital Beach, Kings Ballroom with the salty swimming pool, where many a romance flourished.

The Wind Mill root beer stand on 33rd and O Street, the most eastern limits then ... car hops to flirt with while ordering. The Tastee Inn ... still there with those buns in a tube back then.

Graduated Dental College ... more intellectual capers which I will not get into, undergraduate and graduate activity are understated, memorable times riding up the State Capital front steps in the old time Jeep and toasting the Sower.

I served with SAC during the Korean conflict for two years. The first tragic encounter was identifying the remains of B 29 members, who crashed while on their way home for Christmas, one was a friend from my college days, I was going to surprise him on his return to base, a Nebraska man, pilot of the bomber. On my first weekend on hospital emergency calls a three-year-old girl had been run over on the base, and I was holding her when she looked up at me, and asked, "am I going to die?" She died; I have always felt that this was my reason, why I have always had a love affair with all three-year-old children during my practice years.

I practiced in Wymore, Nebraska ... my highlight was when I appeared on the Johnny Carson show. "Who Do You Trust" in New York. I knew John from college. In New York the comments on the show had to do with Jodie, myself and the Awgawan capers, we rehearsed our lines, put it to bed and went to our hotel for the evening. At five a.m. the next morning a frantic call came from Johnny's staff member. Have you read this mornings Time? Hell, I was still asleep, the Walter Winchell column stated Johnny and Jodie were getting a divorce. A limo came to pick us up and we redid the script. Lots of fun covering college days and a review of our capers.

Tony and Luigi's, what an Italian eating place that was. Their high booths, where you and your date could hide. In Lincoln now there were Spencer Steak House on South Street, and Kings Hamburgers, pig's feet at the Royal Grove pool games and shuffleboard to boot. The Senate Bar ... no age checks there. The Corral at the Capital Hotel with 10¢ glass drafts ... Straight Pipe Kugler acquired his reputation there ten glasses for a dollar. Playing golf at Pioneers Park, but looked forward to stopping at Lee's for a beer, but more especially his off the wall chicken an unnoticed item on the menu, except those of us who knew the truth. The old Runza stand on the way to the park ... pick up food to get you by the first few holes. Ever been locked in at Pioneers? Don't lie. What were you doing there late at night? Did you ever golf at the Vine Street sand course, and jump into the ditch on the first hole to retrieve your ball? Remember 48th Street when it was an unpaved road and there were few cars on campus.

More reformed now, after all, this is Lincoln again ... no more capers ... Jaycees without any capers! Check the skies to see if a new star has appeared in the east.

I once woke up and found a street meter was in my front yard, embedded in concrete. Egads, what do you do now ... cops to ask what's this thing in your front yard ... get rid of it quick ... called friends I could trust ... had a good idea who did the act. I invited friends for an early breakfast to watch the house across the street. During the night I went over and used the longest nails I could find and nailed his garage door shut! Presently my neighbor comes out of his house, goes to the garage door, pulls on the handle ... surprise, the door stayed in place he tried and tried but no luck. He finally started to look around and lo and behold it took a full day to remove the 100 or more nails.

Ever eaten spiked watermelon ... vodka ... at a picnic and watched your lovelies get stiff? Ever had an office party ... wife decides the party is running too long ... drops by so you can take her out for the rest of the evening ... finds her roommate dazed, with someone holding a towel to the head?

Riding a horse for the first time ... requesting an older horse, not too spry. Old Starr is his name ... two r's please. Estes Park ... instructions given ... a two hour journey into the heavens. Keep a firm hold on the reigns please. Man I was frozen to that saddle ... kick Starr, you are falling behind. Hell, Starr was so sagged in the middle, that it took him several steps to clear his stomach from the ground. Kick Starr ... sure, when pigs fly! It started to pour everyone put on rain jackets, not me ... let's don't break Starr's rhythm ... we ate, saw the scenery ... anything that Starr wanted, he got. The group was far gone no sense in pushing old Starr he won't get lost, meanwhile I am retaining the waters of the Colorado skies. People coming down the trail have the right of way ... sure ... Old Starr and I never budged; we incurred the wrath of all those seasoned riders. Let them climb out of the way. Hell, I stopped looking over the edge, when I realized there was an edge to my left and right. I wanted to cross myself for salvation and redemption, but I was too afraid to let go of the ropes, or whatever you hold on to. God that horse crapped a lot! He would tremble every time, which made me hang on for dear life. I asked him to give me a warning, but he no speakedda the Greek ... resorted to my mother tongue, for I thought the end was near. Trail seems to be going down now … God I hope he wasn't looking for a stray mare … I hope that's what a female horse is called, for his stride was picking up a bit. What to do if we come across a stray whatever … I'll just ride it out … hell, I'm an old hand now … three hours and counting … if Starr had a chance, why not! Hell! I just hope he moves off the trail a bit so he doesn't get too excited and slip … I can see the three of us … spreading out, and making like birds of paradise! Still moving, a corner coming up … eyes are closed, please turn Starr … I'm with you. He turned … hello … people shouting ahead … "There you are!" Home is about ten blocks ahead … riders coming up the trail … were you lost? "We were getting ready to come looking for you, but we were waiting for the rains to stop. What a comfort they were. A snake hissing would have been more welcome. Hell, it rained for a week … Old Starr and I would have been part of the Thompson Canyons rivers!

Steak Jerome

By Jerry Mapes

About ten years ago, the governor of the state of Nebraska was Kay Orr. Her husband Bill was of course referred to as the "First Gentleman." Bill Orr is a man with an outgoing infectious personality. He came up with an idea one day of a First Gentleman's Cookbook, the sale of which would pour thousands into the state treasury which would in turn enable the Governor's mansion to be remodeled with no taxpayer expense.

Bill got all of his friends and a few notable national personalities, like Dick Cavett, Johnny Carson, etc. to contribute recipes. Being a good friend of Bill's, I not only contributed a recipe but also money, so that the publishing and printing could proceed. There was a group of about twelve that kicked in, which entitled us to come to several progress dinners at the mansion.

The book did a little better than break even. My recipe was as follows:

Steak Jerome

    1 pound U.S. choice beef tenderloin (or prime)
    3 cloves of garlic chopped
    1 cup sliced mushrooms
    4 green onions sliced crosswise
    ¼ pound butter
    1 8oz. can beef broth
    ½ cup Madeira wine
    4 oz. flour and water mixture
    salt and pepper

Preferably in an electric fry pan, so the heat can be quickly adjusted, melt the butter and sauté the onions and mushrooms for two or three minutes, then add the garlic bits. Now add the beef broth and simmer on medium for two minutes. Turn to medium high and add the beef tenderloin, which you have previously sliced in to ½-inch slices and pounded down to about ¼ inch for ultimate tenderness. The bubbling mixture will cook the beef in three minutes. At this point, add the Madeira wine and simmer for another two minutes. Thicken the mixture to gravy consistency or a little less with the flour and water whisked in.

This is a very impressive dish and can be served with Margaret Mapes' spinach potatoes. As follows:
Instant mashed potatoes for 10 (6 potatoes)
¼ pound butter
1 tsp sugar
2 tsp salt and pepper
2 tbsp chives or green onion tops
2 tbsp dill weed
1 pkg of cooked frozen spinach (chopped)
Bake in greased casserole for about twenty minutes.

'The Day of Infamy'

By Charlie Wright

January 29, 1958 is the "Day of Infamy" in the memory of most Lincoln residents who were born prior to 1945. Lincoln's Chief of Police was Joe Carroll, its Sheriff was Merle Karnopp, Bennett S. "Abe" Martin was mayor and Victor E. Anderson was our governor. At 2:00 p.m. on that date, Charles, the 19-year-old son of Helen and Guy Starkweather, was disarmed by an unarmed geologist on Highway 87, west of Douglas, Wyoming, ending a mass murder spree that left 10 victims in the vicinity of Lincoln and a final victim in Wyoming. Apprehended with Starkweather was 15-year-old Caril Fugate, who had accompanied him on the murder spree. Thus ended a reign of terror, shock and uncertainty that gripped everyone in the city. Grief for the innocent victims and their families lingers to this date.

Lincoln was a prospering city of approximately 130,000 souls which enjoyed the presence of the University of Nebraska and the State Capitol. It had excellent leadership in city government and in its business community. The business leaders were often referred to as the "O Street Gang." Among the great ones were Nate Gold, George Holmes, A.Q. Schimmel, Clarence Swanson and Abe Martin.

On Wednesday morning, the 29th of January, the Lincoln Star reported six persons who had been recently shot or bludgeoned to death in the Lincoln–Bennett area. Starkweather was the prime suspect and law enforcement agencies in an eleven state area had no idea where he was. Rumors were rampant. By midday, tension reached an even higher level when the brutal killing of prominent residents Clara and Lauer Ward and their maid, Lillian Fencl, was reported on the radio and in the Lincoln Star.

Governor Anderson called out the National Guard to patrol Lincoln's streets. Armed guardsmen were visible at 13th and O streets. Sheriff Karnopp deputized large numbers of armed citizens to assist his department. The

Lincoln radio carried reports of house to house searches and occasional neighborhood sightings of Starkweather, who had red hair.

At that time, I was in my fourth and final year at the Nebraska Law College. One of my good friends and classmates was Sidney H. Sweet, from Hartington. Sid and I were attending law school under a two and four year program. After two years of undergraduate study, and the requisite 56 passing hours, we were admitted to law school in our junior years and were to receive our degree at the end of four years study at the law school. However, since the Korean War was still active, and each of us were enrolled in an ROTC program, Sid and I each received reserve commissions in the Navy and Army, respectively, spending two years on active duty between our second and third years of law school. Sid married Mary Jane Rooney of Greeley and I married Suzy Oritz of Omaha while I was in the Navy. When Sid and I returned for our final two years of law school, we were fortunate to have the G.I. bill which provided tuition, books and $135 per month. With our hearty approval, Suzy and Mary Jane obtained teaching jobs at the Irving Child Center which was located in Irving Junior High in the vicinity of 22nd and Van Dorn streets. Among Suzy's first grade students were Bob Nefsky, Bruce Elliot (son of Pete Elliot), Edward Sands and Nancy Brickson. I obtained work as a runner, adjusting insurance claims and preparing research memos for the Cline Williams law firm, for which I received $1.00 per hour. Sid worked for awhile adjusting claims for Crocker Claims Service and then found more steady employment with Mayor Bennett Martin's business office. Coming from small Nebraska towns, Sid and I both liked to hunt and, at the time, I was the proud owner of an Ithaca Feather-Light shotgun which I had purchased at the Navy PX for $67. When the news broke about the brutal murders at the Ward home, I phoned Sid and told him that we should move promptly to protect our wives who were unarmed and would be completing their teaching duties at Irving later that afternoon. Sid agreed.

Sid and I went out to our apartments which were located on the vicinity of 17th and Van Dorn streets, picked up and loaded our shotguns, and drove over to Irving Junior High School. We parked the car, grabbed our shotguns, and walked boldly into Irving Junior High School to pick up Mary Jane and Suzy. As we walked through the halls, we received glances from some of the students and teachers but no one seemed to object to our presence carrying firearms. We located our wives and waited until each of their students had a ride home. As we approached our car, I saw Sam Sharpe who was a grade school student and the son of William Dayton "Tony" Sharpe, for whom I had played baseball as an undergraduate student at UNL. We picked Sam up and delivered him to his mother, Ruth, and then proceeded over to the residence of my aunt and uncle, Marian and Flavel Wright, at 24th and Lake Streets.

Flavel and Marian had four children living at home and I believe that Starkweather worked on the truck which collected Flav's garbage. I recall sitting around in Flav's living room, discussing the horrible murders that were recently discovered and the radio reports that Starkweather might then be loose in one of the Lincoln neighborhoods. Flav had no firearms and was glad to see us, shotguns and all. A suggestion was made that perhaps we should take turns standing watch all night or until Starkweather had been apprehended in Wyoming. This ended the feeling of insecurity that prevailed. However, the period of grief and mourning was just beginning. Our sympathy and prayers go out to the families and friends of the innocent victims to this day.

One could imagine what might happen if we were to attempt the same maneuver, entering a public school carrying loaded shotguns, in current times. With the mass killings and civil disorders that have taken place subsequent to the Starkweather incident, loaded firearms in the vicinity of a public school would not be tolerated. Looking back on the incident, some 43 years ago, my feeling is that Lincoln and its citizens behaved in a very level-headed manner when confronted with this horrible and shocking situation. About three months later, I was in the process of investigating a workman's compensation claim when I encountered a young gentleman named Rodney Starkweather. He was the brother of Charles. I could not help feeling sorry for Rodney because he was obviously also badly scarred by circumstances over which he had absolutely no control.

Looking back on the Starkweather matter and comparing it with the killings in Columbine, I believe that there are certain similarities between Charles Starkweather and the two boys who perpetrated the mass murders at the Colorado school.

The Great Oklahoma Train Orgy

By Jerry Mapes

Back in 1950 when the Cornhuskers had experienced their first decent season in years on the gridiron, Bob Reynolds was everyone's All American for Nebraska and Billy Vessels was his counterpart for the perennial nemesis, the Oklahoma Sooners. The big game, the final of the season for the championship, was to be played in Oklahoma.

The Junior Chamber of Commerce, of which I was a member at 21 years of age, decided as a money-making project they would sponsor a train to run from Lincoln, to Norman and we would leave Friday evening about 10 p.m. The event was such a huge success that we wound up running two trains. In addition to football fans there were people along for the big party which has never been equaled.

A card playing group (I think it was gin rummy) formed immediately. There were lots of groups but this one was notable because it included Adna Dobson, Morris Freshman, George Abel and the then mayor, Vic Anderson (later to become governor).

As the game progressed throughout the evening, probably fueled with a little alcohol (though this is not documented) the participants became engrossed in their game and when the throngs (upwards of one thousand) detrained in Norman there was something missing—The Card Group.

As the train left the station for western Oklahoma, no one noticed, neither the anxious fans nor the leading citizens waiting for a "fill" on a four card disjointed run.

About halftime with the fans milling around in and out of the stadium waiting for the conclusion of a very tight game, here come "our heroes" in the back of a pickup loaded with hay and looking rather sheepish. They had commandeered a farmer to bring them back after they figured out their plight.

Reynolds and Vessels shone as expected and Oklahoma edged Nebraska 49 to 35 before a huge crowd of 55,000 (49,998 for the first half).

The Hardin Center and Other Noble Efforts

By Jack Thompson

Almost half a century ago, in 1956, our goal for what was then called the Community Chest was $580,850 but we came up to the end of the campaign several thousand dollars short of what was then a record goal. As was the custom in such a crisis of the campaign, we would ask some underwriters to guarantee the shortfall until additional contributions would come in. I asked Mr. Erle Campbell, then CEO of the great Miller & Paine store, to go with me to see Mr. Tom Woods, CEO of Lincoln Tel & Tel. Without hesitation, the ever generous Mr. Woods said it was no problem because they had planned to underwrite a special contribution needed to replace the heating system in one of the buildings of a member agency of the Community Chest; he would be glad to pledge that "right now, and the goal would be achieved."

Sometime in the 1950s or early 1960s, we organized the Lincoln Industrial Development Corporation to concentrate on attracting new industries to the community in complete secrecy. Industries seeking new locations did not want publicity, which often occurred when competing banks heard their intentions and sought their banking business. Such leaks caused confusion in their home communities.

The LIDC hired a nationally know consultant on industrial development who recommended that we establish an Industrial Park, a new idea to us at that time. This was to be an attractively landscaped area with curved streets, ample grassland and trees on which to locate non-smokestack industries.

As was often our custom, we consulted Nate Gold about how to find an appropriate area and purchased it. He assured us that it was no problem; that he had anticipated this need some time ago and had purchased a large acreage running up the hill on 14th Street from the railroad tracks to Old Cheney Road directly across the street from the penitentiary. He said he had assumed that this tract would not be popular for housing but knew it would be needed for some purpose. Moreover, he would sell it to us at exactly his cost with no reimbursement for having carried this extra expense for a number of years! Today the park is fully occupied with attractive industry.

When the late Joe W. Seacrest was publisher of the Lincoln Journal, Chancellor Clifford Hardin at UNL heard about an innovation at Michigan State called a "Center for Continuing Education." At that time, the structure at Michigan State was the only one in existence and it served as a center for students from all over the state for faculty meetings, seminars and other gatherings sponsored by the University. Chancellor Hardin organized a group of us to go by air to see the center in operation at Michigan State.

We were royally treated, and very much impressed by the structure of the building and its many uses. The friendly governor of Michigan encouraged us to duplicate it. Happily, our governor at the time, Vic Anderson, was part of our party and was enthusiastic about the idea.

On the way back to Lincoln on the airplane, while we were all visiting about our trip, Joe W. Seacrest suddenly came up to the front of the plane and without having discussed the matter with anyone except Chancellor Hardin, he announced we would go ahead with the project and would raise $1,100,000—a major sum at the time—for a structure that could not be expected to pay for itself.

Joe W. believed in action! Without wasting any time, he pointed to the Governor and said words to the effect "Vic, you will be Chairman. Jack, you work with him on that." Joe W. went up and down the airplane assigning different jobs to all of those on board, and by the time we returned to Lincoln, we were a "campaign" organized and ready to go. No one was about to decline a request by Joe W., who was always willing to help everyone else's worthwhile cause.

The structure has more than lived up to its promise and, at long last, it is properly named the Hardin Center.

The Klatch

By Tom Miller

Someone mentioned to me during the evening about some of the O Street Gang doings and that brought to mind the coffee times at the old Lincoln Hotel and 9th and P in the mornings. There was always one table of the guys including Jess Chambers, Emmett Junge, Don Cunningham, Les Strain, Gene Tallman, sometimes John Lawlor or Nate Gold, once in a great while Abe Martin, and very seldom George Abel. After all the B.S. of the morning and the coffeeing was done a game of chance took place. It was usually based on some of the preprinted numbers on the coffee tab. The one who guessed the number got stuck with the tab.

As the numbers began to close in on the real number as we went around the table the game usually got more complicated as there would always seem to be a developing conspiracy to "get" someone. On the days that George Abel was there it was always the desire of the group to get George and he knew it. When they finally had him boxed in so that the only number left he could call was "the" number there would be a howl of satisfaction from everyone but George. He put up the most defensive look and usually muttered something like he was never coming back because he knew somehow they always made him pay for the morning.

One must remember in those days, which for me were the late '50s when Jess was introducing me to all of the downtowners the total bill rarely ever exceeded $5.00. That made no difference to George. He had gotten screwed again!

The Million-Dollar Thumb
By Bill Orr

One of the best things about Ideal Grocery is that you get to know the employees on a personal basis. Over the years I have shopped with one or more of our Lincoln grandsons, there are five. The meat counter is manned by real butchers who weigh and wrap what you are buying. Larry (now retired) had been there for years. When Larry waited on me and one of my young grandsons was along I would ask: "Larry, show them your 'million-dollar thumb.' " It took our young ones quite a few trips to decide if I was referring to the thumb being weighed along with the meat, I assured our young ones I was only kidding and that Larry and the crew were honest.

The Non-Grinch Who Sometimes Delayed Christmas
Anonymous

One of my Christmas remembrances when coming of age in the forties and fifties was the huge Christmas Day party hosted by A. Q. Schimmel, owner and operator of the Cornhusker Hotel at 13th & M Streets. The Cornhusker was the hub of most social activities in Lincoln and old A. Q. put on one heck-uva spread including a mammoth buffet complete with free flowing booze, Egg Nogg, Tom and Jerrys, etc.

The problem was that this impressive Christmas Day lavish feast started early in the day and usually lasted late into the afternoon. Consequently, many of the town's leading citizens would come dragging home usually too stuffed, too tired or too inebriated to participate in their own family doings and usually went straight to bed or if they chose to "fake it out" fell miserably short of making sense of being a viable part of family Christmas time.

My mother, admittedly exercising a minimum of logic, always announced that the whole thing was a Jewish conspiracy to ruin Christmas for as many gentiles as possible. Mr. Schimmel was of Jewish persuasion. My father continued to assure her that he and his friends were men of free will and that Mr. Schimmel's annual bash was a noble gesture of "Good Will Towards Men."

The Outdoor Theater
By Ed Perry

In the summer of 1948, Dick Oslund and I made big plans to take our dates to an outdoor movie. Dick had a date with Agnes Anderson nee Olson and I was with Jo Ann O'Brien nee Cordell. Dick had his own car. It was a Pontiac Coupe with a big trunk. As we drove to the Starview Theater, Dick and I had a brilliant idea. Instead of paying for each person in the car, as was expected, he and I would hide in the trunk and thus only have to pay for two. We concocted this plan as Dick and I were poor, frugal and cheap. Aggie was the driver, however and instead of going to the Starview she drove the car over every bump, railroad track, etc. that she could find in the city of Lincoln which increased the trunk occupants discomfort. The girls were supposed to take us to the theater and let us out when we were in the theater lot. Unfortunately, we did not establish the time interval between our entry into the trunk and our exit therefrom. Time has dulled the memory of the length of the ride in the trunk, but it is believed to be in excess of one hour. One would expect that there was astonishment from the passing motorists who heard loud screaming coming from the trunk and hysterical giggling coming from the front. Needless to say, once Dick and I and our two lady friends settled in for the movie, no one had an amorous thought. Reports of the event discouraged many of our compatriots from being thrifty in this manner.

These Fondest of Memories
By Robert E. Palmer

How vividly I recall driving, with our family, into Lincoln the night before Thanksgiving, 1963, the week John Kennedy was shot and C. S. Lewis had died. We were coming from a ten year pastorate in Santa Monica, California, and I recall someone telling me that "Nebraska is a low-rolling freehold, just to the left of Iowa, where sin swings her handbag in vain, not too surprisingly, though, since the major hotel in the capital city is called "Cornhusker."" From that star filled night, till nearly a quarter century later when I last saw the "Pinnacle of the Plains" disappear in my rear view mirror, our family lived the happiest years of our lives.

As I look at the five fingers of my left hand, holding the pen as I write, I think of five reasons why I can make such a statement. First, *The Character of the People.* We were met upon arrival by the Joyce Ayres' family who made us feel at home that night, and the next day were introduced to a host of new friends at the Country Club who offered to include us in their lives. The list of close friends we made after that grew so long that I hesitate to mention any names. It was whole families that befriended us, but I'll just mention some of the men. I remember Wilbur Wiedman, who always made house calls for our family; the three Earls: Carter, Lamshire and Luff, who pledged to help in rebuilding Westminster Presbyterian Church; Ted Maude, who became our family dentist; Chan Tyrrell, who provided us with flowers and smiles; Dick Thompson, Art Smith, Don McLeese, and Jerry Mapes who practically adopted us, and many, many more.

Second, *The Accessibility of Opportunity.* The entire community, as we knew it, consisted of a growing circle of friendships, with no social, economic, cultural or religious barriers. People in every walk of life were just a phone call or short drive away. Every door seemed to have a "welcome" sign on it. Downtown was the one place to shop and do business. Stores and companies seemed personalized by the names and faces of people you intimately knew: Magees was "Elmer," Miller and Paine was "Bob," Golds was "Nate," Walts was "Ed," Banker's Life was "George," Ideal was "Gardner," and the Lincoln Hotel was "Abe." A part of my call to Westminster Church consisted of two tickets to all the football games for 23 years, and Avery Forke saw to it that I would attend out of state games. Most weeks there was an invitation to speak at one of the fraternities or sororities, and three or four busloads of students on a Sunday morning seated in the front pews, was not unusual. Civic organizations provided countless opportunities for service and friendship, and social opportunities had to be limited. Van Duling gave us the opportunity of taking groups of friends abroad and to the Holy Land every other year.

The Quality of Life is one of the main factors that attracted us to Lincoln from southern California. They say "it takes a village to raise a child," and living in Lincoln afforded our four children the kind of supportive, yet challenging, sense of community in which the spirit of neighborhood, the excellence of schools, the opportunities for self expression and development, the privacy of home life developed qualities in each that equipped them for making significant contributions in their chosen professions and communities. It was amazing to see the number of people who would informally visit us, and how our large Piedmont house was daily filled with our children's friends who felt they could just walk in and visit at any time. In fact, we never once locked our home during those years.

I especially appreciated the fact that though our family was not native to Lincoln, no barriers were raised to make us feel like outsiders, and abundant opportunities were available to us. *A Sense of Accomplishment.* Three of our children attended the University of Nebraska, and all four have successfully established themselves in their chosen professions, two lawyers, one doctor and one who owns an advertising firm. I was made the chaplain of the Legislature, invited to be a Professor of Education Administration at the University and our family felt included everywhere. My wife Mary Lou earned a Ph.D. from the University and a position with the State Department of Education. The church we served had the kind of support that enabled it to become one of the largest in the country. Although, initially, we planned to stay only a few years to get our church back on the right track, we quickly decided that this was the best place imaginable to rear a family. Not until our youngest graduated from East High did we move to Naples, Florida. In retrospect, I feel that our life had been like a book, with an exciting first chapter in Santa Monica, California, and a final satisfying chapter in Celebration, Florida but the major story consists in our fulfilling chapters of life spent in Lincoln.

When the invitation to contribute to this volume came, it suggested the inclusion of a few stories, so I'll close with *These Fondest of Memories.*

First I recall an exciting mid-week flight to Northern Minnesota where Jerry Mapes, Tommy Ludwick, Tom Smith and I spent several days one winter snowmobiling and socializing in a snowbound cabin. At week's end we needed to return for church. We were to fly back in a single engine Cessna. The temperature was 10 degrees. About five minutes after takeoff, a warning light came on and our pilot, Tommy, decided to bank the plane back toward the airport since we were over an extensive forest. About that time, the engine exploded, sending debris flying and covering the window with oil. Tommy spotted a snow-covered lake and decided to glide toward it. We hit with a resounding thud, skidded for a couple hundred yards, and spun around just before we reached open water. We all jumped out and ran to safety and offered prayers of gratitude. By the time we returned to Lincoln, I was hoping no one knew I had been away. Wrong! It had been announced on the radio and television that we had crashed, and someone even called our home with the news that I had been killed (greatly exaggerated). A photograph of the crash scene appeared on the front page of Sunday's *Journal*. With my fellow crash victims sitting in the front pew, I'll never forget my feeling of gratitude as I faced a crowded congregation on Sunday, without my sermon, and preached extemporaneously on Psalm 139: "If I take the wings of the morning and dwell in the uttermost part of the sea, even there thy hand shall lead me."

Another memorable reminiscence was when I was sued, while Chaplain of the Legislature, by Ernie Chambers and the ACLU for breaking down the wall between church and state. The legislature had voted to have my daily prayers printed in their journal. At year's end, these prayers were printed, at state expense, in booklets, which the Senators used for complimentary distribution to their constituents. The federal judge in Lincoln decided in Ernie's favor, but Paul Douglas, the state's Attorney General, decided to appeal. There were encouragement's to do so by others, from the armed forces to the U. S. Congress, since it appeared my case would be regarded as a precedent against chaplains elsewhere. The appellate court was no help, so it finally went before the U.S. Supreme Court, which decided in my favor. The decision came while our family was vacationing at Dick Thompson's cottage at Lake Okobojii in Iowa. There ensued a flurry of phone calls from *Time Magazine* and the major television networks, which sent photographers and reporters for the story. An interesting sidelight came years later when our son Robert, was taking the national bar exam in California, and 12 years later, when our daughter was taking her bar exam in Florida, that a question twice appeared concerning their father's experience with the law.

Again, I recall, just recently, when the Huskers won their most recent National Championship in the Orange Bowl by defeating Tennessee. Our entire family had traveled to Miami for the game. We just couldn't seem to leave the stadium when it was over, and as Tom Osborne walked off the field, he looked up at us and waved (a photo, which later appeared on the cover of Sports Illustrated). Our family all broke out spontaneously in a rousing chorus of "There Is No Place Like Nebraska." For us, it was a telling and tearful reminder of just how much Lincoln will always mean to each of us as: Huskers at Heart!

Update On My Feature Page Debut
April 25, 1992

By Jerry Mapes

About nine years ago the *Journal Star* gave readers a "shot" at writing an article which I believe came out every Saturday. I was allowed to do an article which I thoroughly enjoyed doing. The following was my submission.

When I learned that my old ex-employer (the Lincoln *Star*) was going to give me a crack as guest editorialist, I figured all my conservative friends would bar me from their coffee groups if I didn't jump on some "Rush Limbaugh" band wagon and tear into the animal rights activists, the feminists or the militant environmentalists.

However, it is my observation that subjects such as these tend to either anger the writer, the reader or, more likely, both. Besides all serious matters such as these are better articulated by angry people and I have difficulty getting exercised over these matters because nobody ever changes anybody's mind.

I was going to touch on the "sensitivity" issue and how I think it has gotten so far out of hand, but I'm not in the mood for this either. They tell me I have another shot at this column on July 4 so maybe I can get worked up by then.

Then I decided to do a *Reader's Digest*–type article on "The Most Unforgettable Character I've Met." Well, for me that dubious honor would have to go to Ralph "Alex" Johnson, a Uehling, Neb., original, later to move to Lincoln, then to Wilmington, Del., and finally retirement near Sebring, Fla.

Axel is my most favorite insane person. The fact that he is now 70 years young, lost his legs when he was 3 years old (he says they fell off in his sleep one night) and is totally irreverent doesn't detract from his uniqueness. In fact, I think it helps.

I've seen him wear his legs backwards, stick ice picks in them in front of startled patrons when he tended bar at the old Elk's Club at 13th and P and the bar he worked every summer in Grand Lake, Colo., and even let one of his legs drop out of his sweatpants while circling a Mexican beach in a parasail harness.

I decided against an "Axel column" because people have either heard of him already or they don't want to hear about him or—you've got the idea.

Now that I have used up about half of my allotted space on what I am not going to write about I decided to tell you about a remarkable group I belong to right here in Star city. We call our selves the Jayceeniles. We consist of ex-board members of the Junior Chamber of Commerce, who served during a certain period of the '50s.

The name "ceenile" was supposed to add a touch of humor to the fact that were all over 35 years of age. Now, however, the designation is entirely appropriate since our group of 24 individuals ranges in age of 55 to 70.

I said we were a remarkable group not because of the membership, although we have doctors, lawyers, judges and one candlestick maker. We are remarkable in the sense that not one of our number has expired since the formation of the group over 30 years ago. We have had strokes, bypasses, heart attacks and numerous other maladies, but we cannot get rid of anyone, I went to a high school 40-year reunion about three years ago and 25 percent of my classmates have gone to their great reward (or other appropriate destinations). Not this bunch. They refuse to budge.

Fifteen ears ago we elected a "Bereavement Chairman" and have selected a new one each year since. Absolute boredom to bereave!

Oh, it's not lifestyle for heaven's sake! We've got fat ones (about 80%), ones that drink too much (about 95%) and ones that don't ever exercise (about 90%). Maybe the dues are paid so far in advance, that nobody wants to miss a prepaid dinner.

Our group performs no functions, rings no bells, donates no eyes and serves no positive contribution other than the propagation of the myth that we are indestructible. I suppose one of our numbers will unceremoniously "bite the dust" before publication and we'll have to scrap my article. This would be a typical thoughtless touch from a Jayceenile.

To add a little "twilight zone" chapter to the group's history, we have had a couple of members move out of town and quit the club. You guessed it, Taps! It's been many months since I've been to our get-togethers (usually the third Tuesday of the month at one of the local eateries and drinkeries), but I have never once considered paying my dues. Not on my life!

Post Script—May 1, 2001

As my friend Ralph "Axel" Johnson who appears elsewhere in this book, died February 1, 2001.

As far as my "indestructible Jayceeniles", we have now lost four fine gentlemen since the article was written. Some say, with tongue in cheek, I hope that it was I that broke the string by writing the article. Like telling a pitcher that he has a no hitter going.

We have lost Reihold Wilhelm, Gaylord Blanc, Donn Davis and Charles Casper from the original group which now consists of: Jack Andrews, Charles Arnold, Frank Barrett, Mark Buccholz, Jack Campbell, Henry Cech, Bob Diers, Paul Douglas, Paul Galter, Greg Kallos, Ted Kessneer, Norm Krivosha, Don Leising, Jerry Mapes, Jim Nissen, Bob Peterson, Lyle Reighard, Bob Taylor, Harvey Traudt, RodVandenberg, and John Zimmer.

If I had to guess who would someday sip from the "last man's brandy" I have to put my money on Zimmer or Traudt since they are the youngest of the group.

The bottle of Cognac sits proudly beneath our group photo on the back bar of the Legion Club.

Lincoln's 'Un-Rapid Transit' of the '60s

By Bob Ammon

Ah yes, without question, it isn't too hard to wax nostalgic over yester-year's picturesque local trolley system, and who hasn't admired brownstone photos depicting bucolic scenes of trolley cars making their steady-and-sure way down Lincoln's Sheridan Boulevard and other notable arterials. They are about as "Norman Rockwell" as you can get.

Alas, time marches on, and by the mid-'40s, gas and diesel busses had shoved electric jitneys to the sidelines. Nostalgia aside, Lincoln City Lines did a superb job of providing the capital city with clean, reliable bus service for the better part of two decades, in spite of dwindling ridership and slipping revenues.

A fleet of sparkling new busses arrived in April of 1972, complete with new colors, air conditioning, and a new name, Lincoln Transportation System, now known as Startran. For the first time, service took precedent over the bottom line, and the resulting improvements were evident to one and all. It was and is, a system that well—justifies the minimal tax dollars that keep it running.

A now nearly forgotten era preceded the city takeover that was probably the low point of our local transit history. Once Lincoln City Lines determined that the only way was out, it curtailed much in the way of short and long-term maintenance, becoming ever more conscious of its shrinking profitability.

Engine overhauls became infrequent, bodywork was neglected, and the busses became rolling accidents waiting to happen. Counting on them to get you to work on time was a joke, as in-service breakdowns became the norm rather than the exception. The misery wasn't limited to just the riders, as anyone stopped behind a bus at a stoplight will attest to. Once the signal changed to green, the cloud of black, smokey soot that enveloped your car was the stuff of legend as the bus slowly gained momentum. One of my wife's earliest memories of Lincoln, after moving here in late 1971, was being all but suffocated by one of the big green buses, truly an "exhausting" experience, pun intended.

The accompanying photos tell it all, so next time you are caught behind a bus in busy traffic, consider yourself lucky, that its not a scene from 30 years ago, when it was life threatening, rather than just inconvenient.

My most dubious memory of bus riding as a boy occurred in the late '50s when my neighbor and best buddy, Scott Stuart and I boarded the Randolph bus at 48th and A Street, headed downtown to, where else, the Stuart Theatre. We were the only two passengers that hot afternoon, and decided that a bit of tomfoolery might be in order. We soon busied ourselves, attempting to do pull ups on the overhead pipe that was normally reserved for standees to grab a hold of.

As we ground to a halt at 40th and Randolph, I knew we were in trouble. The dour, aging driver pulled on the emergency brake, arose from his seat and make his was to the back of the bus. We'd had it!

Well, after a lengthy lecture about rider etiquette, coupled with a stern threat of expulsion if it happened again, we finally resumed our passage. I'll admit to our referring to the driver in very unflattering terms, albeit under our breath, but the whole thing left such an impression on me that I still remember that the bus was number 2955.

A day of infamy! A bus of infamy! Thank goodness we were young.

The Absent-Minded Professor

By Larry Vaughan

It was the best of times and the worst of times. It was October 1957. I had recently been extended a teaching contract by Nebraska Wesleyan University and was just beginning my 27-year career there. My mother had died in 1954, and my father had a very serious heart problem. Dad couldn't walk very far without it being stressful. His heart problem was so serious that he died of a heart attack a year later—but that's going beyond my story.

In September 1957, I stepped into a college teaching job with no preparation and with only one month's notice. In October I began to realize the magnitude of my situation and burned the midnight oil on many occasions just trying to keep ahead of the students in my classes. That first semester of college teaching was quite a struggle for me.

My father was rather proud of my being named an Assistant Professor at Nebraska Wesleyan, after eight years of public school teaching. He liked to "show me off" to his friends and colleagues. Halfway through my second month of teaching classes at Wesleyan, my father asked me to be his guest at the downtown Optimist Club's luncheon. He was a prominent member of the club. I accepted the invitation knowing that he would showcase me. I rather enjoyed the attention I got from it.

My teaching schedule required that I be back on the Nebraska Wesleyan campus by 2:00 p.m. to teach an Educational Measurements class. That really wasn't a concern of mine, because I figured that the Optimist Club luncheon should be over by 1:15, and I would be able to drive to the campus in 15 minutes. The day came for the luncheon engagement. I phoned dad in the morning and said that I would pick him up at the courthouse, were he was Register of Deeds, at 11:30 a.m. I was aware of his heart problem, and I didn't want him exerting himself walking quite a distance to the hotel. He appreciated the suggestion and said that he would be ready, standing on the corner when I arrived.

All went according to plan. I got away from Wesleyan on time and picked up my father at 11:30 a.m. We got to the Cornhusker Hotel where I dropped him off before I parked the car. Parking a car close to the hotel was out of the question, so the best I could do was to park three blocks away. I walked back to the hotel, and dad and I went to the Optimist Club luncheon. The luncheon speaker was rather long-winded. By the time the luncheon was over, and Dad had introduced me to many of his old cronies, it was past 1:15 p.m. I knew I had to hurry. As we were walking down the hotel steps, going to the street, I told Dad that I would go get the car, pick him up on the corner, and take him back to the courthouse. That would save him a brisk walk and hurry things us for me. He agreed that would be fine.

What happened next is what makes this an absent minded professor story. I still can't believe it. I hurried out of the Cornhusker Hotel, ran across 13th Street jogged along M Street for three blocks, jumped in my car, and drove to Nebraska Wesleyan. I was so obsessed with what I had to do when I got back to school that I forgot all about my father. I managed to meet my class on time, counseled a few students, went to a committee meeting, prepared for the next day, and went home at about 5:00 p.m. Never once did I think about the noon luncheon or my father.

When I got home I relaxed, read the Lincoln Journal, helped get the evening meal, and sat down to eat. During the meal my wife, Ruth, and I made small talk but neither of us reviewed the day's happenings. Following supper, Ruth and I did the dishes. She washed and I dried. As I wiped the water off a saucepan, it suddenly dawned on me I forgot to pick up dad. I exclaimed, "Oh my God, I left my dad standing on the corner at the Cornhusker Hotel." After a moment of amazement, Ruth said, "You had better call your father." I said, "No siree, you don't know my dad. We had better go over to his house and see him" and that's what we did.

Ruth and I drove to Dad's house at about 6:30 p.m. The day was still quite warm, a nice, quiet, fall evening. My father was sitting in a wooden swing on the front porch of the house as we approached. Dad saw us coming, and before I could say anything, he began to sing the popular song of the day, "Standing on the Corner Watching All the Girls Go By." That broke the ice. Thank goodness. After my profuse apology for leaving Dad standing on the corner, we all had a good laugh. Dad didn't seem to be any the worse for wear. We learned that a friend of Dad's drove him back to the courthouse after Dad had waited about 30 minutes. What a relief.

As the saying goes, "All's well that ends well."

The ATO House and Other Assorted Vignettes

By Jack Hoyt

All young people should be so lucky as to be exposed to an acerbic fraternity experience, a coffee group and a Lion's Club that "suffered no fools." Hans Jack Thorne, the Hasting Mayor, when he was running for Congress, visited our group at the Cornhusker and told me later, after I got to know him, that it was his most caustic experience on the campaign trail. Needless to say, many of the Lion's Club speakers and guests fared no better.

My good friend, Kenny Younger rode off into the sunset with the Younger Gang and I miss him a lot. Evell Younger, ATO and Nebraska Law School Graduate was LA County Attorney and California Attorney General, has also died, as did Federal Judge "Hungarian" Fred Metheny, five battle field medals. I lived with Ken just after his divorce when I came out to LA. Kenny said, "my kids have more money than God." He had a splendid home, pool and view in the Hollywood hills where steaks, Dungeness crabs, giant avocados and Chivas Regal were the order of the day. If you remember him, he was no nonsense, so when he asked, I knew it wasn't pity. Irsfelt, Irsfelt & Younger was the largest firm in the Hollywood area, no movie people; mainly contractors, road builders, developers, corporations, banks, insurance companies, etc. We had many long lunches through out the years. On trips, Magda was always amazed at his libation capacity. I used to tell him that his old age would be content, since I made him a reservation at the "Old Swedes Home," in Axtell, Nebraska, where the old ladies are especially svelte and erotic.

Sometimes, Bobby "Mike" Hunt, who lived in Pasadena, but was with St. Paul Fire Insurance Company in the Wilshire district, would join us and sometimes Big Bob McNutt, then a law professor at Cal State, Northridge. When you walked into a bar with Kenny and Bob, people did a double take. I used to have lunch with Bob at his fancy Faculty Club. The no campus liquor rule was unheard of in there. He retired and moved some time back.

Christmas—Cocktails at 9am—Robt McNutt—Lincoln Room—Cornhusker Hotel. I think you put that on the bulletin board. I used to see Neuman Buckley CPA and Lawyer in the Bay Area. He told me Charley Toogood was one of the founders of Taco Bell, and that Jack Heckinlively came to him to help set up two of their restaurants. The ole Nebraska Phi Delta connection? However in California, you lose track of people, unless you office or live in the same area. Magda asks me, "How do you remember all of those Nebraska things when you can't remember my only son's birthday?"

Regardless, as super clever Gary Owens, local D.J. and former Omaha D.J. used to say, "I have been insegrevious too long." On a personal note, I have beget at least three daughters, eight grandchildren, and three great-grand-children. They all live near their great mother who lives in Littleton, CO, except Christi's eldest (with three children), who live in Stillwater, OK, where her husband is an Assistant Instructor of Chemistry, working on his Doctor's Degree at Oklahoma State, he is one of the few people in our family who really understands me, of course, we have never met!

One thing that I meant to include in the letter to Norrie, during the dissertation about Notre Dame, was to mention that Nebraska stunned the country (vaulted the Cornhuskers into national fame) when their 1915 undefeated team upset D.D. 20–19! Lum Doyle was on that team, as was ATO Guy Reed who became President of Harris Trust, Chicago and worked for Harvey Rathbone first as a real estate salesman, and Harold Cory, who became President of Hormel Meat Packing.

The recent death of Wilt Chamberlain: In 1958 or 59, I got caught in a very bad snow storm near Sioux City. I stayed at the only downtown hotel. Old but comfy, I checked in and was going downstairs to eat. The small elevator stopped at my floor, the door opened and whoa! ... here was an enclosure that was full-up with giants. I froze, then came a booming laugh and a voice saying, "get aboard partner, plenty of room." It was Wilt and players from the Harlem Globe Trotters, in town for a game. You ain't lived until you've been in a 6'×6' space with five towering Globe Trotters.

I leave you with my recollections of a unique and unforgettable character: Jack Cawood, who was to me, wittier than John Carson (as were some of our other peers) and who saw the world in terms that would make even George

Carlin scratch his head … who, in 1945, as the first to call his raincoat the "Mitch," … when I asked him why he didn't take to two sport, All State and highest scoring in the test for West Point (in Kansas city history), Mac Robinson, who became treasure of Shell Oil, he replied, "He lies like a Hoover, he sucks up other people's personality." Every time Mac would walk by, Cawood would make a sucking sound … who took the last of his money had Geo Ayers build him a pin-striped double breasted gray suit with space for a heater and with no money, hitchhiked to the Omaha Aksarben Races where he just stood around and looked menacing like Bogart … who would wake me up and say, "Let's Drum out," we would walk in below zero temps to get an ice cream Drum Stick at the 'steel-built all-night diner' at 13th and Q … who would, as Bob Wholers was sleeping, put newspapers in a waste basket, steal his artificial leg, light the paper and yell fire, laughing as Wohlers was hopping frantically to the basket … who was told by "Square Root" Palmer that unless he passed the statistics final he would flunk and probably be kicked out of school. As he walked into the ATO House several people came running up to him yelling excitely: "Jack, we got the final from Judge Thone." He looked through the pages and then calmly handed it back and said, while walking off, "I don't need the questions … what I need are the answers!"

As the great sportscaster Jim Healey used to say, "Hey pally, I don't make them up." Billy Wilder went to the doctor and complained that he could hardly pee anymore. The doctor asked Bill his age. He told him, "80 years old." The doctor replied, "don't worry about it … you've peed enough!"

So, we'll go no more a roving
So late into the night,
Though the heart be still as loving,
And the moon be still as bright.   —*Lord Byron*

California is a great place to live—if you happen to be an orange.
—*Fred Allen*

Northeast High School … 50 Years Ago

By Ray Griffin

It should have been the best of times, and probably was, and yet it was probably the worst of times when looking back over the 50 plus years that have methodically marched past.

Just 18 years old, a mid-year senior in high school, a new school building to help initiate, new friends to meet and make and an entire life spreading before me and many other teen-age niceties. What more could anyone ask?

But in the fall of 1941 things weren't all that rosey. Hitler was headed for Russia after sweeping over Europe and somewhere in Japan a little man was busily planning an air attack on Pearl Harbor, which would throw the United States into conflict with that country also.

Northeast High School, located centrally between three Lincoln suburbs, would bring together arch rivals Havelock, Bethany and Jackson (University

Place) under one roof. There were those skeptics who said it would never work. But work it did.

There remain many fond memories of that first year, although for myself and 23 others we would only have a little over three months to enjoy what some were calling "one of the finest school buildings west of Chicago."

Foremost among those memories are the muddy treks across fields to either the front or back door of the new edifice. Then the continuing battle to remove that sticky Nebraska soil before entering the gleaming hallways. There were times, after a rain or snow, when the halls resembled pig pens.

Northeast, dubbed the "Rockets" by a vote of the student body, took off quickly on the Nebraska prep athletic scene. In the schools first basketball season the team finished second to Lincoln High in the state basketball tournament and suffered only two defeats in nine games—plus a tie—in football.

The football loss, which hurt the most, was to Lincoln in the fourth game of the season. Never had one of the suburban schools challenged the downtown school on the gridiron. And so it was a game, which was awaited with anticipation.

Some 7,500 fans gathered at the Lincoln High stadium that evening and there were probably upwards of 50,000 more who claim to have seen the game. The Rockets led 6–0 at the end of three quarters, but the Links scored 13 points in the fourth quarter to prevail, 13–6.

Coach Cy Yordy (Jackson's contribution to the Northeast staff) took the Rockets to a second place finish in the Mid-East conference, losing to York on a pair of trick plays in the title game, 12–7.

Stand outs on that team included the Knight brothers, John and chick, Rex Mercer, Cliff Squires, Bill Tincher (who died in World War II), Bob Watson, Ed Wilson, Ed Delaney, Bill Laub and Bernie Lehman.

Havelock basketball coach Cliff Bosley put together a cage team, which not only amazed the fans and student body, but had the sportswriters digging up new adjectives.

During the regular season the Rockets split with Lincoln High and then finished second in the regional tourney to earn a berth in the state at the Memorial Coliseum on the University of Nebraska campus.

Led by Squires, Mercer, Laub and Max Long, the Rockets used newcomers Frank Meyer, John Johnston, Keith Sutton and Dick Ward to topple Columbus 25–20 in the first round and sneak by Omaha South 16–15 in the semifinals.

Lincoln and Northeast then met in the championship game and the Links prevailed 35–27 to win the rubber game of the season's three game set.

Although the initial graduating class from the school is listed as 1942 (spring of), it was on January 23, 1942, when we gathered (of all places) at the Lincoln High Auditorium to pick up our diplomas.

The remainder of the Class of '42 had to stick around and sweat out the draft until late May. Personally, I escaped until March of '43 before being called to duty in the Air Force.

But on that January night in '42 we really had little hope of escaping Uncle Sam's clutches.

Cotner Terrace
By Richard Lutz

Cotner Terrace Restaurant, located at 225 North Cotner Boulevard, was opened by Mary Lutz on January 15, 1947.

At the time, Cotner Terrace was one of the largest restaurants in Nebraska, seating over 1,000 people. Diners were treated to fantastic food and a variety of nightly entertainment. Johnny Carson was a regular performer with his magic and ventriloquist act.

Celebrities and dignitaries from around the world were served Mrs. Lutz's famous chicken pies, prime rib dinners $1.85 and steak dinners $2.25. In addition to the in-house service, Cotner Terrace was the industry leader in home delivery of complete meals. As a result of her culinary skills and community involvement, Mary Lutz was recognized as America's Outstanding Restaurateur in 1956.

Cotner Terrace closed its doors in 1962, but for those fortunate enough to dine there, the memories of Nebraska's finest dining establishment remain.

Community Chest/Lincoln Foundation
By Don Frey

I can think of a lot of stories about old friends in Lincoln, most of which are probably not printable. For example, who had a hotel room rented full time in order to have a place to meet his girlfriend? I remember so many of the "old timers," eg. Jim Stuart, Albert Held at the bank, Harry and Bob Simon, Nate and Bill Gold, Jim Ackerman, Tom Davies, Louie Finkelstein, etc. etc. When Jim Stuart used to go to out of town conferences with us, he'd pack his clothes in his Army V-6 bag that had Capt. James Stuart stenciled on it.

Louie Horne was the first Community Chest executive from the 1920s until around 1955 when he retired. Louie moved to Columbus, but came back a lot to help build the Lincoln Foundation Building at 15th and N Street. He officed with us and I helped him on that project and others. He used to come into the office and say, "I haven't had an argument in a week." Then he'd pull out his address book, pick a name, get on the phone, and in a few minutes he was in the middle of a big argument. In about 1958 Louie and I went to Chicago to meet with Frank Woods to try to get a challenge grant from him to build the Lincoln Foundation Building. We came back with the grant. Later, after I moved from Lincoln, I got a package from Frank which contained a complete set of blueprints for the Lincoln Foundation Building along with a nice letter from him saying he wanted me to see the results of our meeting in Chicago. He was a nice man. The building was dedicated in 1964.

I also recall the terrifying days when Charles Starkweather was on his rampage. He was our garbage man. In Lincoln at that time, garbage men came into your basement and carried out the garbage, so he had been in our house dozens of times. He killed one of our board members, his wife and maid, about two blocks from our house. Police thought that he was still hiding in the neighborhood, so all the men went home from work. I loaned out my spare guns and we started searching all the garages in our blocks. They called out the "Sheriff's Posse," a sort of honorary group for parades, and were going to do a house-to-house search. Scared the heck out of me since I just knew someone would get trigger-happy, shoot at a cat or something and WWIII would start. Luckily, they found out that Starkweather had left town so the search was called off.

Automatic Pilot

By Bob Askey

I was born in Lincoln, established a career in Lincoln broadcasting, and later moved to Longmont, Colorado in 1966. When Johnny Carson quit his KFOR job in October 1951 to go to the big time at WOW Omaha, where he later got his first taste of television, I was offered Johnny's nighttime radio position. I had been at KOLN (now KLIN) since the summer on 1949, writing commercials and doing some work as a disk jockey (a term coined by the newspaper columnist Walter Winchell).

My radio evening shift had the most listeners, because very few Lincoln homes had TV sets. Television had just begun in the area, with Omaha's KMTV Channel 3 and WOW-TV Channel 6 beginning their broadcasts in 1949. To receive television an elaborate outside antenna, which few Lincolnites bought, so my radio career at KFOR blossomed.

KFOR was an ABC affiliate, and carried great half-hour and full-hour programs from 6:30 to 10:00 p.m., including "The FBI in Peace and War," "Mr. District Attorney," "The Adventures of Ozzie and Harriet," "America's Town Meeting of the Air," "The Greatest Story Ever Told," and, of course, "The Lone Ranger."

> *With his faithful Indian companion Tonto, the daring and resourceful masked rider of the plains led the fight for law and order, in the early western United States. Return with us now to those thrilling days of yesteryear. From out of the past come the thundering hoofbeats of the great horse Silver! The Lone Ranger rides again!*

While all this was going on, I was preparing the 10 p.m. newscast, the climax of the evening programming. People tuned in for the Lincoln news, weather and sports at the conclusion of the dramatic shows. Radio, not TV dominated the Lincoln evening activities.

At that time KFOR was a dual operation station—me as the announcer and a rotating-shift technician as the engineer—rather than a combination station, where one man did everything. So while the dramatic programs were in progress, about 7:05 p.m. I would leave the engineer in charge, and slip out of the KFOR studios, on the 6th floor of the Stuart Building at 13th and P Street, and head to the Tastee Inn on the northwest corner of 13th and Q Street. There I would buy loose-meat burgers for the engineer and me.

Summertime evenings, the inside doors of the Tastee Inn were open (no air conditioning) and I simply opened the fly-covered screen door to get into the little shop. Some people said the flies were on the inside of the screen door, pleading to get out.

Winters, I would hustle down there through cold and snow to have them double-bag the sandwiches to keep them warm. Then I'd buy a couple of glass bottles of Coca-Cola.

Let me explain: in 1951 there were no employee lounges, no microwaves, no refrigerators. Workers brown-bagged PB&J sandwiches with a thermos of coffee, and that was it, so much for employee amenities.

When I returned to the studio at 7:25 p.m., just in time for the 7:30 p.m. station break, the daring and resourceful engineer would then put the hot sandwiches in the equipment rack above the dozens of vacuum tubes that ran the broadcast. This would keep them hot. Then the engineer would take a piece of heavy twine and tie one end around the neck of each Coke bottle and secure the other end around the window handle inside. The Coke bottles would hang a few feet below the windowsill on the west side of the Stuart Building. The freezing winter would keep the drinks cold.

After I had finished voicing the big newscast, at 10:30 p.m., the engineer and I would sit and relax, enjoying our late supper as he segued records so that I could rest my vocal cords. The sandwiches were hot, the drinks were cold, and all was right with the world.

I don't know if station owner Jim Stuart ever realized that for a quarter hour or so, between 7:00 p.m. and 7:30 p.m. each evening, his radio station KFOR was on automatic pilot.

The Lincoln Depot in Its Heyday

By Nina Bryan Rohlfs

Life revolved around the trains in my early childhood. I was a railroad kid—my father worked for the CB&Q (later Burlington Routes, still later Burlington Northern) as a dragline operator in those days, making railroad bridges. We lived on a train, in an orange bunker, and traveled all over the Midwest. But no adventure in our travels could match that of the Lincoln Depot.

On its tracks, in the glory days of the train (notably the late 1940s), one could see all manner of rail transport, from black steam locomotives, billowing smoke as they pulled into the station with a shrill whistle announcing their arrivals, to the sleek, silver, glass-domed Denver Zephyr, with throbbing power sounds emanating from its diesel portholes, and a distinctive sound blasting from its matching sets of massive silver horns.

The brick boarding area between the tracks and the depot yielded a scene unlike any other—glad hugging reunions for disembarking passengers, tearful goodbyes for those embarking via little silver steps manned by uniformed conductors who intoned over and over again, "Watch your step, Miss." Trying to maneuver in the midst of these crowds were those in charge of the large wagons carrying mail sacks, luggage, and other cargo—"Coming through, please," they called.

Inside the magnificent Lincoln Depot's cavernous marble walls, there were constant crowds and much movement. People waited in line at the wrought iron fronts of the ticket counters that lined one wall. The eye-catching ceiling was of an architectural style that made distinguished-looking men look up and nod in approval, and the huge chandeliers complemented it perfectly. In the corner was an interesting, artdeco marble water fountain that was a major attraction for children.

The floor area of the depot was enhanced by row after row of massive, contoured oak benches that were often filled to capacity. In one corner, a large ladies lounge with sturdy leather couches and rocking chairs were inhabited by mothers and their babies. The ladies restroom was at one end of this lounge. It cost a dime to operate the mechanism that opened all the stall doors, and an attendant handed out towels, etc. for a nickel or dime tip.

A reminder of earlier transportation stood along another wall, with velvet ropes to deep curious would be climbers at bay—a perfectly preserved, yellow painted, Overland Freight stagecoach. Throughout the entirety of this cavernous depot were marvelous echoes of loud voices and clicking footsteps bouncing off the marble floors and walls. No echoes were finer, or done with more style, than those that came from the speaker system activated by the conductor, in the hallway. Each conductor had his signature rhythm and voice inflection when announcing arrivals, departures, and the stops made by each train. Their theatrical sing-song hinted at faraway magic lands I wanted to visit in the worst way!

On the other side of this hallway was the restaurant, open 24 hours a day. There were oak tables and chairs as well as a marble counter with stools and steaming chrome urns of coffee. Neon signs beckoned travelers to have a snack while they waited for their trains. Near the boarding gates and the restaurant was the newsstand, full of newspapers, magazines, cigars and chewing gum. They did a brisk business, too.

Roving between the track area and the front doors of the depot were a mass of travelers, followed by "Red Caps," the men who toted their luggage outside to their waiting taxis. Surveying the whole scene were always one or two "special agents," the railroad security men. They answered questions, escorted drunks outside, and calmed lost children, among their other duties.

What can today compare to such an impressive scene? A busy airport might come close, but even it could never measure up to the wonders of the Lincoln Depot I once knew, during the splendid years. I'm so grateful that this historic structure is yet today maintained and appreciated. I still like to visit the old depot, and in a reverie, dream of all the wondrous sights and sounds those mammoth and majestic walls once knew. Those bygone days, and awesome Lincoln Depot, are etched in my memory as rare treasures.

Bob Martens' Coffee Club

By Van C. Duling

One of Lincoln's premier coffee clubs was founded in 1970 by Bob Martens.

For no particular reason, save his dynamic leadership, Bob was appointed the Unofficial Chairman. To this day the lofty title remains firmly in place. He is certainly the driving force of what has evolved into a daily (except Sunday) meeting of some of Lincoln's finest. Fellowship and frivolity abound.

The first meeting place—1970 was Scott's Pancake Shop at 13th and L.

After the closing of Scott's the group moved to Soups On at 14th and M ... thence to Dennys at 9th and R. Saturday mornings found the group meeting Kay's in the Piedmont Shopping Center.

The last and present-day meeting place has been The Pantry at 48th and Van Dorn. The daily average attendance is about 12 members.

The highlight of the year is the Annual Christmas Party which has been held in various members homes as well as the Country Club of Lincoln. The highlight (or lowlight) is the Coffee Club Jazz Group featuring the likes of deceased member Russ Gibson, Jerry Solomon, Tom Allman, Mac McCune and Van Duling. Christmas carols are always abundant plus outstanding culinary delights proferred by Mary Martens, club poster girl.

Bob Martens' Coffee Club's Christmas Party is shown December 17, 1994.

The Last Trolley Ride

By Marylouise Bookstrom

As a reporter for the Lincoln Star, I was assigned to cover the story of the last streetcar ride in Lincoln. It was soon after WWII ended and the city was using buses instead of the street railway, but the trolley still ran to College View.

I boarded the car along with a group of city VIP's in down town Lincoln. It was my first and last ride on a streetcar as it swayed and clacked it's way down A Street, then finally to Sheridan Boulevard where a youngster was excused from class at Irving to pull the trolley from the wire which of course stopped the car until the motorman reattached it as he had done countless times.

It marked the passing of an era in public transportation in Lincoln but maybe we will see the rebirth of electric and rail transportation as we enter a new era.

It Was Fun To Be Young

By Keith Heckman

I grew up in the University Place area during the 1950s. My fondest memories are the experiences and people of that time. We lived near the corner of 48th and Orchard Street. We were about the last house on the street. To the east our playgrounds were cornfields and open lots and Dead Man's Run. A little farther east was the community of Bethany but that was too far for our young travels, 56th Street was the limit.

When I was about five years of age the decision was made to pave our street. What a grand time we had watching the crews and machinery. The work was done in July. Mother would make up several pitchers of lemonade every afternoon and let me take them out to the workers. The men became friends during the project and later I felt a real sense of ownership in having helped with the paving project. It also greatly improved the sledding the following winter.

During the summer months our neighbor, whose property faced 48th Street would rent a part of his lot to an old German immigrant who would sell watermelons. Mr. Kliner would pull his small trailer up from central Kansas and park it on the neighboring lot. About once a week Mr. Kliner's son would drive a big truck full of melons up from Kansas to restock the stand. I would spend the hot afternoons sitting and talking with this fascinating man. His stories about his German heritage were always a treat. As his assistant I got to load the watermelons into the customers cars. During his Lincoln stay, my mother would keep Mr. Kliner well supplied with fresh baked goods, probably as payment for keeping me occupied all day. It was always a sad day for me when the last melon was sold and the trailer went back to Kansas. Later in the year (December) a new trailer would show up on the neighboring lot. This time we had four weeks of Christmas trees. After school and weekends I would spend hours in the little trailer huddled around the gas heater talking to the lady that sold the trees. I would load the trees into trucks and cars for the ride to their new homes. At the end of the week I would get 10¢ for every tree I loaded. A fortune to an eight-year-old boy at that time.

During the rest of the winter months my time was spent scooping for the neighbors. Hard work but often softened by big cups of hot chocolate.

When the weather warmed, my attention turned to the local Dairy Queen store. This was run by a retired couple who would spend their winters in Arizona. Several mornings a week I would harvest a bouquet of flowers from my mother's garden and present them to the proprietors of the drive in. I was always rewarded with a Green River, a wonderful mixture of lime soda and lime syrup. Later I would pick up the litter from the parking lot and wash the windows. The rest of the morning was spent at the UNI Place pool.

This was a great time to be young. There was always something to do. We didn't need money to entertain ourselves. Good thing. We didn't have any. We could explore our neighborhood with no fear. Everyone we met was our friend. Neighbors watched out for us. Their doors were always open to us.

Sounds different from 2001, doesn't it? If we could only return to our memories ...

The Pickup Ride

By George Howard

In the fall of 1999 the annual meeting of the University Foundation was held at the SAC Museum. I asked Daisy and Gates Minnick to ride with me. When we arrived at the entrance a light on the dash cam on indicating "Hot Engine." I parked in the lot thinking the car would cool off while we were at the meeting but when I started the car, the warning light came on immediately. I picked up Daisy and Gates and we looked in the owners manual. It said you could drive 50 miles with the light on. I thought there might be a full service station open in Ashland but only convenience stores were still open. We decided to drive back to the Greenwood interchange on I-80 where there is a large truck stop at the Conoco Station.

When we arrived we checked under the car and there was a pool and still dripping. I went inside and asked the man at the cash register if there was a mechanic on duty and he said no. A man standing nearby said he knew a little about cars. He followed me outside and checked underneath, then went to his pickup for more coolant. He put it in the coolant tank and immediately it came down on the pavement. He said we had a broken water pump. Daisy, Gates and I started talking about what we were going to do. Since it was getting late, after 11 o'clock, they hesitated to call their son Mike to come and pick us up. The fellow with the pickup asked us where we wanted to go. We told him we lived in Lincoln so he then offered to take us. But first he had to take his brother home. The Minnicks wondered if he was going for help to rob us, but after a while, he returned and we started to get into his ? ton pickup.

Daisy had trouble getting into the cab so Gates pushed her on the fanny with both hands. She finally made it and moved to the center of the cab next to the driver who was 6'4" and about 240. Then Gates got in and told me to come in and sit on his lap. I put one foot over his leg and knew right away there wasn't enough room for all of us in there. I told them that they used to have rooms for truckers in the station and I would try to get a room. Gates said no and that he would sit in the back of the pickup on a toolbox. With those three in the cab I doubt whether they would have been able to close the door anyway.

Gates got in back I got in the cab sitting on one cheek and away we went. Cars passing us on I-80 flashed their bright lights when they saw someone in the back of the pickup. When they saw a man in his "funeral suit" and white shirt with his tie flapping in the breeze, they wondered what was going on. Some of them had attended the same meeting and recognized Gates I am sure and especially wondered. It was cool back there too.

Meanwhile, back in the cab, Daisy and I were listening to the driver. His name was Landers, like Ann Landers, and he was working on a project on Saltillo Road driving a dump truck. He was from Cairo, Nebraska, northwest of Grand Island. He had heard of the Butlers, Lee Tyners parents, who used to have a dairy there.

Next, as usual, was the family history. I don't remember whether his first name was Lennie or his son's. Anyway his son was a sophomore in high school and played tackle on the football team. Already he was 6'5" and weighed around 275. Daisy and I wondered about his story that coaches and recruiters were already interested in him. Later I checked with a couple of them and they said they look at a few sophomores if they think the player has lots of potential. I didn't read anything about him last fall when he would have been a junior.

Finally we arrived at Bishop Square. Since there were no lights on any of the units he asked if it was an old folks home. We told him yes it was mostly but not organized that way as such. When we got to the Minnick's unit he came around and helped Daisy and me out of the cab. Since I felt responsible that my car caused this whole mess, I thanked him for the ride and gave him a hundred-dollar bill. He went around to the other side and helped Gates out of the back. Gates thanked him and gave him a fifty. Neither Gates nor I knew what the other had done, but the driver didn't say anything about it. When Gates and I compared notes, we could have had a cab come and pick us up and the bill might have been cheaper.

'The Most Unforgettable . . . '

By Bill Swanson

In my almost 60 years as a resident of Lincoln, these old eyes have been cast upon some amazing situations and characters but none more unforgettable than a young man named Axel Johnson.

Axel, a farm boy from northeastern Nebraska, lost both of his legs in a farm accident when he was three years old. Such a loss would have devastated most of us, but not the plucky Mr. Johnson. Although he walked slowly and sometimes painfully on his two artificial supports, he moved easily in every social situation and was an avid sports fan. To my knowledge, Axel never attended the University, but he was a very well known "man about campus." Following World War II Charley Thone, later known as the Hon. G. Charles Thone, and I shared a rental house at 3401 Otoe Street in Lincoln. Our home was a cheerful gathering place for many young Lincolnites and returning veterans.

One summer, Mr. Thone and I took a short vacation to Estes Park in Colorado. While there, Charley said, "We've got to go over Trail Ridge to Grand Lake to see a friend of mine." We made the drive without mishap and went to the Pine Cone Inn, a Grand Lake drinking establishment frequented by scores of college kids who spent their summers working in the mountains. It was there I was first introduced to the area's best known bartender Axel Johnson, who treated us well as patrons of his saloon.

I move ahead now to September of that year to a day I returned to our Otoe Street abode to be greeted at the door by Charley who announced, "Axel is here to spend a few days with us." Our mansion was a 2 bedroom, 800 square foot house with a small living/ dining area. Charley used one bedroom and I had the other. I said, "It's fine to have Axel here, but where is he going to sleep?" "Don't worry," said Mr. Thone, "He'll just sleep on the living room sofa." And that's just the way it was. Axel was our house guest until late spring, when he returned to Colorado.

With Charley's friends, my friends, and Axel's friends, our house was a lively spot not totally appreciated by the neighbors who were largely young marrieds with kids, who sometimes were kept from early bedtime by sounds of good cheer emanating from 3401.

One episode from those days bears repeating. In early spring the door bell rang and Axel, who was sleeping on the sofa, dropped to the floor and trundled to the door on his stumps. The postman who had a postage due letter for us, took one look, turned white as a sheet, dropped the letter and took off. Needless to say, all future postage dues were dropped in our mailbox with a note from the postman.

I am happy to report that Axel went on to a successful business career, was married and retired in Florida. Ralph "Axel" Johnson died February 1, 2001.

The Airplane Crash of 1982

By Tom Smith

Tom Ludwick, Jerry Mapes and Tom Smith thought it would be a great idea to invite our beloved Pastor Bob to go on a snowmobiling trip to our cabin on Lake Vermillion in Ely, Minnesota. We decided on a date that wouldn't conflict with Bob's Sunday sermon. Bob agreed it would be fun and a new experience for him and an opportunity to better understand the personalities of the three parishioners who had invited him. The date was set, February 18th–21st, Wednesday through Saturday.

Tom Ludwick, being an experienced pilot and airplane owner, offered to fly us to Ely International Airport as he had done so many times successfully in the past.

Our cabin on Lake Vermillion consisted of three separate units, a lodge and two smaller cabins owned by the three of us and Larry Blevins, Ted Maude and Bob Sherwood. Many fun vacations had been spent on the island, yes this was on an eight acre island in the middle of the lake. Most everyone loved the winter snowmobiling even though it was usually very cold, temperatures would range from –60 degrees to +10 degrees Fahrenheit.

As the four of us prepared for our trip north we made grocery lists and generally were preparing for some cold weather fun. Bob Palmer had offered to bring along some Myers Briggs personality questionnaires he thought would liven up our evening discussions and while Lud, Jerry and Smith were packing some evening libations, which they thought would also liven up the discussions. Fortunately, we owned some snowmobiles so all we needed to do was show up, organize our food and begin our great adventure.

Wednesday came and we left early from Duncan Aviation in Lincoln en route to Ely, Minnesota. It was a three hour plane ride and the weather was cooperative, although cold. Upon our arrival at Ely we proceeded to Tom Ludwick's lake car, a 1967 Buick station wagon that had seen it's better days. We packed our gear, including the many cookies and goodies our wives had sent along, into the car and proceeded to Mud Creek Road where after a nine mile drive we would be at the lake. Our friend, Bob Stockdale, who ran a camp at the lake, had plowed a road out to our island so we could drive over the ice and move our groceries and gear into our little haven for the next three days. We moved in and got comfortable by late afternoon. We began preparing for an early dinner so we could go snowmobiling later the first evening. I recall looking at the thermometer at 5:30 p.m. and it was –12 degrees. We cooked up a big dinner, had a few cocktails and then suited up for snowmobiling. Bob Palmer was a novice, so we all spent some time getting him acquainted with the snowmobile and how to handle it on the lake and in the woods. About 7:30 pm we took off on one of our favorite trails and bounced around the woods for about an hour. We decided to head back across the lake to save some time. Bob was lagging a little behind, when we ran into some lake slush; this stuff could bog you down if you panicked at all. Well, Bob panicked, his machine was hopelessly stuck in the slush about a foot deep. We tried to free it but the slush was running into our boots and the cold was beginning to get to us. We decided to let it freeze in and come back on Thursday and dig it out. It was a good thing we did, as we were totally exhausted and very cold.

On Thursday we were able to dig the frozen snowmobile out of the ice and enjoy a beautiful day on Lake Vermillion snowmobiling. That evening we did the Myers Briggs personality tests and enjoyed analyzing each other under the able tutelage of Dr. Palmer.

Friday was again a day of riding snowmobiles and exploring the forest and trails around Lake Vermillion. That night we cooked up a big dinner and packed our gear and got ready to pack the old Buick and head over to the Ely airport about 9:00am that next morning. It was uneventful as we sat around and laughed about our experiences the last three days and the pleasant thoughts of our journey back to Lincoln on Saturday.

Saturday morning came with clear sky and a temperature of –22 degrees. That would not have been a problem. We cleaned up and put the lodge in good shape for the next visitors and proceeded across the lake in the 1967 Buick, back up Mud Creek Road and over to Ely, Minnesota where we would begin the next segment of this journey.

After arriving at Ely Airport, we unloaded our gear, parked the Buick back in its original snowdrift and began to make arrangements to fly home. Due to the extreme cold that morning people at the airport pulled Ludwick's plane inside the hanger to put some heat on the engines so that we could get it started. That process lasted about 45 minutes, but it gave us time to load the plane and get ready for our trip back to Lincoln.

Dr. Palmer had his sermon for Sunday's church service out and doing some minor revisions when Tom Ludwick said that we were ready to take off. Jerry Mapes and I took our seats behind Tom Ludwick and Bob Palmer in the plane and we taxied out to the runway and headed south for take off. Once we were in the air you could look out and see the forest. A few small lakes were the only openings and clear spots in the forest around Ely. We were at 1200 Ft. and climbing when Tom commented that the oil pressure gauge was not working. He thumped it a couple times to see if the needle was just stuck but nothing happened. At that point I began to smell something "hot" and Ludwick commented that he was leveling the plane off and making a left turn to head back to the airport to see what the problem was. Almost as soon as the left turn was completed all hell broke loose. The airplane warning system went off with a siren like noise and the oil hit the front windshield of the plane blocking any view that Ludwick, our pilot, might have had. At that moment the engine had blown up and there was no longer any engine noise. Fortunately for us Tom did not panic, but said to us he was putting the airplane into a steep dive to keep our air speed up. All of this had happened in about thirty seconds to a minute. I looked out my side window (panic had set in) to see what we were going to hit, the good news was we were headed for a frozen lake. Tom asked to let him know when I thought we were twenty feet from the ground so he could try and level the plane for the crash. Our landing gear was still down from takeoff so I knew we would have a big jolt when we hit.

During this minute or so that had gone by, Jerry had put on his coonskin hat over his face for fear it might be hit. The cookies we had left were in flight and for the most part there wasn't much talking going on.

We were braced for the crash and at the precise moment Tom pulled the nose of the plane up and we hit on one wing and did a 360 degree spin before coming to a stop. We were in a hurry to get out of the plane for fear of a fire or explosion, but the main thing was nobody seemed hurt as we opened the doors of the plane. I was the first person out and Bob Palmer was next. We were each next to the doors. I got thirty yards away from the plane pretty quickly.

Soon we were all out an away far enough not to get hurt if a fire occurred. About then Bob exclaimed he had left his sermon in the plane and Jerry said he was very cold. A few minutes had passed and it was apparent that the worst was over. Bob went over to the plane and got his sermon while Tom and I took pictures. Jerry quietly went over to the plane and put on some fresh long johns. Five minutes later snowmobiles from the airport arrived, they had seen the planes engine blow up, they whisked us back to the airport to make arrangements for getting the insurance people to the plane and getting the four of us back to Lincoln.

We ended up driving the 1967 Buick to Minneapolis and flying commercial from Minneapolis to Omaha were Bill Cintani picked us up and drove us to Lincoln. We got home at 10:00 pm Saturday night.

Bob Palmer abandoned his prepared sermon and told the congregation of Sunday morning about our amazing grace. After it was said and done we were very lucky to be alive and in church that Sunday morning in 1982.

Airline Trails

By Bill Carley

United Airlines resumed air service to Lincoln after World War II, on August 1, 1946. This is where I began my post war travel career, as an employee with United at the Lincoln Municipal Airport.

The building used for a terminal in those days had previously been a non-com officers club on the airbase relocated to an area between two hangars on the west side of a large tarmac (called a parking ramp in those days). In front of the terminal were a few light poles used to illuminate the ramp area for night operations. Paralleling the airport property, a half-mile or so away on the east side of the airport, was the Burlington Railroad tracks.

Night Train Greeting

A friend of mine, Dave Baker, was an engineer for the Burlington and had the early morning run to Columbus about daylight. As the train chugged by, I would blink the ramp light and he would give a couple of short blasts on the whistle, or visa versa, as we acknowledged greetings.

Lucy and I were having dinner one evening with Dave and his wife Evelyn when Dave, a storyteller and sometimes practical joker, said "I've got a new fireman riding with me tomorrow. I'm going to tell him about this phenomenon, that when I give two short toots on the whistle the ramp lights in front of the terminal building come on for a short time. I'll bet him a buck if he will take me up on it. Watch for this." The next morning he did his routine three times and I turned the lights on each time for three seconds. Dave called after he returned from his run and said it worked perfectly and he made a buck. I told Dave the agent working with me the next morning did not know how we greeted each others and let's reverse the procedure—lights on three times and each time respond by blowing the train whistle. I wagered a 5¢ bottle of pop (station agents didn't make much money). It went off on schedule, as Dave tooted back each of the three times. I'm sure the agent went to his grave still amazed at how that miracle came about.

The Goober Gobble

There was no control tower at the Lincoln airport the first few months of operation in 1946 after reopening for commercial air service. The United Airlines staff handled communication to the incoming flights through the company radio and provided wind direction and altimeter setting. The flight would call in for this information when about ten minutes from the airport.

We frequently carried our lunch in those days and on one occasion I forgot to bring mine. I called Ralph Anderson at his home and asked him to throw a sandwich together and I would have the mail messenger pick it up and bring it to me at the terminal building. Andy forgot about it until the mail messenger knocked on his door. Andy quickly grabbed two slices of bread, applied an over generous amount of peanut butter, threw it in a sack and sent it with the messenger. I sat down at the radio desk to eat about the time the flight was due to check in. Took a big bite of the loaded peanut butter sandwich just as Flight 24 called in for landing information. I opened my mouth to respond and that gobby peanut butter stuck to the roof of my mouth. All that came out was a noise that must have sounded like a message from outer Slovakia. The captain responded with "Lincoln, Lincoln, repeat that transmission. You came in extremely garbled." Little did he know how garbled it really was!

Snow Job

The winter weather of 1949 was quite severe—lots of snow about January 1st. A big storm hit the area from Denver through Chicago with blizzard conditions, but Lincoln was somewhat spared with less snow and wind. This enabled flights to operate from the Lincoln Airport though Omaha, Denver and Chicago were closed.

One westbound flight destined for Los Angeles landed at Lincoln and was to be held for improved enroute weather west. One overly anxious passenger said he couldn't wait for improvement and had us arrange a rail routing to Los Angeles. We put him on the 9:00 p.m. Burlington to Omaha and there he took a berth in the "set out" Pullman car for the Union Pacific City of Los Angeles, which was due out of Omaha about 1:30 a.m.

About noon the next day, the man showed up at the Lincoln Airport ticket counter again. We naturally asked what went wrong. He replied, "I got to Omaha on schedule last night, had a big drink, went to bed in the "set out" car, had one of the best nights sleep I have ever had on a train with no sudden stops, no click of the rails. About 8:00 a.m., I raised the blind expecting to see the wide-open country of Wyoming. Instead, it was the wall of the railroad station. So I called the porter, who advised that all roads west were also closed by the blizzard and didn't know when the train would leave. So I hopped on another Burlington train and here I am." His original flight was cleared for departure shortly after that and he was on his way to Los Angeles!

Beutel To The Rescue

By Dale Tintsman

In World War II, lawyers were good "Front Line Fodder."

The University of Nebraska 1940 Law College starting class of '40 was the last to graduate before the Law College was closed. There were only a few that were able to stay until May of 1943 to complete the three year course.

As a result of calling ROTC 2nd Lts. to active duty, the draft and enlistments the 1940 class was decimated thus the Law College was closed in May of 1943.

Sometime in the spring or summer of 1945, Chancellor Gustafuson started preparing to reopen the Law College. Dean Harry "Pappy" Foster had retired and the remainder of the old faculty had departed. Dean Fred Beutel was chosen and in a few short months, he was able to put together a totally new faculty.

When we all started to return, Dean Beutel found that some had one semester remaining and others fell between that and having two years in order to graduate. The faculty did an amazing job of arranging schedules to accommodate all. The college reopened January 6, 1946, and continued continuous classes until all that were capable had graduated.

It is an interesting story as to what can be done if the desire is present.

'Buy You A Beer Buddy?'
The Lodge

By George E. Easley

After prohibition, the city of Lincoln permitted only beer to be sold in taverns located in the "beat area" of downtown and Havelock. This was the area where the Lincoln police routinely walked door to door checking out the local businesses.

Both on-sale taverns and off-sale liquor stores were in the downtown area. Liquor and wine were only allowed to be consumed in "bottle clubs" from 1932 to 1967. So, beer was the spirit of choice, and The Lodge was the number one tavern in beer sales for the better part of four decades from 1932 to 1967.

George Easley converted an old livery stable and blacksmith shop on 22nd and O Streets into The Lodge. The Lodge is still operating today at its original location and with very few interior changes.

The Lodge opened at 6:00 a.m. six days a week and was packed with railroaders and blue-collar workers throughout the day. Two other taverns in Havelock vied for number two and three in beer sales—Bob's and Arnold's Tavern.

The dominant beer was Storz beer and number two was Falstaff, both breweries in Omaha. Storz had 30–40% market share and Falstaff 15–25%. Other regional brands like Hamms, Goetz, and Pabst were very popular until the national brands of Budweiser and Miller took over in the 1970s.

In the late 1960s, Lincoln opened up both on and off-sale licenses. The city had restricted the number of liquor licenses since prohibition, so there was a premium on all the existing licenses. Also, the city permitted liquor establishments to move or open new establishments throughout the city. And last, the city allowed liquor by the drink at all on-sale licenses.

When a "beer war" started in the early 1960s, The Lodge dropped its prices near cost. From 1961 to 1963, The Lodge was in the top 10 of beer sales in the United States. With the major changes in the late 1960s, the glory days of The Lodge reigning as number one in beer sales began to falter.

George Easley died in 1950, and the Easley family sold The Lodge in 1977—when son, Robert Easley and grandson George Easley, got the Coors beer distributorship. The Easley family had the longest continually held retail license in Lincoln—45 years.

The Knolls

By John Boosalis

Prior to his retiring in 1980, John Boosalis was involved in the development of The Knolls Restaurant and Country Club in south Lincoln. Following are some of his recollections:

Marv Shaffer, former State Engineer, first opened the Knolls Golf and Restaurant in the early '60s. Although physically vastly different from the facility seen today, the original business included 9 holes of golf, a maintenance shop, clubhouse and restaurant. Shaffer also had living quarters in the restaurant building and showers for golfers, all space which was later converted to party rooms.

In 1966 Bud Feerhusen and Dick Knight agreed to purchase The Knolls. I was brought in as a partner because of my restaurant background.

Dick Knight wanted to get back in the family store business. So Feerhusen and I purchased his share. At that time, Rine Rebensdorf, who had just retired as chef at The Cornhusker Hotel, came in as a third partner. After a few months, Rine decided to sell his shares as he did not believe the facility could succeed, since it was located so far away from Lincoln (considered outside of city limits in those days). After Rebensdorf left, I sold my other restaurant, The Colonial Inn, formerly located on Cornhusker Highway.

Because capital was needed, Jorgie Jorgenson and George Albin then bought into The Knolls as partners. At this time, a swimming pool and two tennis courts were installed. In the later sixties we had come to an agreement to sell The Knolls to Jim Francke, who operated the Esquire Club, however the deal did not finalize.

With a limited seating capacity of approximately 40 people in the small restaurant (now the area used as the lounge), as well as costly resurfacing needed to improve the crushed stone parking lot, Feerhusen, Jorgenson, and Albin all wanted to divest themselves of their interest in the business. It was at this time my wife Catherine and I decided to buy out the other partners and proceed with the upgrading of the facilities.

We added a new dining room, which dramatically increased the total seating capacity, and enlarged both the kitchen and front entrance. We also decided to purchase additional land from Marv Shaffer to add the west nine holes, and added a second lap pool for swimming as well as a third tennis court.

As I reflect back on the early years of The Knolls, it's remarkable to think there were no homes yet in Southwood. One could literally see Highway 2 from the restaurant, and my sons used to hunt pheasants in the fields where the second nine holes currently stand. It's also amazing to note that the wells on the golf course used to supply enough water to the few homes originally built around The Knolls golf course.

Part of the secret of The Knolls as been the dedication to changing with the times. Even since my retirement, another party room overlooking the golf course has been added, the pro shop has been enlarged and the maintenance shop facilities have doubled in size. My son, George Boosalis and his wife Janice who now own and operate the business, have followed the tradition of continually upgrading the facility. It's what has made The Knolls a gem of south Lincoln for over 35 years.

The 1948 Primary

By Mary Louise Bookstrom

During the Nebraska All Star Primary election of every Republican who ever thought about running was entered and many including Dewey campaigned throughout the state. I rode on Harold Stassen's campaign but for two days hitting every town we could in eastern Nebraska. As I recall Stassen won here but Dewey was nominated. Truman won but the press's infamous headline, gave the victory to Dewey until all the votes were counted.

I believe this primary story won a Pulitzer Prize for the Lincoln *Journal Star* and its editor Ray McConnell.

The Great Colorado Debacle

By Stan Portsche

The President
The Stanley Hotel & Conference Center
Estes Park, Colorado 80517

Dear Sir:

This is to advise you that we are contemplating legal action against your company springing from egregious, illegal and unconstitutional discrimination by your representatives. The stated action is based upon the following facts: basis for our suit follows.

In February 1946, three young men returned home to Lincoln, Nebraska, after serving in World War II. They were glad to be alive and had great plans for the future, now that the world was again a safe place to live. They arrived home too late to enter the University of Nebraska that spring and they knew the GI Bill would not start until fall of 1946, so in the mean time they had to find some way to make money.

Someone suggested they go to The Stanley Hotel in Estes Park and seek seasonal employment. Because jobs were tight in Lincoln they pooled their meager resources and decided to give it a try. In late April 1946, they bought a 1930 Studebaker President, six cylinder, for $100.00; they did a little fixing up and searched several junk yards for extra tires as tires were scarce so soon after the war. Preparations were completed by the end of April, so one early morning in May they kissed their girlfriends goodbye and set out for the magnificent Stanley Hotel.

The first fifty miles were uneventful. Then without notice the "old Pres" chugged to a stop and refused to budge. After much lamentation and wringing of hands, it was discovered that the distributor rod had slipped out of its slot in the camshaft. In order to get the Pres to run again it was first necessary to remove the distributor, then remove the front spark plug, run a coat hanger in the hole and turn the crank until the piston reached the high point in the stroke. The distributor and spark plug were reinserted, and the "Pres" was given a little pat on the rear fender and they went happily off again. This was to happen several times before the trip was over, and they got quite proficient with the procedure.

Their joy was short-lived. About twenty five miles further down the road they had their first flat tire. That was all right since they had two spares, but it took them an our to change the tire because they had never changed a wheel that had "spring rims."

A couple of hours later they were on the road again and were naïve enough to think they were doing all right because they still had one spare tire. Speeding along highway 6, at the enormous speed of 45 miles per hour (they had been told going any faster would blow the engine), spirits were high, and they made 100 miles in just under 4½ hours. Their elation was fleeting. The second tire blew out. They still had a spare, but this meant there were only the four tires on the ground. Panic set in because they knew they must find another spare and that size tire was not easy to find. They stopped at the very next town but the tire shop and junk yard didn't have a tire that would work.

The junk yard man said he heard that the junk yard in the next town would have a tire. What to do? The only option was to continue on and take the chance of being stranded out in the middle of nowhere. The next town had no tires so they pushed on. Finally, after stopping at each little town they found a tire that wasn't the right size but it could be made to work. They paid the junk yard owner the grand sum of $1.00 and started on their way again. They never passed another junk yard without searching for extra tires.

After six more flat tires and several more distributor fixes they were nearing the Nebraska/Colorado border. In the meantime because of all the flat tires, with funds getting short, they hit upon an idea to stretch their money. They would merely shut off the motor and coast down hills and thus save gas. Only trouble was that they discovered there aren't that many hills in the sand hills of western Nebraska. But when they did come upon a hill they would turn off the motor and coast. Then, near the bottom of the hill, they would turn on the ignition and let out the clutch. The Pres would come back to life. That worked a few times but then as they were nearing the bottom of one hill they let out the clutch, but this time the Pres had a surprise for them. Gasoline had built up around the carburetor so when contact was made there was an explosion and the motor caught on fire. They were miles from any fire department, but they had enough presence of mind to pull off the road. It was hot and one was asleep in the back seat and while one roused him, the other pulled out a white WWII US Navy blanket and started beating the engine. The fire was out before it caused too much damage. They turned the key and amazingly the Pres came to life once more and they were on their way. That Navy blanket was never the same, and that was the last time they ever coasted down hills.

After all this they finally arrived at Estes Park, somewhat the worse for wear but still excited about reaching their destination. They must first get a look at the magnificent Stanley Hotel, the place of their summer jobs. Next they needed a cheap place to sleep. A little old lady took pity on them and rented her fixed up attic by the day. Their funds were severely low, after buying all those tires. They only had enough to last a few days. But they weren't worried since, they'd heard the Stanley Hotel was hiring young men for the summer, and they would soon be in the chips.

After a fitful night in the hot, fixed up attic, they headed for the magnificent Stanley Hotel dressed in the best post war clothes they had. What happened next are the principal facts, which clearly delineate the discriminatory and callous disregard of constitutional guarantees, which is the raison d'etre of the contemplated legal action.

All three applied for work, and they can still attest to that. One applicant was 6 feet tall and weighed about 165 pound, muscular with a good physique and very handsome. Another applicant was also 6 feet tall but only weighted 139 pounds, was frail and had a big nose. The third applicant was 5'10", weighted 150 pounds, had a good physique but looked like he was only 14 years old (even though he had been a gunner in Italy during WWII).

Then the worst cast of "looks" discrimination took place. The tall, good looking, well built applicant was offered a job. The slim applicant, with the big nose, and the applicant with the good physique, but who looked only 14 years, were told that there were no other jobs available. The good looking , well built applicant, with a good physique, and very handsome who was offered a job, in righteous indignation, told the magnificent Stanley Hotel person, who was responsible for hiring, that all three applicants came as a matched set. If the other two applicants were not acceptable, he could not go along with such gross discriminatory practices and would, therefore, not accept a job either. Humiliated, embarrassed and shamed, the three applicants departed the magnificent Stanley Hotel to look for other suitable employment, but alas, there was none to be found.

After such devastating psychological trauma, the only option was for the three applicants to crank up the Pres and return home. The trip back was not unlike the trip out. Flat tires and distributor slippage galore. The applicants were indeed fortunate to reach home as they had only four tires on the road and no spare, and one tire on the rear wheel was smaller than the rest, so they looked like a dog running down the street. Fortunately, all three applicants made it home safe, but wary, worn and distraught. They had traveled 1200 miles, had 13 flat tires, had thrown away 9 tires, and fixed the distributor uncountable times, and were completely broke.

It is impossible to assess the damage caused by Stanley Hotel's outrageous gross and unlawful discrimination. Even though this was a traumatic experience for all three applicants, in the end, all graduated from the University of Nebraska, and all have been relatively successful in their life's work. They are now in their seventies, with several little applicants and grand applicants. When any jury deliberates, it will undoubtedly agree there was egregious discrimination. It will at a minimum, award the three applicants the cost of their trip which was the huge sum, of say, $200.00 (including cost of the Pres, the Pres was worn out after the trip and had to be junked).

On the other hand, they jury might see things as they may have been but for the Stanley Hotel's unconscionable acts. Things may have been quite different had the applicants all been hired. They might have met rich young things (at least the good looking one) and been set for life in the father's big businesses. All three applicants might have pooled their earnings from the small salary, but big tips and wisely invested in IBM, AT&T, or some other sure-fire money maker. The value of such an accumulation staggers the imagination.

Additionally, the Stanley Hotel might have profited even more had they hired all three applicants. When work got around the handsome applicant would have, in all probability, attracted many young things with rich fathers. The other two applicants would have been available for all the not so beautiful young things with equally rich fathers. The possibilities are limitless. It could have been "Fiddler on the Roof" right there in Colorado.

It seems everyone is filing law suits these days and unquestionably this suit is as valid as most others being filed.

Although some things have certainly changed in fifty years, it appears from your brochure that the Stanley Hotel and Conference Center is still a magnificent place with "An Historic Tradition." Then there are the applicants. Applicant (1) still has a big nose but weighs considerably more now; applicant (2) the one that looked 14, is in his seventies now looks around 18; applicant (3) the good looking one, still is.

Incidentally, our attorney is taking this case pro bono, and he thinks we should settle out of court. Perhaps I can get the others to agree, but you might have to dig up that personnel guy and have him send us a letter of apology.

Sincerely,
Leonard E. Durham (The author, the one with the big nose)
Richard E. Lewis (The one who looked 14)
Stanley L. Portsche (The handsome one and still is)

P.S. We had though about repeating our trek on the 50th anniversary but will not do so for two reasons. First, we can't find a 1930 Studebaker President and second, you probably wouldn't hire us now cause we're too old. Then we'd have to file an age discrimination suit. Where will it all end?

At left Rich Lewis and Stan Portsche, on the right Leonard Durham and Stan Portsche in Estes Park, Colorado 1946.

The Ice Storm

By Chuck Deuser

The worst ice storm I ever encountered in my 71 years happened when I was attending the University of Nebraska in Lincoln between 1947–52. Back then, I might add, you went to the football games to watch Bobbie Reynolds make great plays and nothing more. I even played taps once before a game.

Now back to the storm. Freezing ice covered everything. The winds were blowing at almost gale force. As you drove you crept along because just to stop became an experience. I was coming back to the Kappa Sigma fraternity house at 1141 H Street after a class and stopped at O Street for a red light. Another car was stopped next to me. With no warning a strong gust blew the back end of the Chevrolet I was driving into the back fender of that car next to me. Neither of us was about to get out of our cars in those conditions so we each rolled down a window and exchanged information and then went on our way.

When I arrived at the frat house some of the guys thought it would be fun to jump into a car and drive around to see what was happening. I think we thought that a loaded car would provide great traction and be skid proof. Wrong, we slid all over the place on the glare ice, but we slowly drove around observing the damage and watching pedestrians trying to make headway against the elements.

There was a car dealership, Buick I believe, just south of the campus. A man was on the south side of the building trying to round the corner and go north towards the campus. He would start running along the south side of the building, turn the corner, hoping his momentum would carry him north against the gale. Alas, his traction was poor at best. Now, I guess you could say he appeared to be doing Michael Jackson's "moon walk." His feet looked like they were moving him forward but the wind was moving him in the opposite direction. In his backward journey he grabbed a light pole and hung on for dear life, preventing him from going into the street. We saw him try several times before we slowly moved on.

As I recall the strong winds that day blew a person under a bus, but with no serious injuries. I also recall that some insurance companies were telling their client stores to break out their windows before they would shatter and injure someone.

Speaking of insurance companies, after the weather had cleared I made a trip to the Lincoln headquarters of Union Fire, the insurance company carrying the coverage on the car. My father was an agent of theirs for more than 50 years, in addition to his primary profession of farm management and real estate activities. I sat down and explained the whole incident as the man listened intently. The damage was not major. When I had finished he looked at me and said, "Really, is that what actually happened?" When I told him yes he said they would take care of it, and they did. I'm sure they hadn't heard many stories like that one before.

My 'Hood in the '50s

By John Strope

From ages five to fifteen, my life was spent in one neighborhood—the area bounded by 30th to 36th Street and Randolph to J Street. Within that boundary, there were 30th, Marshall, 31st, 32nd, Elmwood, 33rd, 34th, and 36th Streets going north-south, and only one east-west street, Laura Avenue, which runs only between 34th and 36th. We lived at the corner of 30th and Randolph.

Life was simple. I went to St. Teresa's School and Church at the far end of my neighborhood—36th and J. In the 'hood we played football, kick soccer, baseball, and dodg'em in the street on Marshall. When we got more organized, we all trooped up to Roger's Tract, a great undeveloped expanse now known as Wood's Park.

Remember how we used to know how to play without adults around? If we wanted to play baseball, we went to the area at Marshall and J Street. Over the years base paths had been created by the constant wear of running feet. For a backstop, we put a bunch of our bikes together.

For players, we used anyone, even girls! We probably had a five-year range of kids playing together. We played "workup"—a game where you worked your way up to bad by moving through the various positions, or best of all, by catching a batter's fly ball. And, can you imagine, we played all day and did not have uniforms.

The biggest treat in those later years was when Gary Haas came and hit balls to the guys. Gary was a famous athlete at Lincoln High School and we couldn't get enough of his "playing" with us.

Then, there were the local "dairy stores"—Dorothy's Place at Randolph and 29th (the building still stands) and the one on the north side of Randolph between Marshall and 31st. 3-V Cola came in 16oz. bottles, and we had to pay a deposit on the bottles. Pieces of candy were a penny.

I remember the man with the old pick up (or did he have a cart pulled by a horse?) coming around selling fruit and vegetables in the summer. If we begged the milkman enough, he would toss out some chunks of ice for us to cool ourselves during some of our street games on Marshall. A sweet treat came when Danny's dad appeared with goodies from Kraft foods. He would toss out handful after handful of caramels.

Then, there were all the kids: Dick and Diane, Tim and the older sister he antagonized (or did she antagonize him?), Ronnie, Doug, Anita, Sara Sue and Pat and Mike, Danny and Christine. Whatever happened to these childhood friends? I have had a couple of contacts with Sara Sue over the years. I chatted with Danny on the phone when I was switching planes in Dallas a few years ago. The others still live in my childhood memories.

Most special was my best friend, Ralphie. We loved baseball so much that for several years we met every summer day (except Monday because there were no game on Monday) to keep our scorecards of the Mutual Network Game of the Day broadcast on the radio. I've never seen him since he moved to Pueblo, Colorado in the mid-'50s.

We even had our "mystery" neighbors, Iris and Ingrid, the DPs who lived on the corner of Marshall and Randolph. If my memory serves me well, they and their parents escaped from Czechoslovakia about 1955 and, as displaced persons, settled in Lincoln. For sure, we, their new neighbors did no have much of a world-conscious view.

In that neighborhood, I delivered 85 copies of the Lincoln Journal for a year or so. All the boys had a paper route sooner or later. That first job netted me about $30 per month. A vivid memory still remains of the afternoon my Aunt Irene picked me up at school and took me to deliver all my papers. It was the afternoon all of Lincoln was paralyzed—Charlie Starkweather was on the loose.

I never ventured far from the 'hood. When I did, it was usually by bike or bus. The bus stopped right beside my house and Earl, the driver, would deliver me safely to 11th and N Street where both my aunts worked at Gold's.

By bus, I would venture off to the baseball fields north of Lincoln High School where I played for the Muny Park midget team. Sometimes, a bunch of us would ride down to Antelope Park and ride the paths or visit the Zoo. I bet I'll never get that nasty, nasty zoo smell out of my nose.

Finally, in the 1950s, I remember that all the adults in my 'hood were old and that all the houses were big. We moved in 1960. We stayed in Lincoln and my aunt lived in the 'hood until 1995 so I kept up with news about the people. Best I can tell, everyone is gone, but when I get home for a visit, the 'hood still looks the way I remember it.

Of Interest to Nebraska Readers...

Bipartisan Efforts and Other Mutations by **Paul Fell.** Political cartoonist for the Lincoln *Journal Star* collects the best of his political cartoons from 1984 to 2000. Humor, pathos and politics in a thought-provoking volume. "If somebody's not mad at me, I'm not doing my job."
8½"×7"   84 pages   41-3 $9.95

A Black Hills Lady: The Cinderella Horse by **W. H. O'Gara.** Born in a sod house, the author was the son of Irish immigrants. Stockman, farmer and legislator, his hobby was training harness horses. Here he tells the story of his favorite horse, Black Hills Lady, an extraordinary animal, beautiful and swift. He loved her best of all.
9"×6"   78 pages   12-X $8.95

Daniel and Agnes Freeman Homesteaders by **Beverly S. Kaplan.** The first homestead in the U.S. was filed by Daniel Freeman on land in southeastern Nebraska. This chronicle of that homestead and the life he built there with his wife tells of the courage, stamina, and pluck of the early settlers through drought, depression, and disease, yet were ever ready to help a neighbor.
8"×5"   187 pages   26-X $9.95

Frontier Steamboat Town by **Glenn Noble.** This account of the settlement and early history of Nebraska City from the arrival of the first steamboat and the establishment of Old Fort Kearny is rich with anecdotes. Nebraska City was one of the state's earliest towns, an early port of the Missouri River, and a jumping-off spot for westward migration.
8½"×5½"   257 pages   35-9 $9.95

The Good Old Days by **Jerry Mapes and Van Duling.** 150 Nebraska "old timers" reminisce about life in the Great Plains in the 1920s, '30s and '40s when gasoline was less than a quarter, summers hotter, winters colder and the pace of life seemed a whole lot slower.
6"×9"   224 pages   45-6 $16.95.

Havelock; A Photo History and Walking Tour by **Jim McKee** with walking tour by **Ed Zimmer.** Established in the late 1880s and incorporated in 1893, Havelock, Nebraska was soon home to a Burlington Railroad locomotive assembly and repair shop. In the 1920s the largest aircraft manufacturer in the world located here. Heavily illustrated with old photographs, the book tells of the village's growth and ultimate annexation by Lincoln.
8½"×11"   96 pages   33-2 $12.95

How Cold Is It? by **Roger Welsch with cartoons by Paul Fell.** Tall tales about Midwestern winters collected by folklorist and humorist Welsch and amusingly illustrated by cartoonist Fell.
8½"×5½"   101 pages   34-0 $6.95

In All Its Fury: Great Blizzard 1888 by **W. H. O'Gara.** These firsthand accounts of heroism and courage were collected in 1947 from survivors of one of the country's worst weather disasters. The Great Blizzard of 1888 roared down from Canada at 50 miles an hour, dropping temperatures 36 degrees in a few hours, and killing more than 1,000 people as it ravaged the central third of the nation.
9"×6"   343 pages   04-9 $9.95

Innocents on Broadway by **Flavia Waters Champe.** This delightful collection of letters home tells the story of a teenage dancer on the vaudeville circuit in the 1920s. Getting parental approval with difficulty, Champe took to the road with a group of dancers even younger than herself under her wing, to perform avante-garde modern dance. Suitable for teen readers.   5¼"×8¼"   272 pages   0-939644-24-X $9.95

The Lay of the Land: A View From the Prairie by **Brent Olsen.** A heartlander writes from the heart in this collection of carefully crafted gems. Heartwarming and funny, this is a farmer's view of life in the rural Midwest. He talks about family, about friends, about what really matters in life. Savor these essays one at a time or wolf them down at a sitting. You'll laugh. You'll cry. You'll want more.
5¼"×7⅛"   172 pages   36-7 $11.95

Liars Too by **Roger Welsch with cartoons by Paul Fell.** A humor collection gleaned from the author's *Nebraska Farmer* column, "Liar's Corner," these tall tales and just plain ol' lies are the sort that have kept pioneers sane and farmers laughing through decades of hard times.   5½"×8½"   116 pages   32-4 $5.95

***Lincoln: The Prairie Capital* by Jim McKee.** Hundreds of old photos illustrate this history of Nebraska's capital city. McKee recounts Lincoln's past from the tiny village of 30 with "no water power, mines, fuel, no other so-called natural advantages" to the late-20th-century city of nearly 180,000. Facts and formalities are punctuated with how-it-happened anecdotes in this lively history.

8½"×11"   124 pages   07-3 $17.95

***Luther North, Frontier Scout* by Jeff O'Donnell.** Frontier scouts helped bring the railroads to the prairie by finding meat for the workmen, heading off hostile Native Americans, scouting the route, and protecting railroad personnel. Luther North's life of adventure as a scout gives the reader a glimpse of one important link in the winning of the West.

5½"×8½"   216 pages   10-3 $13.95

***Miss Adams, Country Teacher* by Treva Adams Strait.** In 1928, Treva Strait, age 18, began teaching in a one-room schoolhouse, converted from a cowboy's shack, 35 miles from town on the western Nebraska prairie. The life of a teacher, hardly older than her students, combined with a look at life just before the Depression make this an enjoyable read.

6"×9"   139 pages   25-1 $8.95

***Nebraska Our Towns—Panhandle* by Jane Graff.** Volume 1 of the 7-volume series covering the history of incorporated towns in Nebraska, divided geographically. Each volume captures the images of each population center in words and pictures from its beginning to the present. Includes Banner, Box Butte, Cheyenne, Dawes, Deuel, Garden, Kimball, Morrill, Scotts Bluff, Sheridan and Sioux Counties.

8½"×11"   132 pages   42-1 $29.95

***Nebraska Our Towns—North, Northeast* by Jane Graff.** Volume 2 of the seven volume series covers Antelope, Boone, Boyd, Cedar, Dakota, Dixon, Holt, Knox, Madison, Pierce, Thurston, Wayne and Wheeler counties.

8½"×11"   212 pages   43-5 $29.95

***Nebraska, Where Dreams Grow* by Dorothy Weyer Creigh.** Nebraska reminiscences from sod houses and chautauqua to center-pivot irrigation. A charming history of the state told in terms of what people did in their everyday lives.

8½"×11"   156 pages   15-4 $12.95

Nebraska's Five Seasons: The Best of Paul Fell. The Lincoln *Journal Star* cartoonist has collected over 100 of his favorite "Sketchbook" pieces, taking on everything from parking problems, dieting, home repairs, and Father's Day to Midwestern winters and Nebraska's own fifth season, football.

8½"×11"   94 pages   24-3 $8.95

***Nebraskaspeak: How to Talk Like a True Nebraskan* by Paul Fell.** Cartoonist Paul Fell is at it again. This time he's put together a comical look at Nebraska's take on the English language. Check here for proper pronunciations of Beatrice (Bee-a-trice) and nuclear (noo-cue-lar). Cartoon illustrated, of course.

5½"×8½"   74 pages   17-0 $5.95

***No Gun For This Lady! The Story of Hulda Roper, First Policewoman of Lincoln, Nebraska* by Lilya Wagner.** Relates the story of a woman who pioneered for other women in a profession dominated by men. In the 1950s she was a uniformed officer, investigating domestic disputes, but refusing to carry a gun.

8½"×5½"   89 pages $5.00

***Oh Grandma, You're Kidding, Memories of 75 years in the Great Plains* by Gladys S. Douglass.** Born in 1901, Douglass' life spanned the better part of the 20th century. With humor and interesting detail she tells what it was like growing up in an earlier time. Here's a sampling of the 30 chapters: Before Radio and TV; Womans' Work; Baked Beans on Washday; Riding the Train; Dollar Day at the Fair; Omaha's Easter Tornado; and Seeing Halley's Comet. Retrace your own memories or share the past with a young person. Enjoyable reading.

6"×9"   110 pages   00-6 $7.95

***Omaha Tribal Myths and Trickster Tales* by Roger Welsch.** 70 Omaha tribal tales, originally collected in the 1800s, are retranslated here with explanatory notes. These fables will help the reader to appreciate the rich culture of the Omaha before "civilization" was forced on their people by white soldiers and missionaries.

6"×9"   285 pages   11-1 $14.95

***Perkey's Nebraska Place Names* by Elton A. Perkey.** In addition to origins of place names, each entry includes peak population, dates of establishment and discontinuance, circumstances of the founding of counties, and notes on the origin of towns, railroad stations, Pony Express stations and other stage line points.

8½"×11"   226 pages   19-7 $12.95

Pinnacle Jake & Pinnacle Jake's Roundup, as told by A. B. Snyder to Nellie Snyder Yost. Recollections of the life of a cowboy on the Great Plains at the turn of the century. If you've ever wondered what real life on the range was like, here's your book. "One of the best books I have read..."—Frank Dobie. Great Plains history buffs and Louis L'Amour fans will love this fascinating volume. 8"×5" 340 pages 28-6 $12.95

Postcards From Nebraska: The Stories Behind the Stories by Roger Welsch. Welsch shares the behind-the-scenes stories which made his spot on "CBS News Sunday Morning" with Charles Kurault one of the show's most popular segments. The book covers everyone's favorites from overalls to pickup trucks. Humorous and heartwarming. 8½"×5½" 160 pages 40-5 $13.95

Remember When . . . Memories of Lincoln by Jim McKee. Over 100 vignettes of Lincoln history from Jim McKee's weekly Lincoln *Journal Star* "Memories & Moments" column, collected with historical photographs. 8½"×11" 23-5 105 pages, indexed $12.95

Satterfield on the Loose by Leon Satterfield. A practicing curmudgeon collects the best of his humorous, entertaining, and biting columns from the Lincoln *Journal Star*. "...Funny, self-deprecatory, far-ranging, opinionated, curmudgeonly, and wide."—Kent Haruf 5½"×8½"" 117 pages 39-1 $11.95

Seems Like Old Times: The Big Bands of the Midwest by Loren Belker. From 1935 to 1955 the Midwest was home to dozens of small traveling dance bands. Vocalist, band member and director Loren Belker recalls these regional groups—how they came about, lived and became a part of the local scene. Dozens of historical photographs. Just a few chapter headings to whet your appetite: The Humor of the Musician, The Girl Singer and the Boy Vocalist; The Panic Band; Love Life—Love in the Trenches; Puling a Creep; and Holding Out for $3.50 per Man. 8½"×11" 131 pages 30-8 $16.95

The Sod-House Frontier; Everyday Life in Kansas, Nebraska and Dakota, 1854–1890 by Everett Dick. Everyday life in pioneer days is vividly described in this scholarly work that is also a fascinating read. Contains much on the development of agriculture, the beginning of towns, social life on the plains frontier, road ranches, sod houses, river towns, The Grange, schooling, homesteading and more. 6"×9½" 550 pages, indexed 38-3 $12.95 hardcover

Sod Walls by Roger Welsch. The sod house has all but vanished from the Great Plains, where once it was one of the most common dwellings. On the vast, treeless expanse the settlers found when they came to the Midwest, they built their homes of the only material readily at hand—"prairie marble." Here Welsch tells the story of the soddies from site selection and sod cutting to roof construction, windows, doors, and interior design. Illustrated with over 100 drawings and photographs. 6"×8" 208 pages 27-8 $12.95

Starkweather; A Story of Mass Murder on the Great Plains by Jeff O'Donnell. Details the Starkweather killings. In late 1957 and early 1958, 19-year-old Charles Starkweather and his 14-year-old girlfriend Caril Ann Fugate went on a killing spree that left a trail of 11 dead bodies. 5½"×8½" 31-6 208 pages $10.00

True Nebraskans by Paul Fell. Cartoonist Paul Fell tackles the definition of Nebraskan with wry observations. "True Nebraskans think a good auto sound system is one that plays 'There Is No Place Like Nebraska' on the horn." "True Nebraskans listen to the noontime commodities reports . . . and understand what they mean." 8½"×5½" 18-9 94 pages $5.95

Union Pacific and Omaha Union Station by Carla Johnson. Johnson covers Omaha's early history, the railroad's impact on the city and its passenger depots from the beginning to the construction of the amazing 1931 Art Deco Union Station through local preservation efforts beginning in 1973 to today's amazing Durham Western Heritage Museum. 8½"×11" 84 pages 44-8 $24.95

You Know You're a Nebraskan . . . by Roger Welsch and Paul Fell. Lincoln *Journal Star* political cartoonist Fell and folklorist Welsch team up to produce a laugh-filled collection of gems: "You know you're a Nebraskan . . . if your ancestors arrived on the Burlington, not the Mayflower." This revised edition is a great gift for any native, displaced Nebraskan, or newcomer to our state. 7"×8½" 09-X 80 pages $5.95

Available from: **J&L Lee Company**
P.O. Box 5575 • Lincoln, NE 68505 • Phone (402) 488-4416 • Toll Free 1-888-665-0999
E-mail leebooks@radiks.net • **www.leebooksellers.com**